RECONSTITUTING

THE AMERICAN RENAISSANCE

NEW

AMERICANISTS

A Series Edited by

Donald E. Pease

RECONSTITUTING

THE AMERICAN RENAISSANCE

Emerson, Whitman, and the Politics of Representation

JAY GROSSMAN

DUKE UNIVERSITY PRESS

DURHAM AND LONDON

2003

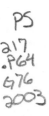

IN MEMORY OF MY PARENTS

CONTENTS

∾

ACKNOWLEDGMENTS

I have been more than fortunate in the mentors and colleagues who have shepherded me through the research and writing of this book. Over many years, Betsy Erkkila has generously shared with me her insights not only into American literary and cultural history, but also into what makes research, writing, and a career in literary studies valuable. Margreta de Grazia's influence and support have been enduring, and have meant everything to me. Carl Smith read the manuscript with great care, then gave me permission to ignore his comments wherever I chose; the book is significantly better for his attention to it. Jay Fliegelman was one of the first readers of the manuscript, which has—as have I—benefited in innumerable ways from the profound depth of his knowledge and his even more profound generosity. I am grateful to Donald Pease for his attention to this project, his acute commentary on the manuscript, and his support of its culmination in print.

This book and I have also had many supporters and perceptive readers at several institutions; I hope these friends will understand all that is meant by an unembellished listing of their names: Tom Augst, Michèle Aina Barale, Nicola Beisel, Lawrence Buell, Jack Cameron, Chris Castiglia, Rhonda Cobham-Sander, Jodi Cranston, Ed Folsom, Judy Frank, Albert Gelpi, Teresa Goddu, Roland Greene, Bill Handley, Andrea Henderson, David Herman, Patrick Johnson, Suvir Kaul, Jack Matthews, John McGreevy, Alice Mitinger, Susan Mizruchi, Stephen Orgel, Dale Peterson, Ken Price, Michael Prokopow, Lisa Raskin, Karen Sánchez-Eppler, Geoffrey Saunders Schramm, Martha Nell Smith, Marc Stein, the late Jan Thaddeus, Kim Townsend, Kevin Van Anglen, Lynn Wardley, Eric Wertheimer.

My appreciation goes to my students Joe Gerber, Coleman Hutchison, and Marcy Dinius, all of whom have been a sounding board for ideas in this book, and to Dana Bilsky, who also diligently proofread the manuscript. Hunt Howell conducted the primary research on Whitman's time at the *Daily Crescent* in New Orleans, and I thank him for this, as well as for the index. James Lebeck researched and produced the map of New Orleans used as figure 5, and answered the call on innumerable other occasions with accuracy and enthusiasm. Russell Maylone, Curator of Special Collections at the Northwestern University Library, and Dan Traister, Curator for Research Services at the Annenberg Rare Book and Manuscript Library, University of Pennsylvania, both provided bibliographical as well as timely photographic assistance. My thanks to Reynolds Smith for his guidance, and to Sharon Torian, Pam Morrison, Katie Courtland, and the staff at Duke University Press for all their support.

My deepest appreciation goes to Julia Stern, Wendy Wall, Jules Law, Andy Parker, and Meredith McGill, all of whom have been—and are—incomparable readers, colleagues, and friends.

My sister and brother and their families have in innumerable ways made all of this possible.

Jeffrey Masten has given me not simply the benefit of his acute intelligence, but also of his uncanny ability to read through to the core of this book's argument and its consequences. He has done all of this (and countless times) while sustaining me with his patience, his wit, and his affection.

Through some curious nurturing mix, I spent many summer days of my childhood in a clubhouse my father built, underlining words in storybooks: this was what I apparently understood at the time to constitute work. *Mutatis mutandis.* This book is dedicated to the memory of my parents, whose love has never left me.

I gratefully acknowledge the material support I have received from the Andrew W. Mellon Foundation, first in the form of a Mellon Fellowship for graduate study (including a fifth-year dissertation fellowship), and later a Mellon Postdoctoral Fellowship in the Humanities at Stanford University.

Materials pertaining to the construction of Emerson Hall are used by permission of the Harvard University Archives. Manuscripts and drawings by Christopher Pearse Cranch are used by permission of the Houghton Library, Harvard University. Sections of chapters 2 and 3 originally appeared in *Reciprocal Influences: Literary Production, Distribution, and Consumption in America*, edited by Steven Fink and Susan S. Williams; I thank the Ohio State University Press for permission to reprint.

ABBREVIATIONS

∽

References to frequently cited works appear within the text in parenthesis along with page numbers. The abbreviations for these works appear below. Where I have not used original editions, I have usually cited the easily accessible Library of America editions of Emerson's and Whitman's writings.

1855 LG   Walt Whitman, *Leaves of Grass*, 1st edition. Brooklyn, 1855.

1856 LG   Walt Whitman, *Leaves of Grass*, 2nd edition. Brooklyn, 1856.

1860 LG   Walt Whitman, *Leaves of Grass* (1860), facsimile edition, ed. Roy Harvey Pearce. Ithaca: Cornell University Press, 1984.

AR   F. O. Matthiessen, *American Renaissance: Art and Expression in the Age of Emerson and Whitman*. New York: Oxford University Press, 1968.

Corr.   John Adams and Thomas Jefferson, *The Adams-Jefferson Letters: The Complete Correspondence Between Thomas Jefferson and Abigail and John Adams*, ed. Lester J. Cappon. Chapel Hill: University of North Carolina Press for Omohundro Institute of Early American History and Culture, 1987.

DC   Bernard Bailyn, ed., *The Debate on the Constitution: Federalist and Antifederalist Speeches, Articles, and Letters During the Struggle Over Ratification*. New York: Library of America, 1993.

EL   *The Early Lectures of Ralph Waldo Emerson*, ed. Stephen Whicher et al., 3 vols. Cambridge: Belknap Press of Harvard University Press, 1960–72.

EPF   Walt Whitman, *Early Poems and Fiction*, ed. Thomas L. Brasher. New York: New York University Press, 1963.

F/A   J. R. Pole, ed., *The American Constitution For and Against*. New York: Hill and Wang, 1987.

GF   Walt Whitman, *The Gathering of the Forces: Editorials, Essays, Literary and Dramatic Reviews and Other Material . . .* , ed. Cleveland Rodgers and John Black. New York: G. P. Putnam's Sons, 1920.

I Sit   Walt Whitman, *I Sit and Look Out: Editorials from the* Brooklyn Daily Times, ed. Emory Holloway and Vernolian Schwarz. New York: AMS Press, 1966.

JMN   *The Journals and Miscellaneous Notebooks of Ralph Waldo Emerson*, ed. William Gilman et al. 16 vols. Cambridge: Belknap Press of Harvard University Press, 1960–82.

LAE   Ralph Waldo Emerson, *Essays and Lectures*, ed. Joel Porte. New York: Library of America, 1983.

LAW   Walt Whitman, *Poetry and Prose*. New York: Library of America, 1982.

LG   Walt Whitman, *Leaves of Grass*, ed. Sculley Bradley and Harold W. Blodgett. New York: Norton, 1973.

NUP   Walt Whitman, *Notebooks and Unpublished Prose Manuscripts*, ed. Edward F. Grier. 6 vols., 1984–. New York University Press edition of *The Collected Writings of Walt Whitman*.

WWA   Walt Whitman, *Walt Whitman of the* New York Aurora, ed. Joseph Jay Rubin and Charles H. Brown. State College, Penn.: Bald Eagle Press, 1950.

WWWC   Horace Traubel, *With Walt Whitman in Camden*. Vol. 1: Boston: Small, Maynard, 1906. Vol. 2: New York: D. Appleton, 1908. Vol. 3: New York: Mitchell Kennerley, 1914; rpt. New York: Rowman and Littlefield, 1961. Vol. 4: Philadelphia: University of Pennsylvania Press, 1953. Vol. 5: Carbondale: Southern Illinois University Press, 1964. Vol. 6: Carbondale: Southern Illinois University Press, 1982. Vol. 7: Carbondale: Southern Illinois University Press, 1992.

One of the most signal weaknesses of
the historical method as applied to the study
of American letters is the ever-present tendency
to resolve the past into a series of personalities.

CLARENCE GOHDES,
"Some Remarks on Emerson's *Divinity
School Address*," from the inaugural
issue of *American Literature*
March 1929

REPRESENTATIVE STRATEGIES

Rhetorical figures . . . are thus of a piece with the deep, buried, invisible presuppositions of every world view.—FRANCO MORETTI, *Signs Taken for Wonders*

In *Department of Commerce et al., v. United States House of Representatives et al.*, the United States Supreme Court upheld a lower court decision "permanently enjoin[ing] the [Census] Bureau's planned use of statistical sampling to determine the population for purposes of congressional apportionment."[1] In its opening sections the Court's decision addresses the question of standing—whether the Indiana citizens who submitted the affidavits and brought the suit had met the legal requirements to justify their claim for remedy. A "distinct interest is at issue," the Court explains:

> With one fewer representative, Indiana residents' votes will be diluted. Moreover, the threat of vote dilution is "concrete" and "actual or imminent, not 'conjectural' or 'hypothetical.'" . . . There is undoubtedly a "traceable" connection between the use of sampling in the decennial census and Indiana's expected loss of a Representative, and there is a substantial likelihood that the requested relief—a permanent injunction against the proposed uses of sampling in the census—will redress the alleged injury. (*Commerce* at 774)

Thus the justices define the injury the appellees were likely to suffer if census sampling were permitted in terms of how "their votes will be diluted vis-à-vis residents of counties with larger undercount rates" (*Commerce* at 767). That is, counties in other states with larger undercount rates will be more "fully" counted, resulting in higher total census populations and thus a redistribution of representative seats in their favor. Counties whose rate of undercount is presumed to be lower, and thus whose sampling supplement will be lower, will be unable to overcome this numerical supplement: thus Indiana in general, and these appellees in particular, suffer the "injury-in-fact" of "expected intrastate vote dilution" (*Commerce* at 775)—the loss of a congressional seat.

Reconstituting the American Renaissance necessarily takes the long view on cases like *Commerce* and the questions regarding representation that they raise. Indeed, despite the justices' assurances, this introduction begins with two questions that go unanswered (or only tacitly answered) in *Commerce*: first, what kind of "personal injury" (*Commerce* syllabus at 767) does vote dilution constitute? Secondly, what is the system of representation presumed to be in place that garners for this lawsuit the attention of the nation's highest court and a finding of "personal injury"?

Rather than directly answering these questions, however, *Reconstituting* argues first and foremost for their genealogical significance and historical persistence, finding in the census debates over sampling a recent example of the nation's persistent conversation on the nature of political representation. (This is a "conversation," of course, that has not always been carried out verbally.) This book takes as axiomatic not only what has been called a second American Revolution in the Civil War, but in its focus on writings produced largely between these two epochal events, it traces the persistence of the Founders' theme (and scheme) of representation as a sometimes explicit topic and a sometimes implicit yet structuring rhetoric for subsequent generations.

Reconstituting also takes as axiomatic another dimension of the recent census case that may seem less apparent, but that is no less foundational for this book's reading of representation and its discontents between the Revolution and the Civil War. As framed by the Supreme Court, the dilemma in *Commerce* is, like many cases in constitutional jurisprudence, as much dependent on language's plural meanings, intentions, and the worlds that words are assumed to represent as it is on resolving a matter of political representation in any very traditional sense. Explicitly at stake in the case are two phrases from the Constitution's original instructions regarding the census: that "the actual Enumeration shall be made within three Years after the first Meeting of the Congress of the United States, and within every subsequent Term of ten Years, in such Manner as they shall by Law direct" (Article 1, Section 2). What is an "actual Enumeration"? What is the relation between the two phrases "actual Enumeration" and "such Manner"? Just how strictly is one to apply the adjective "actual" to the seeming insistence on "Enumeration"? Does "Enumeration" modify "Manner," and thereby specify the only sanctioned means for counting? Does "actual Enumeration" leave room for statistical sampling, even if such mathematical procedures were not known or practiced at the time of ratification? What does, or did, "actual" mean, and how should the term be reconciled in light of the ambiguous language everywhere in the Constitution—ambiguities that reflect the compromises that permitted its initial adoption by (most of) the delegates of the Philadelphia Convention? The Constitution lacks in any number of places any very explicit instructions for dealing with, among other matters, the exponential growth of the nation and its population over, as it turns out, more than two centuries, except to count it, and for Congress to continue, in some "such manner," to represent it.

Reconstituting the American Renaissance argues for the ubiquity and persistence in the American context of this cohabitation of the linguistic with the political, even, as the sampling case suggests, up to the present day. In so doing the book expands Brian Seitz's analysis of the significance of the Bill of Rights in relation to the Constitution's claims to interpretive preeminence. The adoption of the first ten amendments to address the Philadelphia document's ambiguity— or plain silence—on matters of individual liberties deemed by some too important for guesswork establishes the Constitution's peculiar status as a constituting text that "ambiguously affirms its own transgression, . . . its writing is a rewriting, and its final truth that its truth is not immutable but always open to modification and never final." Indeed the promise of amendment at the time of ratification was not initially mere afterthought, as the term improperly suggests, but was instead the very condition of Constitutional enactment and ratification.[2] In this ongoing supplementarity, as a "law that gets more definite in its development" (Seitz 83), the Constitution contains within itself a method for its own amendment, as well as an "elastic clause" as a rhetorical (though potentially profoundly instrumental) "escape hatch" for issues it fails to address explicitly. In these ways it announces its interpretive instability—its virtuality (I return to this complex and persistent term below)—not as an exception, but as its very (literary) mode of being, requiring in perpetuity the continual, if precedent-based, exegesis formalized when Chief Justice Marshall articulated the Court's preeminent right of judicial review in *Marbury v. Madison* (1801). Somewhat tautologically, Marshall justified such review precisely on the grounds of the Constitution's own preeminent authority. The peculiar fact of the rule of law by legislative statute in the United States (as opposed to the precedent-based, customary dictates of the common law) revolves around a text that itself (self-) generates endless texts, cites other texts, indeed, incites other texts.

Such a condition of "constituting"—which may also be called "writing"—and/as supplementarity has profound implications for understanding texts produced in the United States between the Revolution and the Civil War. It is one of the governing assumptions of *Reconstituting the American Renaissance* that the distinction between the political and the literary is itself profoundly complicated in an American context in which language-making and nation-making are so profoundly inter-implicated. Turning in later chapters to writings by Emerson and Whitman, the book argues for the atavistic peculiarities of Romantic writing in the United States that never quite sheds its profoundly material origins in the revolutionary political/imaginative texts that both described and produced the break from Great Britain. As John Adams famously described it to Jefferson, the Revolution occurred first and foremost "in the Minds of the People" (*Corr.* 455)—that is, as an effect and a consequence of language, political rhetoric, and representation: from broadsides and *Common Sense* through declaration, constitution, and amendment. "Constituting" is understood in this book's title and in the founding documents it begins by analyzing as a profoundly performative, collaborative, instrumental, and collective act.[3]

Thus this book's placement of the Constitution and the ratification debates as its "origin," the documentary and interpretive contexts that establish not simply the rules of governance of American polity but also the inextricable connections in the American context between two discursive realms that retrospectively, from the perspective of the advent of American Romanticism in the nineteenth century, have come to look distinct—namely, the political and the literary. I wish to extrapolate from this recent U.S. Supreme Court sampling case a mode of reading useful not only in demonstrating the alignments between the political and the rhetorical as these persist into the twentieth and now twenty-first century, but particularly for situating the centrally important relationship between Emerson and Whitman within the context of the broad historical conversation about representation that their writings both implicitly and explicitly engage. In contradistinction to important studies derived from F. O. Matthiessen's *American Renaissance: Art and Expression in the Age of Emerson and Whitman* (1941) that separate the eighteenth century's Revolution from the nineteenth century's Renaissance, this book posits a specifically American version of the "long eighteenth century" by chronicling the ongoing political and literary repercussions of the debates over representation that catalyzed the Revolution and that continued to swirl at the time of the Constitution. The book demonstrates the extent to which Emerson and Whitman inherited different dimensions of these debates over representation, even as they treated as significant different aspects of the multiple meanings of the Revolution and its complex and sometimes contradictory legacies. This project, which began as an examination of Whitman, and then of Whitman and Emerson, has expanded into one in which a wider historical scope tracing continuities and discontinuities back to the Founding has seemed to offer the greatest promise for new insights about Emerson and Whitman as well as fresh understandings about the American literary history in which they play such central roles. Thus the book seeks to specify the scope of these similarities and differences in the service of a new understanding of this crucial nineteenth-century (non)pair.

Through-Lines

If starting with the debates over Constitutional ratification nevertheless seems somewhat arbitrary, it may be in part because the discursive traditions this book both depends on and traces are manifold, having multiple antecedents arising from a variety of cultural sites and rhetorical and political traditions. To take an obvious example: the notion of "the people" on which the Constitution depends as both its authorizing voice ("We the people") and as the referent for its "actual enumeration" has a history that stretches back at least to the seventeenth century, as Edmund Morgan has shown. As a consequence this study follows the methodological principles laid out by J. G. A. Pocock in *The Machiavellian Moment*, "identifying certain conceptual vocabularies" and "examining the process by which these conceptual systems, their uses and implications, changed over time" (57). Alternately placing the polyvalent concept of representation in its political and literary dimensions at the center of its analyses, *Reconstituting the American Renaissance* offers a genealogical account for the plight and fortunes of what chapter 1 calls "the representational arts" in the first seventy-five years of the republic.

Starting with the Constitutional debates is in this particular instance both salutary and instructive. For one thing, the selection of these debates for thinking through, among other things, the peculiarities of Emerson's and Whitman's Romanticism/transcendentalism has the advantage of specifying the discursive contexts out of which the period known as the Renaissance emerges. This is in opposition to the standard model derived from Matthiessen in which the abundance of the Renaissance springs, Athena-like, out of the head of an Emerson-

Zeus ("the cow from which the rest drew their milk," as Matthiessen so memorably put it [AR xii]). Thus *Reconstituting* intervenes in the standard periodization that has governed our readings of American literary history at least since Matthiessen—dividing Revolution from Renaissance—by looking backward to the nation's founding for a renewed understanding of the intersections between the political and the literary, especially as these evince consequences for the Romantic writing produced out of such complexly interwoven discursive terrain. It reads Emerson and Whitman anew within discursive milieus structured by the concept of "representation" in its multiple senses, only partially stabilized in the complex disagreements of the Founders, reenergized (and so newly destabilized) by the election of Jefferson in 1800, and complicated yet again by Andrew Jackson's "common man" rise following his stunning military victory against the British at New Orleans in 1815.

Part of the work *Reconstituting the American Renaissance* performs in complicating our understanding of these originary relations between the political and the literary also complicates our sense of the act of "constituting" on which so much depends. For instance, it is not at all clear that the kind of institutional and interpretive supremacy invoked today with reference to the written Constitution was the presumptive case at the time of its production and ratification. Rather, as Guyora Binder and Robert Weisberg demonstrate, "eighteenth-century ideas about constitutional interpretation were even less formed [than those concerning contracts], because written constitutions were novel and stood in uncertain relationship to the customary model of law that shaped legal method."

> On the one hand, custom was clearly a source of fundamental law that could authorize not only judicial review of, but also popular resistance to, legislation. On the other hand, the eighteenth century witnessed a movement throughout Europe to codify custom. Hence, the mounting enthusiasm for written constitutions may be seen as part of an impulse to codify rather than repudiate custom, and thus it was not clear whether the new written constitutions were to be construed against a background of customary norms or as substitutes for custom, exhausting its authority. (37–38)

Among its other effects, this insight into the contingencies of the Constitution's production makes apparent that even that document's status as a national "new

beginning" is complicated, for its own relation to previous traditions was precisely what was at stake in securing an interpretive paradigm for it. Not only is
the question of political representation not settled with ratification but the
status of the document supposedly settling the status of representation is, from
the start, unsettled. Thus the Bill of Rights announces not simply the virtuality
of the Constitution's interpretive essence—perpetually subject to interpretation
and amendment (that is, to an always proximate supplementarity), as Seitz
argues.[4] But also, as if to codify the Constitution's uneasy relation to past
interpretive models and circumstances, the Tenth Amendment secures unspecified rights "to the States respectively, or to the people," a final addition ratified
in 1791 that echoes nothing so much as the second Article of Confederation—
the very document the Constitution had been designed to supplant.[5] Clearly,
finding a beginning within this history opens out a pattern of potentially
infinite regress.[6]

The very status of what it meant to "constitute," Binder and Weisberg suggest, was initially uncertain, especially with regard to the relation of the new
written text to previous modes of both oral and written governance, codifica-
tion, and legality. If constitutionality as a concept and the supremacy of the
federal are categories more or less taken for granted today, though still contested in relation to particular legislative initiatives, Binder and Weisberg's
formulation recalls an original foundational fluidity (if such a useful oxymoron
will be permitted). This book seeks to unravel further and to reread this lack of
absolute legibility; "constituting" is in this book as much a matter of uncertainty as of clarity, as much of circulation as of reification. Like the declaring by
a previous assembly of Philadelphia delegates, "constituting" always carries
within itself a highly polemical, situational charge. The debate over the Constitution and then its ratification put more issues, and more aspects of these
issues, into circulation than simply the text of the Constitution and those of the
"winning" Federalist side; moreover, the passage of the Bill of Rights called into
question almost immediately the finality of just what the Constitution had
constituted in the first place. Ratification thus marks a way station of temporary
resolution within a much broader terrain of contestation. There is a hint of
this even before Marshall enunciated the Court's right of supreme interpretation, when "the people" like Daniel Shays and his supporters in western Massachusetts fought against what they feared was a dangerously oligarchic translation of revolutionary fervor into an imminent, and too settled, settlement.[7]

Likewise, years later, near Harpers Ferry, John Brown attempted with biblical sanction to resolve once and for all the irreconcilable contradictions he saw at the heart of the originary national covenant.

Crossings

The contests over what the Revolution had wrought and what precisely the Constitution had resolved were persistent; into this tradition in which the status, claims, and validity of the American system of representative governance are never more than temporarily resolved, and amidst the persistent controversies over representation in its manifold political and literary connotations, *Reconstituting the American Renaissance* places writings by Emerson and Whitman in order to generate a new understanding of the nineteenth century's relation to the eighteenth. The choice of Emerson and Whitman as representatives for the Renaissance requires some comment. Shaped by the material practices of their distinctly different cultural and educational "foregrounds," Emerson and Whitman came into the period of their greatest productivity with different conceptions of the functions and political efficacy of the word in the world. *Reconstituting* ranges widely across their writings in order to examine the ways in which not simply their lectures or publications but also the forms in which these writings or orations originally circulated, and the audiences to whom they were originally presented, provide sites and particularities in and through which to discover the elusive traces and wholesale recurrences—textual, political, performative, and cultural—of the nation's Founding dilemmas.

Certainly one could look elsewhere and to other relations to find similarly persistent traces. Orestes Brownson, in his critique of what he reads as a call for an elite intellectual class in Emerson's Dartmouth Oration of July 1838, relies on a rhetoric about representation at least as old as the Sons of Liberty:

> He who disdains the people shall find the people scorning to be his audience. . . . He may prophesy, but it shall be in an unknown tongue; he may sing, but he shall catch no echo to his song; he may reason, but he shall find his arguments producing no conviction. This is the inflexible decree of God. We can make the people listen to us only so far as we are one of them. When God sent us a Redeemer, he did not make him of the seed of angels, but of the seed of Abraham. He gave him a human nature . . . in like manner as those he was to redeem . . . so that he might

be touched with a sense of human infirmities. . . . So he who would move the people, influence them for good or for evil, must have like passions with them; feel as they feel; crave what they crave; and resolve what they resolve. He must be their representative, their impersonation. (21)

Brownson relies in his critique of Emerson here on an unreconstructed notion of the representative as mirror and as "impersonation" under the banner of which the Revolution had presumably been waged. I say "unreconstructed" because, as chapter 1 explores in detail, the Constitution makes a virtue out of the very representative virtuality that the colonists had decried as British parliamentary tyranny. It installs a system of representative filtration in which the very mathematics of representation (the ratio of citizens to House members, for example) assume that "the people" and their genuine interests will be better served precisely to the extent that their representatives in Congress do *not* simply represent or "impersonate" "the people" themselves. There is, then, in Brownson's critique, a kind of time lag, the "literary" following slowly behind in the footsteps of the "political." Brownson engages Emerson in a "literary" context—a periodical review of his published oration—on the status of the representative that has purportedly already been "decided" in the political realm. In so doing, this book argues, he provides additional evidence about the ways in which, in the United States, and from the first, the "literary" and the "political" have been repeatedly defined, in classic binary fashion, only in the (incoherent) terms each can provide for the other.

For certainly there is a politics to Brownson's marshaling the "inflexible decree of God" in order to naturalize his insistence on a "vox populi, vox Dei" worldview, even as there is an explicit politics to Emerson's initial salvo:

Now that we are here, we will put our own interpretation on things, and our own things for interpretation. Please himself with complaisance who will,—for me, things must take my scale, not I theirs. I will say with the warlike king, "God gave me this crown, and the whole world shall not take it away." (*LAE* 97)

How shall we understand Emerson's insistence on the monarchical? What is the place of this rhetoric and its emphasis on the rule of the singularly powerful within the republican rules the Constitution established, or the democratic system toward which at least some revolutionaries of 1776 had aspired? What, finally, does this rhetoric owe to its origins in eighteenth-century political debate, and how should its persistence be reckoned? Constitution or no constitution, this is the play of the literary and the political on which this book depends.

Reading Whitman's polemic on "The Eighteenth Presidency!" (c. 1856) likewise demonstrates some of what becomes available by reconsidering nineteenth-century texts in relation to these founding, eighteenth-century frames. This essay, which may be notes for a lecture it seems Whitman never delivered, formally reiterates a link between orality and print that the ratification debates so clearly exemplify. "Circulate and reprint this Voice of mine for the workingmen's sake," the essay commands, walking a line between the anonymity of print, which Michael Warner has so carefully analyzed as a necessary element in the production of a nationalized public sphere, and an older, more intimate connection between speaker and listener of the kind Whitman's poetry constantly, and often erotically, explores.[8]

Whitman's polemic also pronounces the ambiguous status of the figure of the representative, what Whitman characterized in another context as "both in and out of the game":

> From my mouth hear the will of These States taking form in the great cities. . . . I am not afraid to say that among them [the "millions of mechanics"] I seek to initiate my name, Walt Whitman, and that I shall in future have much to say to them. I perceive that the best thoughts they have wait unspoken, impatient to be put in shape. . . . (LAW 1323)

Blurring the line between speaking *for* and speaking *with*, this passage also alternates the interpretive emphasis between, on the one hand, the initiation of the singular name, and, on the other, the collective "among" that echoes a similar, and similarly alternating, declaration in "Song of Myself": "I troop forth replenished with supreme power, one of an average unending procession" (1855 LG 43). Thus these lines demonstrate in part the central unresolved feature of American representative praxis and the virtuality at/as its core, what Edmund Morgan calls "the ultimate fictitiousness of popular sovereignty," the simple truth that "governors and governed cannot be in fact identical" (*Inventing* 282). Whitman here also contests the sovereignty of the federal nation itself, invoking the older notion of confederation by naming as his subject-addressees the citizen-mechanics of "The States"; in this way he prefigures what will happen after Lincoln's election in 1860, when Southerners secede under the banner of states' rights, refusing once and for all the national model of consolidation that Lincoln's War for Union will be fought to uphold.

To the extent that that war was also fought over the extension of race slavery, the 1999 sampling case also remains a salient example of earlier disputes recurring with uncanny persistence. This is especially true to the extent that twentieth-century notions of vote "dilution" as invoked by the Indiana appellees emerge most starkly in the histories that precede the passage of the 1964 Voting Rights Act. This is a way of saying that the demands for direct representation first raised by would-be American revolutionaries two hundred years ago are not simply the quaint reminders of American democracy's "growing pains" in a distant era. Instead the sampling case's invocation of vote dilution itself calls up a whole history of abuses pertaining to the political status, rights, and citizenship of African Americans in the United States, whose situation, beginning with their voteless and heavily-diluted three-fifths status in the Constitution's "actual Enumeration," reminds us how resistant to final resolution these dilemmas have continued to be.[9] Chapter 4 shows in part how the struggle to incorporate the fact of enslaved bodies into a coherent American ideology functions as a limit-case for the transcendental claims Emerson and Whitman articulate during the years of Matthiessen's Renaissance. Thus the fundamental questions at the heart of this project: what is the nature of political representation? Who shall speak, and for whom?

The Return of the Virtual

Even resonant questions such as these, however, require careful treatment, lest a genealogical inquiry such as this turn into what Catherine Belsey has called "history as costume drama" (*Subject* 2), which eradicates precisely the changes over time that genealogy is designed to highlight. The last question raised above offers a case in point. If the Revolution, at least initially, reverberated to the sounds of a no-taxation-without-representation war-cry against the British Parliament's claims of "virtual representation," there is little doubt that the winning gentlemen-revolutionaries knew both who would do the speaking/representing, and for whom, once independence had been achieved. The newly united states were to have a federal government of the best men, men of standing who would be able from their positions of economic independence to offer the disinterested leadership required to speak the people's best interests. Insofar as this was the case, these newly "free" gentlemen-Americans aligned themselves with Tory apologists like Peter Oliver, who lashed out against what he so piquantly called "daemonocracy" in his 1781 *Origin and Progress of the American Rebellion*. Neither Oliver nor the men of Philadelphia, with at most a few exceptions, would tolerate the rule of the many, which they imagined as the direct representation of the people's too-often moblike or demagogue-directed "interests." To remind ourselves of this widely held and literally demonized status of democracy restores to our understanding the place of the "virtual" as it functioned in the ratification debates.

These central issues were usefully raised by an opponent of the Census Bureau's use of statistical sampling during an interview broadcast on National Public Radio:

> Under the current plan [i.e., with sampling] . . . the Census Bureau . . . will count ninety percent of the population. They will guess at ten percent of the population. That means that they will create twenty-seven million mythical people. They will determine what those twenty-seven million people look like, and they will determine where those twenty-seven mil- lion people live. The moment we start apportioning Congress based on mythical people, we no longer are a representative democracy, but we become a virtual democracy, and that's exactly what the Founding Fa- thers were trying to avoid.[10]

One might have a number of responses to these remarks, and not the least of these might be simply to declare them false. As chapter 1 demonstrates, among the majority of the Framers, a "virtual democracy" was precisely what many of them sought. A "direct" democracy—a "representative democracy," in this commentator's words—was anathema. For every *pre*-revolutionary writer like "A Gentleman in Connecticut," arguing in his 1766 published "Letter . . . To His Friend in London" that "the very terms *representative* and *represented*, suppose likeness between one and the other. To have a country represented by something not like it, must be a wrong representation . . ." (Devotion 17), one can find a *post*-revolutionary Federalist Founder, like Fisher Ames of Mas- sachusetts, insisting that even while

> much has been said about the people divesting themselves of power . . . , and that all representation is to their disadvantage, because it is but an image, a copy; fainter and more imperfect than the original, the peo- ple[,] . . . it will not be denied that the people are gainers by the election

of representatives . . . [,] [the people] become the true sovereigns of the country when they delegate that power, which they cannot use themselves to their trustees.[11]

The evidence for this perspective among those who will come to be called Founders seems overwhelming, though this book is also interested in restoring Anti-Federalist dissenters to their rightful place as founders of a complexly oppositional strand in republican thinking likewise bequeathed to the nineteenth century, and to figures like Whitman—by way of Jefferson, Paine, and Jackson—in particular.

For Philadelphia convention delegates following the lead of Madison and Hamilton, the virtual against which the revolutionary armies had fought comes to stand not for an aberration but for the foundational premise of the endorsed representative system, as Publius makes clear in his famous *Federalist* No. 10, an essay that appears in innumerable American literature anthologies, not only as the sole representative of Publius's complex thinking on the period's resonant debate over federalism but as the single text standing in for the whole of the contentious debate over representation and ratification itself. This is the debate that this book seeks to restore as an origin for its interpretation of antebellum American writing. To the extent that the beliefs of the mass of citizens are, under the Philadelphia plan, to be filtered through the "best men," it may well become an irrelevance just what is the relation between virtual representation and the "mythical" citizens the NPR commentator so abjures: for in this system they represent two sides of the same coin. Looked at one way, vote dilution—which might be defined as the making virtual of the votes of the people through some process of representative filtration—was precisely the goal of Federalist constitutional framers.[12] The manner of dilution took many forms, as Anti-Federalists like the Pennsylvania Minority insisted; some of their most strident objections specified the high number of constituents represented by each member of the House;[13] the small number of citizens elected as special delegates to the Pennsylvania ratifying convention;[14] and the election of the federal Senate by the state legislatures rather than by general election, a situation eventually altered with the passage of the Seventeenth Amendment in 1913. Any uncertainty about the legitimacy of this book's claim for reading Renaissance writings as evidence of a specifically American version of the "long eighteenth century" might be subsumed by another, more principal one: just how long might that eighteenth century legitimately be said to extend? *Commerce v. U.S.*

House and its invocation of vote dilution and virtuality suggest that it might be very long indeed.

Matthiessen's concept of a Renaissance and the canon he included in it have come under increasing scrutiny in recent years, and this book works broadly within the tradition of these revisions. Its genealogical reading reconsiders the rebirth Matthiessen located in American letters in the half-decade starting in 1850, finding in the period's engagement with the swirling issues surrounding representation a renewed and intense engagement in a discussion as old as the republic itself. Indeed, one can take the quest for rebirth—as seen in Emerson's stand against the "sepulchres of the fathers" or in Whitman's insistence that "there was never any more inception than there is now"—as the surest signal of a deeply felt cultural urgency to settle the relation to a past revolutionary age that seemed uneasily to burden the present moment in ways that would not or could not be shaken away. As Russ Castronovo notes, "ambivalence toward national genealogy" is one of the defining features of pre–Civil War U.S. culture (*Fathering* 4).[15] Within this frame Matthiessen's construction of the Renaissance might be imagined as a kind of writing out of these discourses of the political—as Eric Cheyfitz and Jonathan Arac have separately noted—and so a completion of the task Emerson set for himself in staging an imminent and "original relation to the universe" instead of what he found himself contending against: a relation that was always already and everywhere riven with the inherited tensions of his parents' generation.[16] To see Emerson in these terms becomes particularly pertinent, as the opening of chapter 3 demonstrates, when one examines the manuscript books, borrowed from his father, in which some of his earliest writings occur.

Moreover, this book also builds on the revisionist work that has contested as patently undemocratic Matthiessen's canon even as a representative sampling of the works of antebellum white men, many of whom exhibited palpable ambivalence about the "democratic" emergence with which their writings are said to coincide. Emerson and Whitman, for example, professed diametrically opposed views about the future of the nation and the institution of letters at the prospect of any Jacksonian "leveling."[17] Still, arguments such as these have in general not carried sufficient force to shake apart the synthesis Matthiessen represents, now for a third generation of college syllabi, students, and critical specializations: the notion of a distinct, and distinctly American, "literary" emergence in the nineteenth century, an emergence virtually simultaneous with the political consummation of what is now said to be the latent democratic promise of the Founders. Looked at one way, *Reconstituting* tells what happens to this standard story, and to two of its central authors, by imagining that such a democratic promise has been from the start, at best, contingent, and intimately tied to the political languages within which such possibilities have been imagined and described. To see the shifts toward democratic, and away from merely republican, systems of self-representation as a development largely unforeseen by the Founders places us in a position to acknowledge and to investigate the *residues* rather than (only) the disjunctions between Revolutionary and Renaissance texts, and so to reconstruct a genealogy for the discursive or generic discriminations that constitute American Romanticism in general and the writings of Emerson and Whitman in particular.

For example, that the categories of the "literary" and of "Literature" signify a much broader and interdisciplinary realm of written knowledge in the eighteenth century necessarily influences the stories we tell our students, and ourselves, about American literary history—if utilizing that final, catch-all phrase is not already to beg the question.[18] What is the history (instead) of verbal representation in America, and what is the literary history of the American version of political self-representation? For this project it is not simply the case that Matthiessen's sampling, as numerous commentators have stressed,[19] is unrepresentative in relation to the vast scope of antebellum American writing; it is rather that these writings are themselves engaged with, and contesting the very nature of, representation and the representative.[20] *Reconstituting* argues that, though heretofore largely unremarked, writings by Emerson and Whitman differently but consequentially extend and adapt eighteenth-century strategies and concerns; their writings resonate anew with echoes that have their origins in facets of the Constitutional settlement that have never wholly ceased reverberating through American literary history and American historical literatures. To the extent that we have come to recognize a familiar nineteenth century directly through the writings of Matthiessen, we have yet fully to apprehend the extent to which "Art and Expression in the Age of Emerson and Whitman" (the subtitle of *American Renaissance*) and what he calls in the preface "the possibilities of democracy" must be seen as the virtual equivalences they truly represent.[21]

Discipline and Publish

Reconstituting the American Renaissance proceeds for the most part chronologically, culminating in the last chapter with an analysis of texts by Emerson and

Whitman associated with the formal period of the Renaissance. But the book's major structuring device as well as its underlying logic is cumulative; subsequent chapters return to works previously discussed in order more fully to flesh out newly relevant dimensions. Chapter 1, "The Rise of the Representational Arts in the United States," opens by analyzing the rhetorics of constituting—the languages both advocates and opponents of the Constitution utilized while debating the possibility of replacing the Articles of Confederation with the revised plan that emerged out of the Philadelphia convention in 1787. There was, of course, a great deal of contention and disagreement that marked these debates: disputes about which social group or interest was likely to benefit most substantially from the formation of a newly "consolidated" government; about whether the responsibilities of the three branches of power were adequately partitioned; about whether the arithmetics of representation deployed in the composition of the House were sufficient to the scope of the nation's expanding population; about how the "enumeration" of Africans held in bondage should be conducted and what function this population should play in the allocation of congressional seats; and perhaps most significantly, about whether this latest attempt in North America could outlast (or outsmart) history's seeming resistance to republics.

But as compelling as the specific details of these disagreements may be—and there will be a great deal more to say about them—this chapter is primarily interested in the conceptual terms and the material forms within which the arguments for and against the Constitution were argued, reproduced, and disseminated. For whatever their substantive disagreements, the writings of Federalists and Anti-Federalists alike shuttle back and forth between two interrelated aspects of the period's obsession with the question of representation. Letters, broadsides, pseudonymous pamphlets, and even the period's best-known contribution to political theory, *The Federalist*, while ostensibly grounded in the raging debates over *political* representation that instigate the revolutionary break from Parliament, repeatedly intersect with arguments about the representative capacities of language, including the validity—and on occasion, even the very possibility—of its claims to mimetic verisimilitude. Thus these eighteenth-century "political" writings *share* with what have been seen as their more resolutely "literary" cousins a persistent attention to their own legitimacy. (And this attention itself occurs in a context in which the status of the "literary," as noted above, is itself in transition.) One can see these issues at stake when Thomas Paine vilifies in *Common Sense* (1776) "the artful and hypocritical letter which appeared a few months ago in two of the New York papers": his scalding pairing of "art" with "hypocrisy" is effectively redoubled in the word "letter," which points not simply to the epistolary but also to a broader, anxiogenic instability about the referential security of the alphabet itself (107).

Cathy Davidson and Michael Gilmore have independently noted the insecurity eighteenth-century fiction registers about its generic integrity and its discursive legitimacy, and this book's opening chapter examines the degree to which such anxiety recurs in the "political" texts of the era; Gilmore's description of eighteenth-century novelists applies equally to innumerable eighteenth-century pamphleteers, political commentators, and Publius: "uncomfortable with the very fictionality of fiction, . . . novelists called their tales histories and retold narratives whose outlines were widely known from documentary sources. . . . Although authorial protests of factual accuracy reflected the scientific disposition of the age, they also conveyed mistrust of imaginative license" ("Literature" 622–23). Not simply novels but a range of texts we have learned from our post-Romantic perspective to label "political" (in contradistinction to a realm, following Paine, of "letters") share what William Hedges has described as an "acute self-consciousness [that] may come as close to being the essential distinguishing characteristic of American literature as any other one commonly attributed to it" ("Myth" 111).[22] This formulation suggests something of what is gained by rereading Emerson and Whitman through the lens of eighteenth-century textual practices, but also what is gained by rereading the ratification debates with an eye toward Emerson and Whitman.

In the first chapter of his indispensable *Original Meanings: Politics and Ideas in the Making of the Constitution*, Jack Rakove writes about the difficulties inherent in narrating the Constitutional Convention. "In practice," he writes,

> (it is argued) there can be no single story of any event—least of all, so complex an event as the adoption of the Constitution. Moreover, the composition of any narrative history requires decisions as to perspective and dramatic structure that differ little from the imaginative contrivances of the novelist.
>
> Even if a historian confident in his empiricism can dismiss such radical doubts as the mischievous intrusion of overly refined literary theories, the problem of perspective remains crucial. . . . (6)

Reconstituting the American Renaissance interprets the pervasive self-consciousness that Hedges finds in American writings, and that suffuses the writings on the Constitution, as a characteristic that itself crosses the line between the "empirical" and the "literary." It is not the "literary theorist" but over and again Publius the historian and statesman who employs "the imaginative contrivances of the novelist." Likewise, the texts debating ratification and the political questions concerning governance over and again reveal "the mischievous intrusion" of questions about "the problem of perspective." These "literary" concerns show themselves to be central elements of the debates over ratification, which is to say that "empiricism" will not, for the purposes of the present book's analyses, eliminate ambiguity. *Reconstituting* finds in the writings of Constitutional ratification what looks from a later period—that of Emerson and Whitman, and beyond—like literary "self-consciousness." Likewise it finds in texts by Emerson and Whitman recurring vocabularies of the political, such that the distinctions between the literary and the "empirical" that govern Rakove's method in his remarkable book seem not, for our present purposes, to hold.

Rakove throws up his hands in a passage shortly after the one just quoted in which he notes the difficulties inherent in "divining the true intentions or understandings of the roughly two thousand actors who served in the various conventions that framed and ratified the Constitution, much less the larger electorate that they claimed to represent" (6). In *Reconstituting*, the difficulties in "divining intentions" are shown to be complicated enough when only "single" "authors" are considered, like Publius in *The Federalist*, whose writings on the Constitution demonstrate a "mischievous intrusion" of polyvocality and multiple perspectives within themselves—even, that is, before one might, as I will not do here, attempt to parse out the contributions by Madison, Hamilton, and Jay. This is a polyvocality that comes to look like an essential feature of these texts and these voices—so much so that generic distinctions between the "political" and the "literary" collapse. Likewise this book examines the insistently political discourses that inform Emerson's and Whitman's writings—not just the content of what they are discussing, but the relations to their readers that their texts encode, and that necessarily position these works within the debates about the role of "representative men" in the eighteenth- and nineteenth-century United States. Who, we shall see, is more self-conscious about writing non-self-consciously than Publius himself?

Noting how writing of whatever genre in this period inscribes a pervasive ambivalence about its own utility and claims to validity also shifts the standard account of American literary history, often figured as an awakening toward enlightened Renaissance from out of what sometimes seems a benighted "Middle Ages." In opposition to this model, *Reconstituting* asks in what ways the Renaissance rejects the rhetorical traditions and paradigms it inherits from the revolutionary and early national periods, but also in what ways it recapitulates or extends the earlier period's queries, methodologies, and "representative" arguments. Thus this book builds on and diverges from the work of other scholars who have considered the relations between the literary and the political in the period between the Revolution and the Civil War. Many of these scholarly works demonstrate the pervasiveness of the model that persists in splitting off antebellum writing from the texts of the early national period that precede it, which I read in this context as another measure of the profound, and in some sense unexamined, influence of Matthiessen's model of a separable five years at midcentury about which, as he wrote, "you might search all the rest of American literature without being able to collect a group of books equal to these in imaginative vitality" (AR vii). Despite, or perhaps because of, its vagueness, this criterion of "imaginative vitality" has proved remarkably resilient and has for some critics come to seem a category in need of defense.

Thus David Simpson, in *The Politics of American English, 1776–1850*, writes of "two American literatures" with the Renaissance as the dividing line, and fears "demean[ing] . . . as less original" figures like Emerson by reading them in relation to texts produced pre-Renaissance (8). And in what seems a related kind of reflex gesture, Mark R. Patterson divides *Authority, Autonomy, and Representation in American Literature, 1776–1865* into two distinct sections—"The Post-Revolutionary Period" and "The Antebellum Period"—although he seeks in each section to analyze the relation of a number of authors' works to the controversies surrounding the "democratization of American society" (xi). With critics attempting to maintain Matthiessen's period designation against the grain of their own methodologies, it may well be time to ask: what can be gained by undoing this distinction, by reading instead across the century divide and so dismantling the fortress around the Renaissance that has been in place for more than a half-century?[23] Clearly the various answers carry political, literary, and canonical ramifications—ramifications that are, in a word, found repeatedly in this book to revolve around issues of "representation" and the "representative." When Michael Kramer in his important book *Imagining Language in America* seeks to "elaborate further upon the intellectual underpinnings of the political situation that faced the generation of Adams and Jefferson and suggest the imaginative consequences of the fact that so much political significance was placed upon the use of language" (120), this book investigates how the "political" and the "literary" are inter-implicated in this passage and the larger epistemic systems it figures. *Reconstituting* revisits the relation Matthiessen positioned as the subtitle of *American Renaissance: Art and Expression in the Age of Emerson and Whitman* by building on suggestions like Robert Ferguson's that "the American Renaissance assimilated early republican thought and language even as it qualified traditional usage" (*Law* 204).[24] This study expands in a more radical direction Ferguson's sense of "assimilation" and "qualification," demonstrating the persistence, recirculation, and rearticulation of early rhetorics in ways not always intended or seen by their writers. If it has become a critical truism that all discourses may be political, the Constitutional debates reflect a simultaneous and foundational engagement with the corresponding discourses of mimesis, in all its many forms, which extends into the nineteenth century.

A comment is due on the absence from these pages of what might appear a necessary text: Emerson's *Representative Men* of 1850. Because this study is interested in finding the ways in which discourses of representation inform writings by these two central authors even, or especially, in those texts in which such discourses would not seem to be either necessary or expected, I have focused on some of the most familiar, most anthologized essays in the Emerson canon—"The Poet," "Self-Reliance," "Experience," *Nature*—texts at the very center and so particularly valuable sites for contesting traditional interpretations, and for recovering an irreducible historicity.

There is another reason why I have omitted *Representative Men* from these pages, one suggested by Mark Patterson when he reminds us that "given [Emerson's] conception of the representative as an agent of the constituent self, Emerson's autobiographical gesture should remind us that all representation is self-representation. . . . As a consequence, *Representative Men* can profitably be read as an intellectual autobiography, in which Emerson traces the growth of his own mind" ("Napoleon" 240). I find this an extremely convincing account of what is at stake, *for Emerson*, in the lectures subsequently printed as *Representative Men*. But *Reconstituting the American Renaissance* has a more fluid sense of the representative, along with a more pervasive uncertainty about the parameters between self and other, and between self and society: thus this book's methodological invocation of Althusser's interpellation. I have been interested in these pages in complicating our understanding of what evidence has in traditional interpretations tended to "count" in our projections about the "growth" of Emerson's, or Whitman's, "own mind." As a consequence this book looks beyond the narratives of "great men" to find networks of cultural and material practices within which subjectivity is forged, dialectically, relationally, but no less concretely and with important consequences for how we tell stories regarding "representative" American literature.

The Persistence of Representation

Chapter 1 isolates two sets of related issues that connect revolutionary and early national texts to those of the Renaissance. Texts debating Constitutional ratification evince a particularly vexed relation to the linked concerns of precedence, authority, and the status of the New. At the same time they demonstrate that the status and validity of art and the artful are complexly implicated in the broader crises of representation initiated with the Revolution. To demonstrate how these various concerns reappear in Renaissance texts, Emerson's famous line from *Nature* striving for "an original relation to the universe" can be examined as an example of what can be achieved by the genealogical readings this book makes available. Newness has long been heard as a resonant tone in Romanticism's clarion call, but even so familiar a line as Emerson's exposes some of the complications surrounding these issues that derive in part from the Constitutional settlement.

In the first place, Emerson pleads in this famous line not simply for "direct" representation, but for an entirely unmediated relation to Nature's world and work—an opting out of the system of representation entirely. This quest for an absolute mimesis recalls an older Puritan/Protestant wish to escape, at last, and finally, mediation of all kinds. But it also has roots in the early national period's distrust of the artful and the struggle over the very plausibility of verbal representation that arises from within a context in which mimesis and the British claims of proper or effective virtual representation no longer appear to be opposites, but seem rather (deconstructively) allied and aligned, even versions of each other. As Larzer Ziff has noted, "Even the stoutest patriotic opponents of the argument that the American colonists were virtually represented by Parliament came, after the Revolution, to see that the notion of literal representation—of the body of representatives being a replication of the body of the people—was a greater fiction than that of virtual representation" (*Writing* 106).

Such a summary of the political understanding some revolutionaries had reached by the time of the Constitution is duplicated in Publius's excursus on language's inherent limitations in *Federalist* No. 37:

> Hence it must happen that however accurately objects may be discrimi-nated in themselves, and however accurately the discrimination may be considered, the definition of them may be rendered inaccurate by the inaccuracy of the terms in which it is delivered. . . . When the Almighty himself condescends to address mankind in their own language, his meaning, luminous as it must be, is rendered dim and doubtful by the cloudy medium through which it is communicated. (37: 245)

Publius offers this divine analogy in the service of his defense of the Con-stitution, asking his opponents to take the Philadelphia document and its ambiguities on faith. As Kramer says, "Madison inverted—or retooled—the Commonsense critique of language, in which ambiguity disguises design and dissimulation. Here, ambiguity gives way to good intentions" (*Imagining* 134). Many of Publius's Anti-Federalist counterparts imagined ambiguity in much less sanguine ways. Such skeptical accounts of ambiguity—like the demand for a Bill of Rights to spell out what was left ambiguous—reach forward toward "Romantic" artists at midcentury like Hawthorne or Melville, Poe or Dickin-son, whose writings repeatedly stage encounters with ambiguity: Hester's A, the whiteness of the whale, "It's easy as a Sign." Likewise for Emerson in the open-ing pages of *Nature*, the idea of an "original relation" that denies the authority of past accounts while constructing a relation without room for uncertainty recapitulates in the nineteenth century what Jay Fliegelman describes as the late eighteenth century's desire to close the "problematic gulf between intention and statement" (Introduction xxxi), between words and things.

   Emerson's call for a system of representation that would escape the limita-tions of (mere) representation does not, however, escape the politics of repre-sentation—a situation that comes into focus when we inquire on whose behalf Emerson calls for this "original relation"?

> Our age is retrospective. It builds the sepulchres of the fathers. It writes biographies, histories, and criticism. The foregoing generations beheld God and nature face to face; we, through their eyes. Why should not we also enjoy an original relation to the universe?[25]

This passage permits certain modes of mediation while refusing others. The "original," unmediated relation to the universe that the speaker seeks exists alongside a fully mystified relation to the work of both building and writing. Labor is in the passage pasted over: we do not know who is doing the writing of what we are to see as mediated, and so merely derivative, criticism and biographies, nor who does the building of the sepulchres to house this worship of the dead; the subject-actor of these actions is, grammatically speaking, "the age." Emerson's larger epistemology provides one explanation for this peculiar relation to agency, for these obscured agents reflect the notion in "The Poet" of writing as finely tuned aural transcription.[26] Likewise, Emerson's model of transcription recalls, as Christopher Newfield has demonstrated, and as chapter 3 discusses in detail, the highly compromised nature of agency across Emerson's classic essays.

Raymond Williams traces some of this obscurantism around agency to Romanticism's determined efforts to constitute a new mode of artistic production untouched by the determinism of the market or of industrialized, mechanized work.[27] Emerson's rhetoric works here by disallowing agent status for these builders and writers and ascribing to "our age" what it also implicitly reserves for his new Poet-Man. Here the implied addressees of Emerson's *Nature* enter the equation: who is this "we" who "should . . . enjoy an original relation to the universe"? Published anonymously in its first edition in 1836, Emerson's *Nature* presumes a gentlemanly coterie of readers, the "we" to whom its speaker also most assuredly belongs. *Nature*'s foregrounded "we" thus carries some of the same tensions that so vexed some of the first readers of the Constitution, as Patrick Henry made explicit when he asked "who authorised [the delegates at the Constitutional Convention] to speak the language, of *We, the People . . .*?" (*F/A* 116). Who or what authorizes Emerson in *Nature*, and on whose behalf? Whom does this vague but inclusive pronoun include or represent? The same can of course be asked of Whitman. How these two writers manage these claims and their discontents has a great deal to tell us about the continuities across a century of American political and literary history and writing. Thus chapter 1's concentration on the rhetorics of "constituting" prepares the ground for reading Emerson and Whitman anew within a context defined by the interrelated concerns of delegation, authorized speech, and the manifold issues of representation.

Chapter 2 rereads the paper trail of letters, anecdotes, and reviews that underwrites the standard account of the Emerson/Whitman relationship in the terms master/disciple by reframing their relation under the rubric of the "long eighteenth century." Even as *Reconstituting* deploys in its first chapter the debates over ratification as a starting place for reconsidering the Renaissance and its two central authors, "Rereading Emerson/Whitman" purposefully pluralizes the notion of origins, in contradistinction to a literary-historical tradition that persists in locating Emerson as the singular, dominant model and precursor for understanding Whitman's poetic emergence.

Indeed, in introducing the contentious issue of origins regarding Whitman's poetic practice, one might note how contentious has become the choice of a word to describe the publication of the first edition of *Leaves of Grass* in July 1855. Does the book's publication represent Whitman's "emergence"? (From what?) Does the poet Whitman materialize "like a shape from the depths," as Malcolm Cowley put it? *Reconstituting the American Renaissance* argues that the critical consensus on Emerson/Whitman offers largely differences without distinctions, a set of models fundamentally infused with Emerson as the ghost-in-the-machine, driving Whitman toward an Emersonian mode of transcendentalist poetics; even in the mystery, out-of-nowhere model, Cowley presents Emerson as "the man best qualified to understand what the new poet was saying" (Introduction viii).

In its attempt to reimagine how to manage questions of influence both within and beyond the canon, *Reconstituting the American Renaissance* pleads agnostic on the question of Whitman's intentions toward Emerson, and attempts to replace the standard model of Whitman's indebtedness to Emerson as origin by investigating this central relation within the broader frames of the macropolitical discourses and materialist practices put into play in chapter 1.[28] Within this frame, what looks like Whitman's resistance to Emerson is instead a marker for differences that exceed the relatively local details of their relationship, and so provides a valuable and urgent site for detailing the various legacies of representation—political, literary, and canonical—in the United States. Chapter 2 interrogates a range of binarized oppositions (e.g., I/we, poetry/journalism, inspiration/labor) through which the connection between these two central figures is routinely explicated. Moreover, its exploration of these binaries is grounded in a number of features of the 1856 second edition of *Leaves of Grass*: the spine on which Whitman emblazoned Emerson's most famous sentence of greeting, and the appendix in which he reprinted Emerson's famous letter and a lengthy reply of his own. Since the 1856 edition is quite likely the first printed artifact in which the names Emerson and Whitman appeared together, the chapter reasserts the primacy of this site for reading the terms in which a different and more complex relation between these two authors first circulated. In sum the chapter is about estranging Emerson/Whitman by, in part, reading their estrangement as it is configured and published in the pages of the 1856 edition.

Such rereading bears important consequences for reconceptualizing not only the careers of these two major figures but American literary history as well. Reconstituting the Renaissance and American literary history entails interrogating with theoretical rigor the fundamental imagining of literary history in terms of "representative" figures in the first place. Part of the work of reconstituting representation is to interrogate the (commonsensical) standing of representative figures like the two placed at the center of this book, not only by broadening the canon but by unseating Matthiessen's Authors and reimagining them as ventriloquizers of political, literary, and cultural discourses that variously cross and conjoin at the sites of their textual production. One of the alternatives this book puts forward is a broadened notion for thinking literary history through the material production, circulation, and interpretation of texts of all kinds. This is what I take to be at stake in this book's epigraph, which appeared in the inaugural issue of *American Literature* in 1929.

Chapter 3, "Class Actions," traces the divergent legacies in writings by Emerson and Whitman of that nexus of American republican thinking, Publius's charge in *Federalist* No. 10 "to refine and enlarge the public views by passing them through the medium of a chosen body of citizens," thereby ensuring "that the public voice, pronounced by the representatives of the people, will be more consonant to the public good than if pronounced by the people themselves." More specifically, the chapter contrasts the representational strategies and attendant class dynamics encoded in Whitman's early newspaper writings with those present in the lectures Emerson was delivering at roughly the same time. The chapter ranges across a wide range of contemporaneous texts, like John Quincy Adams's first address to Congress in 1825, in its attempts to witness the intricate webs that link nineteenth-century modes of address across various and even seemingly incommensurate genres to eighteenth-century rhetorics of representation.

Thus the chapter foregrounds the genealogical methodologies on which the book as a whole is constructed. Examining notebooks in which Emerson made space for his own compositions by first excising writings by his father, it demonstrates how William Emerson literally prepared a place from which his son could take up a pen and begin to write. Emerson's writings about the preeminence of the orator bound within the covers of his father's notebooks become a fitting emblem for tracing the complicated material and rhetorical legacies through which the prophet of "self-reliance" emerged.

The chapter also engages Whitman's famous poetic catalogs, reflecting on the politics of a poetic form in which the poet-speaker-representative man makes himself temporarily absent in order to represent more "directly" the constituencies of his poetic republic. Taken as a whole "Class Actions" finds a template for understanding Whitman's poetic practice and a context for reckoning its emergence, not only in Emerson's essay "The Poet" (1844), where it has been traditionally located, but with reference to his own complexly working-class political writings as well. Rather than simply re-binarizing Emerson/Whitman around this representational dynamic of filtration, making Emerson the Federalist and Whitman the loyal opposition, the chapter also delineates Whitman's own autocratic tendencies, for he is the poet as Common Man whose initial project nevertheless reads like a variation of Publius's plans for what he tellingly calls Union: "Through me many voices." Thus the chapter sketches some of the complexities, and the historical referents, for thinking the cultural locations of poetry before Romanticism has reified the relation between literature and politics in terms of pure oppositional distinction.

"Representing Men," the final chapter, turns its attention to some of the most canonical texts of the "Renaissance" proper and restores to the literary movement transcendentalism its manifold historical contexts. In so doing, it revisits the Constitution's infamous three-fifths compromise as a means of reckoning the fact of enslaved bodies within the nation as the foremost site of both a political and a literary crisis of representation. It suggests, moreover, that so-called transcendentalist writings by Emerson and Whitman can be productively reinterpreted by recognizing the enslaved bodies that recur in them, and in relation to which the quest for transcendence repeatedly occurs. The chapter restores the transitive verb at the heart of transcendentalism and calls attention to the direct objects—the enslaved bodies—that complicate idealism's itinerary at midcentury. Thus the chapter brings full circle a genealogical reading of Emerson and Whitman not simply as makers, but as at once "made" by, and re-makers of, discursive traditions and epistemological faultlines that have their roots in the nation's constitutive representative dilemmas. Representation thus remains at the center of the book's analytical frame, though it has become by chapter 4 a category deployed less for exploring political representation, and more a heuristic for reconceptualizing the broader narratives of literary history. Thinking the gaps and absences in American literary history through the concept of representation opens to critical examination what has sometimes seemed least available for analysis—the ideal, the transcendent, indeed, the literary itself: "Yet America is a poem in our eyes" (Emerson, "The Poet"); "The United States themselves are essentially the greatest poem" (Whitman, "Preface" to *Leaves*).[29]

In part the work of this chapter is catalogic, its task to enumerate the persistent occurrences of enslaved bodies within these high canonical texts of transcendentalism where the critical tradition has in various ways occluded them. This is perhaps especially the case in Emerson studies, where discourses of disembodiment predominate, following out the logic of Emerson's own insistence that the state of embodiment itself closely parallels that of enslavement: "*That* is morning, to cease for a bright hour to be a prisoner of this sickly body, and to become as large as nature" ("Literary Ethics," *LAE* 102).[30] In its attention to these textual details the chapter extends the model provided by Stallybrass and White, who argue for the "transcoding" of the hierarchy of the bourgeois body. By adopting their central proposition that "body and social formation are inseparable" (145), the chapter identifies a similar transcoding between discourses of slavery and those attached to the bourgeois body. Thus slavery—a word that never appears in the Constitution—amplifies and concentrates representations of the body across a range of discourses, including miscegenation, homoeroticism, and temperance. Moreover, it generates, as only such booming silences can, an echo that sounds louder in the supposedly "literary" texts we have grown accustomed to hearing in registers furthest removed from slavery's resonances.

CHAPTER ONE

THE RISE OF THE REPRESENTATIONAL ARTS

IN THE UNITED STATES

∾

The degree of possible overlap between *representative* and *representation* in their political and artistic senses is very difficult to estimate. In the sense of the *typical*, which then stands *for* ("as" or "in place of") others or other things, in either context, there is probably a deep common cultural assumption. At the same time, within this assumption, there is the contradiction expressed both in the arguments about *representative democracy* and in the arguments in art about relations between the *representational* and the *representative*.
—RAYMOND WILLIAMS, *Keywords*

E pluribus unum, "Out of many, one": dating from 1776 (but originating perhaps with Virgil), the national motto of the United States denotes at once the challenge and the achievement of the Constitutional Convention, the results of whose labors were formally endorsed when New Hampshire became the required ninth state to ratify on the first day of summer in 1788. The motto encodes as self-evident and essential what from a preratification perspective was precisely the defining issue, for the consolidation that the motto simply declaims, the Federal Convention and then the state ratifying conventions hotly debated. Would the United States continue as an aggregate of independent states under the conditions explicitly spelled out in the second section of the Articles of Confederation, and the insistence there that "Each state retains its sovereignty, freedom, and independence"?[1] What continuities had been retained between the Articles and the newly nationalizing instrument constructed in Philadelphia? The "E pluribus unum" that shines out from the face of the Great Seal of the United States occludes these questions, and, in their place, inserts a genealogy as teleology—making of one of a range of possible outcomes the one true outcome toward which all events necessarily pointed.[2]

As Jay Fliegelman has argued, this national motto derives most directly in colonial times from the masthead of the popular eighteenth-century *Gentle-*

men's Magazine and so offers, it is useful to see in this context, another example of the ways in which the "political" and the "literary" interpenetrate in the period.[3] Under the motto's logic—in which nation-making and anthology-making tacitly overlap, and magazines are both printed and militia-ready—the Constitution might be figured as an attempt to adopt a uniform, centralized "editorial" authority where previously separate "articles" had been collected from a wide range of sources and drawn together by little more than their cover. It is not until after the Civil War that "United States" becomes, grammatically speaking, a unified nation (notion?) consistently requiring a singular verb, as the OED and the writings of the ardent unionist Walt Whitman make plain.[4] These minor consequences of the motto's ambiguities begin to suggest the links that remain to be drawn between even this simple analogy about "magazines" and the rhetorical and political issues repeatedly raised by the published contest over ratification.

But the creation of united states is not by any means the only work of consolidation toward which "E pluribus unum" points. For there is another historical consolidation that has taken place since the adoption of the Constitution, one that has rewritten not simply the inevitability of the outcome of the debates that preceded formal ratification, but also the role and significance of the various printed materials debating ratification during the Constitutional episode. The principal documents in this category are the eighty-five essays that comprise *The Federalist*, the first of which appeared on 27 October 1787, in one of New York's five newspapers, the *Independent Journal*.[5] By consolidation, I am referring to a historical process that has over the course of two centuries come to see *The Federalist* as a virtual substitute for the whole of the process of Constitutional consolidation that Publius's essays themselves take as their over-arching subject matter. These essays, concerned at their heart with the necessity of energetic governmental consolidation, now themselves are sometimes seen by scholars to consolidate the cacophony that resonated during the period of Constitutional debate. From the multitude of published essays, letters, and broadsides that circulated as part of the ratification controversy, *The Federalist* often stands alone (as in the latest *Norton Anthology of American Literature*) and removed from this argumentative context. Compared against the late publication date of Herbert Storing's *The Complete Anti-Federalist* in 1981, the first collected *Federalist* appeared simultaneously with the completion of serial publication and essay No. 85 on 28 May 1788; roughly the first half of the series was published in a collected volume on 22 March 1788.[6] Publius seems from the start to have had his eyes on that much larger potential audience called posterity, the same mentioned in the Constitution's preamble.[7] Indeed, as Michael Warner has shown, "through various machinations [Publius] was able to appear simultaneously in four newspapers in New York and another in Virginia, with occasional appearances elsewhere to boot—a strategy of blanketing the public space of print that was warmly resented by his opponents" (*Letters* 113). Thus these multiple sites of reprinted *Federalist* essays reproduce one of the claims about the import of the new Constitution that opponents most feared and against which they declaimed most vehemently; indeed, "suppression of Anti-Federalist writing facilitated ratification in a number of states" (Cornell 104). Out of many (newspapers), one.[8]

Patrick Henry's denunciation in the Virginia ratifying convention, decrying what he understood to be the central change in America's self-definition, addresses just these issues:

> When the American spirit was in its youth, the language of America was different: Liberty, Sir, was then the primary object. . . . But now, Sir, the American spirit, assisted by the ropes and chains of consolidation, is about to convert this country to a powerful and mighty empire. . . . (F/A 122–23)[9]

Henry may well have taken his evidence for these quasi-imperial ambitions from the opening lines of *Federalist* No. 1:

> After an unequivocal experience of the inefficacy of the subsisting federal government, you are called upon to deliberate on a new Constitution for the United States of America. The subject speaks its own importance; comprehending in its consequences nothing less than the existence of the UNION[,] the safety and welfare of the parts of which it is composed, the fate of an *empire* in many respects the most interesting in the world.[10]

Publius's use of the word "empire" importantly shifts the term away from the connotations that had helped to underwrite the break from Britain. Sheldon Wolin has labeled this change the "feudalist" groundwork at the base of the "progressive" American Revolution. In his reading, the confederated states adhered to, and worked to maintain, feudal systems of "imperial" governance marked specifically by "difference, pluralism, and the dispersion of power among several centers" (130) against the imposition, especially after 1763, of increasingly centralized and uniform British administrative measures. As is well known, these measures were warmly resented as attempts by Parliament to legislate more and more intensely about "internal" matters the colonists believed fell outside that body's traditional prerogative.

But with the break from Britain achieved, Publius's use of "empire"—like the Constitution itself—retreats from the revolutionary insistence against centralization and endorses instead a single, defining power able to "extend the authority of the Union to the persons of the citizens—the only proper objects of government" (15: 149) in place of "a number of unsocial, jealous, and alien sovereignties" (2: 91). This is the ground of Henry's fervent objection, which relies on the same definition of empire employed by Dr. Franklin in a speech at the Federal Convention that not only banks on his status as senior sage but also carries traces of the rhetoric of Manifest Destiny that grow only more numerous over the course of the nineteenth century:

> I have lived, Sir, a long time, and the longer I live, the more convincing proofs I see of this truth—*that God Governs in the affairs of men.* And if a sparrow cannot fall to the ground without his notice, is it probable that an empire can rise without his aid? (Madison, *Notes* 209–10)

Thus message and medium coalesce: the imperial publishing strategies of *The Federalist* align with the imperial vision for a consolidated nation that the Papers (in their own "comprehensive" treatment of the issues that themselves comprehend "the fate of an empire in many respects the most interesting in the world" [1: 87]) endorse as the primary justification for ratification.[11]

The word "interesting" in Publius's call for the nation's full attention connotes a range of meanings that taken together also explicate his rhetorical position in the papers as a whole. In the first place, the notion of "interest"—or more precisely, "disinterest"—is tied to the ancient notion of republican virtue on which the success of representative government was said to depend. Despite rumblings in the period that such expectations of a virtuous citizenry were unrealistic within a commercially vibrant and expanding domestic economy that at the time of the Revolution *already* exceeded the scope of Jeffersonian agrarianism, the notion of disinterested virtue opposed to luxury remained a touchstone in the republic's imagination of itself, as the debates over ratification repeatedly demonstrate.[12]

The notion that the imperial fate of the United States is "interesting" also draws on a lesson Publius might have learned from the contest with Great Britain marked first and last by the vigorous disagreement over virtual representation. If the claim that the colonists were virtually represented in Parliament had been so thoroughly deflated by the early 1770s that not even the King's ministers could resuscitate it, in *Federalist* No. 1 Publius is drawing on another aspect of Parliament's argumentative, counterrevolutionary strategy. British theorists argued that the doctrine of shared interests between Britain (or Parliament) and the colonies (or their traders and merchants) justified taxation, on the assumption that Parliament would never upset the harmony of these favorable fiscal relations (see Reid, *Concept* 119, 45). But not even this argument was dependable, as a widely circulated pamphlet by Daniel Dulany observed:

> It is indeed true, that the interests of England and the colonies are allied, and an injury to the colonies produced into all it's [*sic*] consequences, will eventually affect the mother country; yet these consequences being generally remote, are not at once foreseen; they do not immediately alarm the fears, and engage the passions of the English electors; the connection between a free-holder of Great-Britain, and a British American being deducible only thro' a train of reasoning, which few will take the trouble, or can have opportunity, if they have capacity, to investigate; Wherefore the relation . . . is a knot too infirm to be relied on as a competent security. . . . (quoted in Jensen 100)

When Publius recalls the "interesting" nature of the ratification decision that the (white, male, property-holding) citizens of the newly united states have been called on to deliberate, he is also implicitly reminding them that, unlike the spurious doctrine of shared interest Parliament had concocted to betray the colonies, there is in these debates only one genuine "interest": whether "societies of men are really capable or not of establishing good government from reflection and choice" (1: 87). Thus Publius posits universal "interest" as a figure for all the other unanimities *Federalist* No. 2 delineates: "With equal pleasure I have as often taken notice that Providence has been pleased to give this one connected country to one united people—a people descended from the same ancestors, speaking the same language, professing the same religion . . . " (2: 91). Publius's invocation of this universalized notion of "interest" in relation to his nevertheless partisan account of the urgency and necessity of the federal plan may be seen as a touchstone of the consensual mode in eighteenth-century writing, a mode that refigures debate and dissent within a language of consensus and common sense.[13]

These centripetal tendencies also gain significance in relation to the place *The Federalist* has come to occupy in American literary and political history. The consolidation of the dissensus of the ratification debates into the monologic figure of *The Federalist* occurs not only because these essays come down to us sanctioned by the pronouncements of a long line of statesmen and scholars, from Thomas Jefferson to Lincoln to the present. Rather, there is another, profoundly material basis for the prominence of *The Federalist*, related to the publishing monopoly Publius and the network of Federalist printers sought to achieve: as Albert Furtwangler writes, virtually alone among the many documents of the period, *The Federalist* has come down to us as "a bound volume that emerged from the welter of ephemeral debates, one that has endured in a fame reinforced by the long history of the Constitution" (43).[14] The exegetical paradigm that this bound book reinforces comes full circle when, to a greater and lesser extent, the Constitution and *The Federalist* become virtual versions of each other.[15]

But while history may be written by the winners, the story and the interpretation of the texts that comprise it are rarely as straightforward as the aphorism permits; as if to endorse this book's genealogical interest in the shifting interpretations of "stable" texts over time, the uproar of Jeffersonian opposition to Federalist rule at the turn of the nineteenth century produced "a distinctly Anti-Federalist reading of *The Federalist*"; as Cornell argues, "Publius was reincarnated as the first strict constructionist" (244) and became an authority for the party whose interpretation of the Constitution he had originally opposed. Such shifts only gain further resonance in relation to the single aspect of the history of *The Federalist* about which many historians remark: that *The Federalist*, whatever its prominence today, actually seems to have played almost no significant role in influencing the eventual vote in favor of ratification taken at the New York Constitutional convention. Furtwangler calls the impact of the papers "marginal," and the author of a detailed account of the debate in New York uses the word "negligible."[16] Like some of the "literary" texts treated in later chapters, *The Federalist*'s present-day centrality when viewed in relation to its relative insignificance when Constitutional ratification remained undecided calls our attention once more to the shifting nature of canons, both literary and political, as well as the ways in which the impress of "representative" standing marks the contingent work that the present always actively produces out of a usable past.

Naming and Creating

Virtually since its initial appearance in the *Daily Advertiser* on 22 November 1787 (and on subsequent days in the *New-York Packet* and the *Independent Journal*), readers have seized on No. 10 as a pivotal document in which many of the larger concerns of *The Federalist* as a whole have their most fruitful and significant exposition. This assessment dates at least as far back as John Quincy Adams's 1836 "Eulogy on James Madison"—No. 10's presumed author—and in the twentieth century the claims for this number's centrality grew even more insistent.[17] Much of the attention stems from No. 10's very significant subject matter, an extension of No. 9's discussion of "The Utility of the Union as a Safeguard against Domestic Faction and Insurrection" that introduces Publius's concept of representative filtration on which he develops his model for the new government. "A republic," Publius writes, "by which I mean a government in which the scheme of representation takes place, opens a different prospect and promises the cure for which we are seeking."

> The two great points of difference between a democracy and a republic are: first, the delegation of the government, in the latter, to a small number of citizens elected by the rest; secondly, the greater number of citizens and greater sphere of country over which the latter may be extended. The effect of the . . . difference is . . . to refine and enlarge the public views by passing them through the medium of a chosen body of citizens, whose wisdom may best discern the true interest of their country and whose patriotism and love of justice will be least likely to sacrifice it to temporary or partial considerations. Under such a regulation it may well happen that the public voice, pronounced by the representatives of the people, will be more consonant to the public good than if pronounced by the people themselves, convened for the purpose. (10: 26)

Isaac Kramnick explains the passage's significance as a crossroads in American political theory:

> Madison's brilliant achievement was the appropriation of a word ["republic"] with unmistakable populist connotations for a governmental structure which, while ultimately based on popular consent, involved a serious diminution of popular participation. His critics might call the new order aristocratic or monarchic, . . . but for Madison it was republi-

can, as opposed to the discredited direct democracy practiced to such excess under the Articles [of Confederation]. (41)

Thomas Gustafson offers a somewhat less approving account of Publius's accomplishment: "The rhetoric of the Revolution is redeployed to retard the Revolution. The spirit of '76 is killed by the letter of '76 coopted by the elite of '87" (286). However one evaluates the ingenuity that stands behind Publius's renomination—and there have been innumerable evaluations since these words were first published—at the heart of No. 10 is the concept of naming, and so, of representation. To understand fully the rhetorical significance of Publius's founding "achievement," then, it is necessary to consider it within the context of eighteenth-century paradigms for composition and rhetoric. Publius's own attention to definitions—"A republic, *by which I mean*"—offers a starting point for these considerations.

By frankly marking the shift in definitions at the outset, Publius sets on the rhetorical table—much as he might literally have done during the Convention in Philadelphia—the preliminary terms on which his argument depends. Considered this way, there would seem to be in the gesture no sleight of hand: to the contrary, Publius's shift—making "republic" do the work of "democracy"—extends logically from these definitional premises toward an account of the way legislative representation will be adapted (and should be adopted) under the new plan.

But such new definitions bear important consequences for what Robert Ferguson describes as the paradigms of consensual literature in this early national era, which depend on a shared language based in "conformity, preparation, popularity, common sense, and reception" (*Enlightenment* 3). Publius's setting out the new terms of his argument at the outset evacuates any broader, definitional consensus because the redefinition of "republic" shifts the term away from standard usage. As Ferguson explains, Publius's sentence "dramatize[s] the vital tension at work in a consensual literature" (19), between, on the one hand, individual authorship and originality, and, on the other, communal norms, "common sense," and shared assumptions. Indeed, the sentence tries to have it both ways: it first announces the premise on which the new, revolutionary (or counterrevolutionary)[18] paradigm for representation depends, but then retreats by reinvoking the collective and claiming that the redefinition "promises the cure for which *we* are seeking" (emphasis added). The oscillation between authorial ingenuity and larger, communal objectives bespeaks contradictions inherent in this culture around the issue of authorship; the same uncertainties about originality and attribution are evinced by the period's affinities for pseudonym.[19] Indeed the tensions surrounding pseudonymity and anonymity play out in a great deal of ratification controversy and often revolve around elite authors on either side of the debate trying to trade on name recognition rather than allowing their arguments to rise or fall in what was described as the relatively open marketplace of ideas in/and the public sphere (see Cornell 74–80).[20]

Some perspective on the significance of Publius's definitional gesture can be found by placing it in relation to Hugh Blair's *Lectures on Rhetoric and Belles Lettres*, first published in the United States in the 1780s. Blair's *Lectures* was the period's primary authority on the plain style—a foundational element in the consensual mode—and was circulated widely, reprinted multiple times, and adopted as the standard text in U.S. college curricula during the eighteenth and early nineteenth centuries (Hochmuth and Murphy 158–59). In a section on "Perspicuity and Precision," Blair describes the attributes important for the plain style and declaims against the "ostentatious and deceitful" "sort of art," where "ornament [is] substituted in the room of use" and tends "to the corruption, rather than to the improvement, of good taste and true eloquence" (Blair 1: 3). "Propriety," he writes,

> is the selection of such words in the Language, as the best and most established usage has appropriated to those ideas which we intend to express by them. It implies the correct and happy application of them, according to that usage, in opposition to vulgarisms, or low expressions; and to words and phrases, which would be less significant of the ideas that we mean to convey. (2: 187)

Carefully set off against the "vulgar" and the "low," the focus here is "established usage," on which, Blair insists, stands verbal "propriety"; we would not want to overlook the incipient valences of social class that such culturally determined preferences simultaneously (re)articulate and (re)inscribe. "The whole thrust" of consensual writing, Robert Ferguson has argued, "is to mask uglier actualities and to keep dangerous passions below the combustion point" by means of a "public language of shared meanings" "to minimize and control difference" (*Enlightenment* 17).

Thus we may want to consider not only Publius's transparent renomination of the term "republic," but to look as well at unmarked *reticence* or *muteness* that may mask the sharpest dissent or the most radical reconfigurations. The documents emerging from a convention that met in secret and that put forth its sweeping revision demanding an all-or-nothing, up-or-down vote, without the possibility of amendment, carry the traces of dissent, but often only as traces, or as outright silences; "Many Americans," Ferguson writes, "object to the notion of a national federal republic in 1787, so the Constitution, in creating one, never mentions the words 'national,' 'federal,' or 'republic'" (*Enlightenment* 17). Though it looks precisely the opposite—more like a pronouncement of a "personal" preference than a declaration designed to generate or enforce unanimity—Publius's redefinition of the term "republic" can be seen as a part of the same drive toward consensus and unanimity as his positing a universal "interest" in the outcome of the ratification debate. That is, the shift in definition marks a fundamental change in the terms of the argument at the outset. If one adopts Publius's definition—and it looks "reasonable" enough—one simultaneously evacuates a prime position from which the counterargument could be cast. In the consensual mode as a strategy for containing dissent, the gesture toward "coming clean" by announcing the terms within which the debate will take place actually eliminates the possibility of debate itself.

The opening paragraph of No. 46's discussion of how the Constitution changes pre-Revolutionary assumptions about political representation provides another related example.

> Resuming the subject of the last paper, I proceed to inquire whether the federal government or the State governments will have the advantage with regard to the . . . support of the people. *Notwithstanding the different modes in which they are appointed*, we must consider both of them as substantially dependent on the great body of the citizens. . . . The federal and State governments are in fact but different agents and trustees of the people, constituted with different powers and designed for different purposes. The adversaries of the Constitution seem to have lost sight of the people altogether in their reasonings on this subject. . . . These gentlemen must here be reminded of their error. They must be told that the ultimate authority, *wherever the derivative may be found*, resides in the people alone. . . . Truth, no less than decency, requires that the event in every case should be supposed to depend on the sentiments and sanction of their common constituents. (46: 297, emphases added)

Publius in this passage constructs a binary between the proponents and "the adversaries of the Constitution," though it is a division without a true referent, not only because of the great multiplicity of views hidden within the simple opposition Federalist/Anti-Federalist, but also because he takes away any position from which the opponents could argue against the Constitution by marginalizing (with the word "notwithstanding") the only ground on which such a critique could be mounted. Once Publius banishes as inapplicable or unrelated "the different modes in which [the different legislative bodies] are appointed," he sets the terms within which the only right-minded perspective on the subject can be taken, thus effectively squelching the potential for opposition. "Reserving the proofs for another place," Publius claims to be speaking for "truth, no less than decency"—a phrase that signals once again Blair's consensual notion of plain-style "propriety." With the actual exigencies of political representation (the fact, for example, that the Senate will be elected not directly by the people, but by the state legislatures)[21] literally pushed aside, the Federalists and Publius come to represent those who understand and defend the proposition "that the ultimate authority . . . resides in the people alone."

The passage also constructs another important binary/hierarchy through its subtle deployment of the passive voice. When Publius says of his opponents that "they must be told that the ultimate authority, wherever the derivative may be found, resides in the people alone," the sentence seems to proffer an egalitarian leveling, even as it encodes a kind of autocratic ploy, masked by a passive voice ("must be told") through which, of course, Publius alone is doing the telling. Indeed the simple fact that Publius addresses these defenses of the Constitution to "the people" opens out a space between himself and the people whom he claims to represent. This is a complication evident in the pseudonym "Publius," a name that unifies the discordant opinions of the three collaborators Madison, Hamilton, and Jay but speaks for the public, even when/as "he" speaks to them as an "I." It is only one of the ways in which the consensual mode and the plain style are sometimes at odds with each other. As Michael Warner has written, alluding to Publius Valerianus, one of the founders of republican Rome, "the authors of *The Federalist* . . . punningly identify themselves with the public while also identifying themselves with the founding of polity and the institution of law" (113). Likewise Dana Nelson comments on Publius's pseudonymous and "carefully delimited and abstracted group identity (not the least in merging the three identities of the three authors into Publius, 'the people' speaking in the Name of the One)" (39). Who speaks with "ultimate authority"? How and why does the public (Publius) address itself (the people), since its "interest" is its own?

These are not, it is important to note, issues that simply dissolve after ratification. As chapter 2 takes up in detail, the complexity of pseudonymity recurs in the writings of Whitman the newspaper editor who likewise "contains multitudes" when he signs as an editorial "we." And of postratification America Nicholas Rombes notes the persistence of questions about "voice" as precursors to the prohibition of dissent formally instituted with the passage of the Alien and Sedition Acts in 1798. Regarding George Washington's denunciation of the newly formed Democratic-Republican societies in the 1790s, Rombes notes that these disputes "centered on the question of whose voice legitimately represented 'the people,' and who had access to the language that constituted a civic community of discourse" (6).[22]

The complicated play between the many and the few, between the people and their representatives in Publius's essays appears in another of Blair's dicta when he turns his attention in the *Lectures* to related concerns regarding neologism:

> When I mentioned obsolete or new-coined words as incongruous with Purity of Style, it will be easily understood, that some exceptions are to be made. On certain occasions, they may have grace. . . . In prose, such innovations are more hazardous, and have a worse effect. They are apt to give Style an affected and conceited air; and should never be ventured upon, except by such, whose established reputation gives them some degree of dictatorial power over Language. (1: 187–88)

Here "established reputation" occupies the flip side of Blair's earlier "established usage" in a way that recapitulates the controversies over hierarchy that the "Revolution" and then the debate over ratification raise. Like venture capitalist wordsmiths, those who have garnered sufficient cultural power are able, Blair relents, to coin new words, or to use obsolete ones, despite the general proscription against such creativity, figured here in a range of epistemological energies that swirl around this notion of "dictatorial power."[23] David Simpson, citing the work of John Barrell, notes in *The Politics of American English* how grammarians and rhetoricians in the period routinely "fail to specify the exact identity of what they call 'common usage,' which they cite as the authority to be followed," because "any closer definition of this entity would dramatize in an embarrassing way the degree to which what is called common is in fact something rather more exclusive" (35). In linking neologism to power and to decidedly unrepresentative rule, Blair captures the classic republican double bind that is never very far from the surface when the issue of right representation is raised: it is no accident that *dictation* finally "catches up" with the older *dictator* in the early eighteenth century.

This is by no means only a Federalist issue; elite Anti-Federalists, while they embrace the local in a way that Publius's filtration model is designed exactly to evacuate, often do so because any "weakening of state government would erode the patterns of deference." Elite Anti-Federalists, like Blair's men of "established reputation," frame their resistance to the Constitution in distinctly class-based terms, favoring a small, "feudal" republic in order better to manage "the tensions between patricians and plebeians" (Cornell 72).

The same tension between oligarchic and republican values occurs at No. 10's best-known theoretical moment:

> The effect of the . . . difference [between "republic" and "democracy"] is . . . to refine and enlarge the public views by passing them through the medium of a chosen body of citizens, whose wisdom may best discern the true interest of their country and whose patriotism and love of justice will be least likely to sacrifice it to temporary or partial considerations. (10: 126)

In Publius's idealized account the voice of the people is at once diminished and expanded, as if, in a kind of chemico-linguistic clarification, the dross were removed from unguarded, rambunctious opinions until only the pure distillate of "true interest" remains. But a good deal depends on the "medium of a chosen body of citizens" and the relation between this body and the citizens at large from which it is drawn to determine how one in 1787 might read this possibility of "refinement."

Indeed, that final word might itself have raised backs in the Constitutional period. For while there were great hopes that, with the Peace Treaty, once again America would live up to its promise as "a Land refin'd / Where once rude Ignorance sway'd th' untutor'd mind" (quoted in Silverman 444), likewise there were fears that too much luxury, comfort, and European fashion would hasten the end of the virtuous republic, if, indeed, it were not already too late.[24] Richard Bushman in *The Refinement of America* captures precisely the paradox: "At a time when the Revolution had ended the principles of monarchy and aristocracy and the forces of capitalist enterprise were leading Americans into industrialization, Americans modeled their lives after the aristocrats of a society that was supposedly repudiated at the founding of the nation" (xix). It would not be too much to say that the Federalists Bushman describes as pursuing refinement pursued themselves right out of power with the election of 1800, which must be seen at least in part as a referendum on whether the means the Adams administration had employed in ensuring that only properly "refined" individuals ruled the nation justified what looked to some like an organized witch-hunt. Elkins and McKitrick describe the situation with characteristic subtlety:

> But for the Federalists of 1800 this image—that of men of "enlightened views and virtuous sentiments"—had become an obsession. It applied to none other than themselves, a beleaguered company whose robes of authority were being smirched by the advancing forces of insolence, vulgarity, disorder, self-interest, faction, and demagoguery. And it was against these forces that the Federalists, with their sedition law, were now blindly striking back. (703)

If one wanted to read typologically (not to say typographically), one could note the link between the Federalist print monopolies during ratification suppressing Anti-Federalist counterarguments and this crowning gesture of censorship in 1798.

Virtually word by word, then—as this explication of a single, central paragraph from the seminal No. 10 suggests—the lines of contestation between the political and the rhetorical in the debates over Constitutional ratification (but, I have argued, not only or simply Constitutional ratification) reveal themselves.

What's in a Name?

The tensions and contradictions that the preceding explication has uncovered exceed Publius's "individual" stake in the ratification debates, for they reflect instead the broader plight of representation in the years that follow the Declaration of Independence and its confident announcement of "self-evident" truths and a "long train of Abuses and Usurpations" to "a candid World."[25] Indeed when, in 1765, Thomas Whately, one of the Secretaries in the British Treasury, invoked the truism that the American colonists could in fact be taxed by Parliament because, like all Englishmen anywhere in the empire, they were, in his very significant adverb, "virtually" represented by the members of the British Parliament they had not elected, he could not have imagined the chain of events his argument would help to set in motion.[26] The assumption that—Whately and his peers notwithstanding—the relationship between representatives and the represented should rather be arranged according to the trope of a very unvirtual mirror proved sufficiently powerful to organize a disparate group of colonies to declare and then fight for their political independence. As Edmund Morgan explains, "In the course of the dozen years of resisting [Parliamentary] measures the colonists insisted, again and again, that a representative derived his only legitimacy, his only authenticity, his only being from his attachment to and identification with his particular constituents" (*Inventing* 244). Putting theory into practice following the British surrender at Yorktown, Americans continued to rely on these time-honored, and now Revolution-sanctioned, assumptions, increasing the total number of representatives in most state legislatures through a system of essentially one-to-one correspondence between towns and legislative seats (*Inventing* 247).

To a great extent, these assumptions lived on in the debate over Constitutional ratification. As briefly discussed in the introduction, Fisher Ames invoked, *even as he dismissed*, the claims of direct modes of representation when he reminded delegates in Massachusetts that "much has been said about the people's divesting themselves of power . . . , and that all representation is to their disadvantage because it is but an image, a copy fainter and more imperfect than the original, the people" (quoted in Kramnick, Introduction 45). Similarly, the Anti-Federalist Melancton Smith straightforwardly argued to the New York convention that "the idea that *naturally* suggests itself to our minds, when we speak of representatives is, that they resemble those they represent; they should be a true picture of the people" (*F/A* 101, emphasis added). Both of these men, and the others for whom they are standing in, are counting on the fact of shared assumptions governing the notion of representation, although, for our purposes, especially remarkable is the extent to which, even as late as the ratification debates, Federalists and Anti-Federalists alike demonstrated the propensity for speaking about matters of political representation by drawing on the ancient artistic and literary concept of mimesis (in Ames's references to "images" and "imperfect copies," for example).

Without doubt the actual dynamics of political representation were—and remain—a contested, tricky affair, and even as parties on both sides of the Constitutional debate appealed to it, there were reasons to be skeptical about just what was being represented, and how. Brian Seitz recounts some of the early ways so-called direct representation in the colonies was imagined; he notes, for example, that a 1780 Massachusetts law configured the lower house as the "Representatives of the Persons, and the Senate of the Property of the

Common Wealth" (68). "What was represented in the bicameral legislatures," he concludes, "was . . . certainly nothing as fundamentally (or apparently) simple or unitary as 'the people' or 'the public thing'" (69):

> The people who were writing about consent and about the people were not themselves the people, even if they stood in for them, spoke for them, and represented them. The people doing the talking were themselves specific people, points in a power discourse, not the imaginary, potentially univocal universal in the name of whom they purported to speak. (58–59)

This virtual space between representatives and the represented opens out especially vividly, however, following the Revolution, when many colonists came to see that Secretary Whately—and not they—had apparently been right all along. The Anti-Federalist Brutus explains as much, writing in 1788 in the *New York Journal*:

> There is surely a distinction between the people and their rulers, even when the latter are representatives of the former.—They certainly are not identically the same, and it cannot be disputed . . . that they do not possess the same sentiments or pursue the same interests. (F/A 54)

Brutus acknowledges in these lines how some of the assumptions about representation that underwrote the Revolution have given way to another, importantly antagonistic possibility: that "virtuality"—rather than a devious scheme propagated by irate Parliamentarians to deny colonists their rights as free Englishmen—was instead the defining condition of (political) representation.

Not simply "the defining condition," however, the filtration model of representative "virtuality" is made the virtue, the cornerstone, and the guarantor of the Philadelphia plan—the solution, according to Publius and the Federalists, to the riddle of stable nation-making. Virginia's George Mason—to name one of the delegates who refused to sign the Constitution—also refused this renunciation of revolutionary doctrine, insisting that representatives "ought to mix with the people, think as they think, feel as they feel,—ought to be perfectly amenable to them, and thoroughly acquainted with their interest and condition" (quoted in Morgan, *Inventing* 279). But even if, as Morgan writes, Mason believed "it was in the very nature of the national government that it could not be truly representative" (279), it may be important to note how even in this dissenter's notion that representatives "ought to mix with the people," there may already be inscribed a notion of the representative as a class (however defined) apart.

This embrace of a previously demonized "virtuality" as a defining, even saving, characteristic of all acts of representation carries vast consequences not simply in the realm of politics but also for the rhetorics within which the debate over the Constitution was conducted. If Hugh Blair confidently asserts the ideal in his definition for "Precision" that the word "imports retrenching all super-fluities, and pruning the expression so, as to exhibit *neither more nor less than an exact copy of his idea who uses it*" (1: 189, emphasis added), those who contested the meaning of the Constitution from either side could rarely assert so certainly and with such firmness that this kind of mirrored precision in expression was possible. What was to be the basis for discovering and uttering truth when the mechanisms of representation had themselves become suspect? The plain style could surely be of assistance, but what or who was to guarantee its plainness? The practice of politics conducted by verbal fiat, through declarations that hold "truths to be self-evident," reveals in the ratification debates its soft underbelly, where the insistence on "self-evidence" denotes not complacency or confidence so much as a retreat from the contentious linguistic realm within which the possibility of truthful argumentation and unbiased, impartial representation had become by the late 1780s increasingly fraught.

It is a problem the resonances of which long outlast the comparatively local question of ratification. In 1836, in the famous chapter titled "Language" in *Nature*, Emerson reminds his readers that "wise men pierce this rotten diction and fasten words again to visible things" (*LAE* 23)—one of the best-known efforts in what must be seen as a decades-long tradition of American attempts to repair representation's breach. For Emerson's writing in the 1830s follows a long line of like-minded reformers, including Noah Webster, whose own efforts as lexicographer were founded on the widely held belief that "the dictionary could be an armory in the battle against misrepresentation" (Gustafson, *Representative* 321). Countless contemporaneous social commentators would have agreed with Tocqueville's assertion that "when castes are destroyed and classes change and merge, all of the words of a language get mixed up too" (480). To address these problems, for many commentators reminiscent of Babel, Webster, like Emerson, promoted "a standardization that promised allegiance to the rule of a common language perhaps more than it promised an equality of voices unmarked by differences of class and region" (Gustafson, *Representative* 328).

Looked at from this perspective, the way Publius signals his making "republic" do the work of "democracy" also points up the pervasiveness in *The Federalist* of this attention to proper definitions and careful interpretation. Publius repeatedly demonstrates his concern for diction and systematic exposition: in No. 81, for example, he attaches an etymological footnote to the word "jurisdiction,"[27] and in No. 67, he analyzes at length the grammatical relationships between clauses in the Constitution pertaining to procedures for making appointments, in the course of which he observes that "the relation in which that clause stands . . . denotes it to be nothing more than a supplement to the other" (67: 391). Such strategies point up Publius's awareness that a great deal is at stake in appearing to adhere to standard usage with arguments grounded in history and precedent (one effect of acknowledging etymology), and appealing to commonsensical, shared principles of grammar and syntax.

One sees in Anti-Federalist arguments as well this attention to the importance of right naming, as when Federal Farmer explains how the "truth" changes depending on its desired effects: "When we want a man to change his condition, we describe it as miserable, wretched, and despised; and draw a pleasing picture of that which we would have him assume. And when we wish the contrary, we reverse our descriptions" (*F/A* 28). Of course the same conclusion about the indefinite significations of language opens out merely by noting that writers on *both* sides of the debate—some supporting the new consolidating federal plan and others favoring the system of state sovereignty under the Articles of Confederation—utilize the same pseudonym "Federal Farmer."[28]

In No. 7 Publius sketches out probable scenarios of relations between the states if the Philadelphia plan is rejected, and once again his explanation extends to these contingencies of naming:

> Each State, or separate confederacy, would pursue a system of commercial policy peculiar to itself. This would occasion distinctions, preferences, and exclusions, which would beget discontent. . . . *We should be ready to denominate injuries those things which were in reality the justifiable acts of independent sovereignties consulting a distinct interest.* (7: 111, original emphasis)

As Publius portrays it, the discord produced by the independence of these multiple sovereignties is dependent to a great extent on the way things are named within these new and multiple frameworks. The "keener edge" that leads to conflicts that may not be amenable to what he elsewhere calls "pacific adjustment" grows out of a difference in perspective: what from one angle are merely "habits of intercourse" become, from the perspective of competing individual states, "injuries" and effectively "the same inducements which have, at different times, deluged in blood all the nations in the world" (7: 109).

Nearing the end of the series, Publius returns to the issue of right naming when he considers the Bill of Rights that some Anti-Federalists were insisting upon as a condition for ratification.[29] Publius contends that a detailed enumeration of specific rights "is certainly far less applicable to a Constitution like that under consideration, which is merely intended to regulate the general political interests of the nation, than to a constitution which has the regulation of every species of personal and private concerns" (84: 476). His next rhetorical move creates an equivalence similar to the one between republic and democracy in No. 10:

> The truth is, after all the declamations we have heard, that the Constitution is itself, in every rational sense, and to every useful purpose, A BILL OF RIGHTS. . . . And hence it must be apparent that much of what has been said on this subject rests merely on verbal and nominal distinctions, entirely foreign from the substance of the thing. (84: 477)

Kendall Thomas reflects on Publius's equivocation here as it rises to ward off an acknowledgment of the fundamental illegality that must at all costs remain disavowed: that the Philadelphia convention had been charged with amending, not replacing, the Articles of Confederation, and that, in its formula for ratification (requiring the endorsement of only nine of the thirteen states), the delegates had explicitly violated the provision in the Articles that alterations had to be unanimously approved by the states. If, as Thomas says, "the rule of law . . . is the name for a certain radical impossibility" (225), given that the Founding act of these Fathers (like all such foundings) literally founders at the site of this core transgression, it should hardly be surprising to catch Publius's contradiction about the scope and significance of the replacement Constitution.[30]

The Federalists' victory in securing ratification of the Constitution depended in part on their taking advantage of these contingencies of naming. Passage of the Constitution was to a large degree predicated on the Federalists' deployment of the concept of the sovereignty of the people, most famously, and at the time controversially, in the familiar first three words of the Constitution's preamble. As Edmund Morgan explains, "The Anti-Federalists were forced by this line of argument to maintain that the people of the several states had left the state of nature and had by compacts delegated their powers to the state governments and to Congress and could not retrieve them at will. The Federalists could then pose as champions of the people's superiority to their governments" (*Inventing* 281).[31] Insisting on the people's sovereignty—however vitiated that sovereignty had been made—the Federalists were able to respond to critics like Patrick Henry who wanted to know "what right had [the Philadelphia delegates] to say, *We, the People.* My political curiosity, exclusive of my anxious solicitude for the public welfare, leads me to ask who authorised them to speak the language of, *We, the People,* instead of *We, the States?*" (F/A 116). Federalist delegates responded that "the people" were the one true sovereign to whom they had rightly deferred, and this perceived populism helped them carry the day. And yet, as Kendall Thomas notes, there were certainly observable limits to this "deferral"; if history taught that rulers were insatiably power-hungry, then "Americans could look at the decision of the framers to cast aside their instructions as a fresh proof" (Rakove 152). Indeed the very possibility of such "casting aside" of instructions itself denotes the shift in the meaning of legislative representation that had already taken place.

Precedent (I)

For those who found reason to query the Federalists' "populism," there remained the important and troubling fact that convention delegates had far exceeded their convention mandate, for Henry's concerns depended on a vital link for Anti-Federalists between the people and the states. Indeed this crucial belief marks one of the most insistent contributions of Anti-Federalists to the history of American dissent. Its traces can be seen in Jeffersonian/Democratic–Republican thought at the turn of the nineteenth century, and it is the one belief that links Anti-Federalists of all stripes in the eighteenth century, across all social classes and their varying degrees of radicalism, in opposition to Federalism. To the extent that they enunciated a single consistent political philosophy, Anti-Federalists insisted that "the true expression of the people's political will" (Cornell 63) resided in the several states and the manageably small constituent districts within their borders. This is a belief with a long revolutionary prehistory, manifest, for example, in the Declaration's allegation that George III had "called together legislative bodies at places unusual, uncomfortable, and distant from the depository of . . . public records."

The belief in the state as the (imagined) site of genuine, direct representation may seem odd, as Akhil Reed Amar notes, for today the *federal* government usually is seen to defend minorities *within* states against the persecutions of some majority, however defined (1133–34): for example, federal troops in Little Rock, accompanying African American students attempting to desegregate public schools. But a different model and understanding of the dangers to citizens and to democracy is in place following the Revolution and ratification, and there are a number of important consequences that emerge out of the special status Anti-Federalists accorded the (representative) link between constituent-citizens and their states. Most of these have to do with a belief in the state governments as the institution that best retained a connection to the true sovereign power of the people themselves. At this historical distance, when the authority of the federal government is simply assumed, it is remarkable to think about the first half of the nineteenth century as a testing ground for how the competing interests of state and federal governments would be negotiated. I have called this section "Precedent," but it is clear that on this issue no clear precedent existed in 1798, or 1830, or even 1855, to explain how citizens, states, and the national government were to understand their mutually informing relations, except perhaps through models of competing loyalties and conflicting demands. What is today, post–Civil War, post–New Deal, largely a given, was then unsettled, and the status, provenance, and domain of national governance in the figure of Union is repeatedly contested.

The Virginia and Kentucky Resolutions, for example, introduced by Jefferson and Madison in late 1798 to oppose the federal adoption of the Sedition Act as unconstitutional, depended on an ongoing instability regarding precisely who had ratified the Constitution, and for whom. Opponents of Adams's Acts argued that "the people acting in their corporate capacity as citizens of the individual states were the true parties to the compact that created the Union and could serve as a check on the federal government" (Cornell 239). From this premise it followed that the states were themselves duty-bound as the direct representatives of the people to "arrest the progress of . . . evil" (quoted in Elkins and McKitrick 720) by the national government after it had passed Acts that so egregiously violated the First Amendment.

Similarly, in the 1830s, under John Calhoun's leadership, South Carolina prepared for secession when, in arguing against the legitimacy of the federal tariffs of 1828 and 1832, it insisted that the individual states had retained the authority to nullify the actions of the federal government—a right like the one they had practiced in the looser arrangement under the Articles of Confederation. The language of the South Carolina Ordinance of Nullification, dated

24 November 1832, demonstrates the extent to which the relation of the states to the powers invested (by whom?) in the federal government remains contestable after ratification. Although Andrew Jackson utterly and famously rejected all of South Carolina's premises,[32] and though not a single state adopted the Virginia and Kentucky Resolutions, as significant for our purposes is the dilemma itself, the questions about representation and right interpretation that these contests raise, as in the closing lines of South Carolina's nullification ordinance:

> And we, the people of South Carolina, to the end that it may be fully understood by the government of the United States, and the people of the co-States, that we are determined to maintain this our ordinance and declaration, at every hazard, do further declare that we will not submit to the application of force on the part of the federal government, to reduce this State to obedience, but that we will consider the passage, by Congress, of any act authorizing the employment of a military or naval force against the State of South Carolina . . . as inconsistent with the longer continuance of South Carolina in the Union.[33]

The passage merits attention not simply for the way it distinguishes "the government of the United States" from "the people," but also for its interpellation of "co-States," as if no quite settled terminology yet exists for articulating the relations that the Constitution has produced between the "local" administrative entities that preexist the compact of 1789 *and* that somehow also constitute the post-1789 Union. The secession of Southern states following Lincoln's election represents from this perspective not some new mode of protest but rather the last step in a range of practices tied to understandings about the republic that have by 1861 clearly been available for quite some time.

Excursus: Free Labor and Anti-Federalism

> Indeed, the long reach of these nullificationist debates comes across in Whitman's cryptic 1855 poem, later titled "A Boston Ballad." Like Whittier's contemporaneous "The Rendition," Whitman's poem treats Anthony Burns's enforced return to slavery, one of the first escapees sent back following passage of the Fugitive Slave Law in the infamous 1850 Compromise. The poem provides another example of Whitman focusing on something other than the plight of slaves when he writes about slavery. As in "The Eighteenth Presidency!" Whitman's sympa-

thy and attention are directed at the plight of white working-class
men—a displacement carried so far that the text imagines such men
suffering the terrors of the lash in defense of the rights of free labor.[34]
Indeed the only signifier of the black man in the poem may be the
"blackbellied clipper" (1855 LG 90), which, in the poem's diegesis, is
the foreboding ship that returns King George's bones to "rule" the
states, but which might also be seen as a slave trader, its "belly" filled
with the bodies of newly enslaved, and "consumable," Africans suffering the deplorable conditions of the Middle Passage.

What appalls the speaker in this poem is neither slavery nor the
return of fugitives, but that American revolutionary fervor has van-
ished. Arbitrary, nonrepresentative power has returned to rule, not in
the figure of the King and his cronies, but now in the figure of his as-
good substitute: the federal government. Instead of celebrating Evacu-
ation Day with a parade that recreates the British departure from
Boston and the honorific beginning of republican self-rule, the poem
provides two substitutes: the appalling spectacle of uncontested federal power, and the pitiful sight of absolutely passive citizens in the
former home of the Sons of Liberty:

> For shame old maniacs! . . . . Bring down those tossed
>   arms, and let your white hair be;
> Here gape your smart grandsons . . . . their wives gaze at
>   them from the windows,
> See how well-dressed . . . . see how orderly they conduct
>   themselves.
>
> Worse and worse . . . . Can't you stand it? Are you
>   retreating?
> Is this hour with the living too dead for you?
>   (1855 LG 89)

If the poem sustains barely any interest at all in the living body of an
enslaved man being returned to bondage, it cannot take its eyes from
the "orderly," "dead" citizens who stand silent in the face of this clear
imposition against state prerogatives. "You have got your revenge old
buster! . . . . The crown is come to its own and more than its own,"
says the speaker: federal power has replaced the monarchy that the

revisiting "phantoms" had fought so hard to depose. But what also "comes to its own" in these lines from 1855 is the unresolved status of political representation, and on the cusp of the Civil War.

The poem's intervention grows more curious when it is placed beside contemporaneous documents describing how some of Boston's most prominent citizens (Thomas Wentworth Higginson, who was injured in a scuffle, among them) were anything but passive in response to Burns's arrest.[35] The poem explicitly chooses the Burns case and the Fugitive Slave Law as occasions to depict federal power run amok and a citizenry not in any sense attuned to the risks they face in permitting such centralized power once more to rule. For why else revise the "truth" of the response to Burns's imprisonment—what one contemporaneous pamphlet calls "The Boston Slave Riot"[36]—except to demonstrate federal power's virtual nullification of the local control the Revolution had been fought to reassert. Indeed, with its depiction of federal troops "marching stiff" like Redcoats in formation, the poem (like Jefferson) implies that this is a revolution that needs to occur again.

Unanimity and Its Discontents

Whether genuine sovereignty was said to reside in the states or elsewhere, the question remains: who precisely were the people invoked as the ultimate authority? How could their "interests" be known? This issue of where or how the "people's voice" most emphatically or distinctly resounds cannot be easily determined, not least because the notion of "the people," as numerous commentators have noticed, is itself a fiction—albeit one the stakes of which are in these contexts exceedingly high.[37]

Indeed so amorphous is this oft-invoked collectivity that Publius's characterization of them oscillates essay by essay in accord with the local demands of his argument. As evidence, consider the characterization of "the people" from No. 2 as the first of a pair for comparison:

> With equal pleasure I have as often taken notice that Providence has been pleased to give this one connected country to one united people—a people descended from the same ancestors, speaking the same language, professing the same religion, attached to the same principles of government, very similar in their manners and customs, and who, by their joint

counsels, arms, and efforts, fighting side by side throughout a long and bloody war, have nobly established their general liberty and independence. (2: 91)

The question that this passage begs—perhaps not entirely successfully—is the fact of its own context; that is, its very existence in a series of essays, *The Federalist*, striving to *produce* unanimity in the place of an existing divisiveness undercuts the excerpt's wishful projection of a utopian singularity of purpose and unity of "the people."[38]

Other passages in *The Federalist* paint contrary portraits of the nature of "the people." In No. 10, for example, Publius explains why the system of representative filtration is necessary by depicting the civil unrest that the Constitution's filtered system is constructed to avert:

The influence of factious leaders may kindle a flame within their particular States but will be unable to spread a general conflagration through the other States. . . . A rage for paper money, for an abolition of debts, for an equal division of property, or for any other improper or wicked project, will be less apt to pervade the whole body of the Union than a particular member of it, in the same proportion as such a malady is more likely to taint a particular county or district than an entire State. (10: 128)[39]

Before analyzing this passage's account of the nature of "the people," it is crucial to note the utterly nonarbitrary nature of the examples Publius chooses: "a rage for paper money, for an abolition of debts, for an equal division of property." Invoking the kinds of problems raised by the protestors led by Daniel Shays in Massachusetts and by the Whiskey Rebellion in Pennsylvania, Publius's list goes a long way toward substantiating Jennifer Nedelsky's thesis in *Private Property and the Limits of American Constitutionalism* that the protection of property rights was the primary preoccupation at the center of the Constitution's newly consolidating blueprint. Madison and most of the Founders, she argues, "took the principle of consent as a given and turned their attention to the dangers inherent in governments based on such principles. The result was a subtle but important shift in focus from the promise of republican government to the containment of its threats" (4). As Richard K. Matthews notes, Madison's "goal was stability, not the virtue of citizen participation" (201).[40]

Moreover the passage by Publius effectively reverses the categorization of "the people" established in No. 2: the people and the nation then projected as inviolable wholes now require protection from multiple sites of discord that are spreading like so many pox on the body politic.[41] Where there had been unity, there are now members and parts and division, until at the last Publius takes refuge in—of all things—the model of "Confederacy" that the Constitution is specifically written to replace. Where there had been a sense in No. 2 that there did not exist any "particular count[ies] or district[s]," in No. 10 there is the seemingly endless potential for subdivision, marked by a gradual diminution in scale—state is to nation as district is to state—and governed by a significant rewriting of the ancient analogizing of the state to a human body subject to the same "malad[ies]" as a single, corporeal human being.[42]

This plurality of definitions for "the people" is the premier site that unveils the larger crises of representation prevalent in the period as a whole. Publius's definition of the people changes, then, not simply because the demands of his arguments change from paper to paper and topic to topic, but because "the people" can be known only through such representations in the first place. "The people" in whose name and by whose authority the new Constitution is (nominally) adopted is a chimera and a mirage, a construction always of rhetorical negotiation which, as such, can never be said to be either true or not. Rather than grounding a system of virtual representation that has become destabilized, "the people" become instead one more symptom of a representational system without grounding. There is no truth about the people except through the mediations of verbal representation, which turns out to be just another way of noting something else the revolutionary generation alternately acknowledged and denied: that virtuality and representation are not opposites, but synonyms.

To situate our reading of the ratification debates within this contentious realm of rhetorical instability also gives an effective purchase on an emerging debate in U.S. eighteenth-century literary historiography, one that emerges in part out of Robert Ferguson's claim that these seemingly ephemeral ratification pamphlets occupy the very "center of the contrapuntal development in revolutionary thought" (Ferguson, *Enlightenment* 86). Printed and distributed throughout a society with extremely high literacy rates, and driven through printing presses by the foundational belief in the saving value of right ideas, these texts also significantly blur the boundaries between the printed and the oral/aural, not least because, as Michael Gilmore notes, print had not yet overtaken orality as the form associated most closely with factuality.[43] These ratification writings struggle for attention within the period's supercharged political atmosphere as a kind of precursor to modern talk radio, one pamphlet generating further pamphlets according to the genre's rapid-fire "natural responsiveness" (Ferguson, *Enlightenment* 86); taken together these printed texts function as crucial knowledge-disseminating (and -producing) vehicles in an ongoing ideological contest of point-counterpoint.[44]

One might, then, at the material site of these ratification pamphlets link together aspects of two "schools" that have of late arisen around the roles of orality and print in the revolutionary and early national periods. On one side, Michael Warner in *The Letters of the Republic* has persuasively argued "the specificity of *reading* as the paradigmatic public action," to such a degree that "when the virtuous citizen fixes his vigilant eye upon the civic scene, what he is looking at is a printed object" (52–53). In a contrasting view, Jay Fliegelman and Christopher Looby have separately insisted on voice and aurality as the central communicative and ideologically invested modalities of this cultural moment. The titles of their pertinent books point the way: in *Declaring Independence*, Fliegelman seeks to resituate the break from Britain "as a rhetorical problem as much as a political one" (3) that takes place within the context of the period's "intensified quest to discover (or theorize into existence) a natural spoken language that would be a corollary to natural law, a language that would permit universal recognition and understanding" (1–2); in *Voicing America*, Looby articulates "the saliency, in many of the texts of the period, of vocal utterance as a deeply politically invested phenomenon of the social world" (3). Taken together these three studies provide competing accounts of the primary discursive means through which eighteenth-century British North America began to understand itself as different, and then as potentially distinct, from Great Britain.

The quickly printed and issued pamphlets and broadsides that fueled first the new nation's revolutionary fervor, and then its Constitutional deliberations (and apprehensions), straddle these print/orality distinctions in their spontaneity, their dialogic responsiveness, perhaps even in their ardor and their ubiquity. I have not, however, cited the debate between the oral and the printed in eighteenth-century studies to choose between them; rather I want to offer a metalevel critique of both "schools" that has the effect not of invalidating one at the expense of the other but rather of qualifying how these two modes might be usefully conjoined.[45] Viewed for their commonalities, one finds at the center of both models a crisis over representation itself: what will be the basis of right speaking and right writing? Can the truth of rhetoric be grounded and through what mechanisms will its accuracy be assured? Fliegelman sums up the central motivation: "An age preoccupied with efficacious persuasion and with un-covering hidden designs behind the masquerade of deceptive action and mis-leading speech translated a growing distrust of reason and rational persuasion into a wishful faith in an irresistible discourse of feelings" (36–37).[46] One need not cite Derrida's theoretical equivalence between speech and writing to find in the texts of this period evidence that the question of language, figured as the capacity of words to represent the world truthfully, without passion and with-out distortion, recurs everywhere and only becomes more troubled within a context in which the chorus of speakers and writers is growing exponentially.[47] One might see in the period's quest for a "natural" language—a language of sure feeling and instant communication independent of words—a measure of these pervasive uncertainties about linguistic efficacy and reliability.[48]

To reexamine the debates over ratification and representation from within this frame is to catalog the strategies through which writers attempted to ground arguments that seemed groundless, to defend and clarify positions when such defenses and clarifications seemed fruitless. Appeals to the lessons of history, to the consensus authorities of the past, to the presumably plain boundaries of genre occur throughout the ratification writings and mark cate-gories that persist into the nineteenth century. To revisit these strategies and the discourses they underwrite is thus to posit continuities between Revolution and Renaissance, to set the stage for a reconfiguration of the junctures of American literary history that link the eighteenth century to the nineteenth as well as the confederation to its so-called consummation in the federal plan.

Precedent (II)

Put another way: as the Constitution's provisions for representation reveal themselves to be inadequate in terms of the Revolutionary mandate, compensa-tory appeals and justifications need to be motivated. In particular, Publius analogizes in *The Federalist* from selected instances in world history, identifying and examining historical precedents and authorities in order to substantiate the choices made by the membership of the Constitutional Convention.

Of course Publius is hardly the only player in this game, and on occasion the two presumably opposed groups utilize the same examples to support incom-patible positions. In No. 9, Publius laments that "opponents of the PLAN . . . have . . . cited and circulated the observations of Montesquieu on the necessity of a contracted territory for a republican government" (9: 119). Publius goes on to dismantle the arguments that deploy Montesquieu against the Convention's plan; for one thing, in adhering to the letter of what Montesquieu has written, he argues that many of the states in the Union are themselves too large to manage adequately a republican form of government. Moreover he scoffs at those who have suggested a further splitting of these larger states into what he calls "an infinity of little, jealous, clashing, tumultuous commonwealths, the wretched nurseries of unceasing discord . . ." (9: 120). Not content simply to contradict the opposition, though, Publius invokes another authoritative dimension of Montesquieu's writings that "explicitly treats of a CONFEDERATE REPUBLIC as the expedient for extending the sphere of popular government and reconciling the advantages of monarchy with those of republicanism," by quoting six paragraphs from the ninth book of *Spirit of Laws* because, he notes, "they contain a luminous abridgment of the principal arguments in favor of the Union" (9: 120–21).

Federalist and Anti-Federalist documents involved in these debates, however, demonstrate that the name "Montesquieu"—among other similarly utilized authorities—functions as a free-floating signifier whose name recurs but whose particular expert opinions can nowhere be precisely pinned down. What Montesquieu actually wrote seems to matter less than that Montesquieu wrote it, and the result is the blatantly contradictory opinions that writers from opposing camps deploy as the "essential" Montesquieu. A telling example of this phenomenon emerges when the Montesquieu endorsed by the Minority Dissenters from the Pennsylvania ratifying convention is placed beside the Montesquieu-according-to-Publius just examined:

> We dissent, first, because it is the opinion of the most celebrated writers . . . that a very extensive territory cannot be governed on the principles of freedom. . . . If any doubt could have been entertained . . . , it has been fully removed by . . . *Mr. Wilson*, one of [the] majority on this question: . . . "It is the opinion of some celebrated writers, that to a small territory, the democratical; to a middling territory (as Montesquieu has termed it) the monarchical; and to an extensive territory, the despotic form of government is best adapted." (F/A 71–72)

Here, in part for being the only "celebrated writer" named, Montesquieu stands in as the authority defending the full range of these alignments, even though the parenthesis directly attributes to him only the concept of the "middling territory." Taken together these competing citations substantiate Cathy David-son's claim that "both Federalist and Anti-Federalist could call upon the same republican rhetoric to justify contradictory actions, assumptions, and visions of the Republic" (159). (This practice is not exactly unheard of today.)

Within the contentious field of argument around ratification, the net is cast wide for authorities of whatever prominence, and the elevation of Mr. [James] Wilson's contemporaneous testimony (in the passage just excerpted) beside that of the "celebrated writers" only reinforces the conflicted situation in which any argumentative harbor will do in a storm. Certainly there is a local, strategic logic to the inclusion of Wilson's testimony, but even that situation comes to look from within a broader context like one more example of language's utter malleability, such that Wilson's "same" words can be utilized to endorse two diametrically opposed ratification outcomes.

The uses of external authority are further complicated by an emergent American exceptionalism, which threatens the possibility of precedent in any form at all.[49] This refutation of authority—or rather, its nearly simultaneous invocation and refutation[50]—marks *The Federalist*'s intersection with history under the sign of the ineffable but substantive American difference.[51] Within such a context, precedent inevitably shifts and settles under the strain of the overbearing claims of novelty and difference, as evidenced by these lines from No. 1, which look backward to John Winthrop's invocation of a "City on a Hill":[52]

> It has been frequently remarked that it seems to have been reserved to the people of this country, by their conduct and example, to decide the important question, whether societies of men are really capable or not of establishing good government from reflection and choice, or whether they are forever destined to depend for their political constitutions on accident and force. If there be any truth in the remark, the crisis at which we are arrived may with propriety be regarded as the era in which that decision is to be made; and a wrong election of the part we shall act may, in this view, deserve to be considered as the general misfortune of man-kind. (1: 87)

The intrusion of a theatrical metaphor ("the part we shall act") reveals the twinned historical consciousness that inflects much of *The Federalist*, for these are in the grandest sense decisions to be made not just for today, but for all time: America's citizens have broken or must break with precedent and tradition, in favor instead of striking out (like the Puritans before, and the Western pioneers to come) into uncharted geopolitical territory.

But Publius's language of "election" shows just how difficult such a break can be. The American opportunity to "decide" on the basis of "reflection and choice"—as opposed to a discourse of fatedness—struggles in this passage against an older Calvinist language of "election," a by no means fortunate Fall ("the general misfortune of mankind") in which choice plays no part whatsoever. The call to break from the past bears that past in its very discursive roots, and so resurrects the possibility of precedent in the traces of the past from which it would break.

Meanwhile the dismantling of authorizing historical precedent necessarily, categorically, brings with it a diminution even of those precedents Publius would seem to want to maintain. This process emerges most saliently in an account in No. 30 of the difficulties the Continental Congress experienced in securing sufficient revenues to sustain the collective military effort against England; the passage opens with a line that resonates particularly with South Carolina's nullification claims against the tariff thirty years later:

> [The States] have no right to question the propriety of the demand [for money]: no discretion beyond that of devising the ways and means of furnishing the sums demanded. But though this be strictly and truly the case . . . yet in practice it has been constantly exercised and would continue to be so, as long as the revenues of the Confederacy should remain dependent on the intermediate agency of its members. What the consequences of this system have been is within the knowledge of every man the least conversant in our public affairs. . . . It is this which affords ample cause of mortification to ourselves, and of triumph to our enemies. (30: 213)

The passage all but makes any discussion of the proposed Constitution a moot point, for the reason that the fiscal end-runs perpetrated by the states would seem not only to undermine the possibility of Union—any union, in whatever confederated or constituted form—but to render fanciful any hopes of victory in a Revolution *already won*. These fiduciary subterfuges should have ended where the passage ends, with defeat at the hands of the British ("our enemies").

As a whole these various passages exemplify the ways in which the status of precedent and history has become rhetorically motivated and dependent in the

Constitutional era. From essay to essay the ground shifts, and what is depended on in one place—say, the unanimity that God has geographically bequeathed to British North Americans—can in the next be dissolved into a system of discrete, unimaginably ferocious and competing factions. "America does not repel the past or what it has produced under its forms . . . , accepts the lesson with calmness . . . is not as impatient as has been supposed that the slough still sticks to opinions and manners and literature . . ." : thus Walt Whitman confidently writes on the first page of the first edition of *Leaves of Grass*. But how is one to differentiate the "slough" from the "lessons" if they are deployed interchangeably? What are the lessons of the past? Where are they found, and how can they be utilized by the present?

Unsocial Aliens

Another way to look at the contradictions Publius employs in his defense of the new Constitution returns us once more to the unstable status of "the people." Arguing at certain points that only a republic "would be reconcilable with the genius of the people of America" (39: 254), elsewhere Publius appears much less certain about how precisely to define that "genius," or who it is that best embodies it. This concern with "genius" and with defining an American difference carries over into Whitman's writing: in the 1855 "Preface" Whitman distinguishes America on the grounds that "other states indicate themselves in their deputies . . . . but the genius of the United States is not best or most in its executives or legislatures, nor in its ambassadors or authors or colleges or churches or parlors, nor even in its newspapers or inventors . . . but always most in the common people" (*1855* LG iii).

But "the people" whose genius Publius and Whitman variously assert and on whose authority the government is instituted are also themselves the reason a government is needed in the first place, as Publius famously explains in No. 51: "But what is government itself but the greatest of all reflections on human nature? If men were angels, no government would be necessary" (51: 319). Certainly important in these most quoted of all lines from *The Federalist* is the fundamental reliance on the same metaphor of "reflection" and mirroring found elsewhere in this chapter's accounts of representation. Additionally, the passage shows two recurring but contradictory principles between which *The Federalist* generally oscillates: Americans either participate in, or are excluded from, the passions that have heretofore universally controlled the conduct of men in the world.

As pressing is the question whether the rulers placed in charge of the emergent American nation can distance themselves from that same lamentable history. The answers Publius provides are familiarly redoubled; Publius is once again at a crossroads in this passage, which concerns the ways a newly empowered national government would be better suited to adjudicate disputes between the states:

> [The national government] will be more temperate and cool, and in that respect, as well as in others, will be more in capacity to act with circumspection than the offending State. The pride of states, as well as of men, naturally disposes them to justify all their actions, and opposes their acknowledging, correcting, or repairing their errors and offenses. The national government . . . will not be affected by this pride, but will proceed with moderation and candor to consider and decide on the means most proper to extricate them [the States] from the difficulties which threaten them. (3: 97)

This passage illustrates a sentiment that recurs throughout *The Federalist*, and indeed, throughout much eighteenth-century political commentary: that the powers of the government must be entrusted in the hands of "more temperate and cool" leaders who will act with the best interests of the collectivity, rather than themselves, in mind.[53] But Publius's second sentence diminishes the possibility of finding such a cool-headed group, for the reason that, like the individual states, *all men* justify their own actions at the expense of broader or higher principles. In the middle of insisting how the national government and the men who run it will be different, Publius ends up demonstrating the opposite: that as a government of men, the national government will operate on the same principles of human nature that the system of representative filtration is designed to avoid. Thus to address as many critics have done whether Publius is more or less optimistic about human nature—or to decide that he is simply "realistic"—may obscure the larger rhetorical significance that on this issue, as on many others, Publius seems incapable of validating one side of an argument without at the same time acknowledging and thereby validating the other.[54] The arguments for and against the Constitution cannot be grounded in some transcendent notion of human nature, because the "facts" of human nature—like so many of the "facts" cited in these debates—point (or can be made to point) in two directions simultaneously.

These double-sided and self-defeating tendencies reveal themselves in a particularly intensified form when Publius undercuts his own arguments' claims to adequacy while discussing the way factional interests influence social interactions:

> The latent causes of faction are thus sown in the nature of man. . . . So strong is this propensity of mankind to fall into mutual animosities that where no substantial occasion presents itself the most frivolous and fanciful distinctions have been sufficient to kindle their unfriendly passions and excite their most violent conflicts. (10: 124)

Publius's observations about factions function here as a metacommentary on the ratification debates themselves. These debates are their own concrete evidence of the variety of "factional" productions mankind creates, what Publius calls the "different opinions . . . concerning government, and many other points, as well of speculation as of practice."

The applicability of these discriminations to *The Federalist* becomes only clearer as Publius continues:

> No man is allowed to be a judge in his own cause, because his interest would certainly bias his judgment, and, not improbably, corrupt his integrity. With equal, nay with greater reason, a body of men are unfit to be both judges and parties at the same time; yet what . . . are the different classes of legislators but advocates and parties to the causes which they determine? (10: 124)

The exclusion of men from acting as adjudicators for causes in which they are themselves implicated has an absolute parallel in the status of *The Federalist* itself, even as the verbal representations Publius is making on behalf of the proposed Constitution cannot help but be a "factional"—rather than objective—account of the supposed benefits and recommendations of that document. As Matthews argues, "The framers themselves represented a single faction since, at least on the issue of the institution of property, they were of one mind" (59 n. 26).

That this is the case brings us to the heart of the crisis of representation that underwrites (or fails to underwrite) Publius's attempts to justify the new Constitution. When Publius argues that "men are unfit to be both judges and parties," the possibility of representative government and of objective, uninflected arguments is quite literally swallowed up in the scope and the breadth of his original definition:

> By a faction I understand a number of citizens, whether amounting to a majority or minority of the whole, who are united and actuated by some common impulse of passion, or of interest, adverse to the rights of other citizens, or to the permanent and aggregate interests of the community. (10: 123)

Though he attempts with his own pseudonym to mystify the problem, Publius's discourse over and again points out the factionalism that, as he argues here, is the *essence of representation*.[55] Put another way, "the possibility for deception and misapprehension always exists in the figurative space created in the act of representing" (Patterson, *Authority* 50). The breadth of the definition of faction makes apparent that there is not a stable "community" whose "permanent and aggregate interests" can be assessed, for the reason that there is no such assessment—no naming or representation—that does not come from some interested and thereby contingent perspective.

Little Arts

The prefatory disclaimer to the 1788 two-volume collected *Federalist* places the inevitability of interestedness in sharp relief:

> The particular circumstances under which these papers have been written have rendered it impracticable to avoid violations of method and repetitions of ideas which cannot but displease a critical reader. The latter defect has even been intentionally indulged, in order the better to impress particular arguments which were most material to the general scope of the reasoning. Respect for public opinion, not anxiety for the literary character of the performance, dictates this remark. ("Preface": 85)

Elsewhere in *The Federalist*, however, "a critical reader" seems to be precisely what Publius seeks:

> In the course of the preceding observations, I have had an eye, my fellow-citizens, to putting you upon your guard against all attempts . . . to influ-

ence your decision in a matter of the utmost moment to your welfare by any impressions other than those which may result from the evidence of truth. (1: 89)

The Publius who seeks to train attentive readers in this excerpt contradicts the Preface's seeming reluctance to engage its readers over issues of "method": Publius raises the issue of "literary character" at all, he explains, only out of "respect for public opinion." But is this a public of compliant or active reader-citizens whom Publius addresses? Does he imagine "the people" as Lockean infants to be deleteriously (and helplessly) "impressed" by demagoguery? What kind of reasonable readers require Publius to emphasize by repetition "particular arguments which were most material to the general scope of the reasoning"? In Rakove's words, "A nagging skepticism about the basis on which citizens formed their opinions underlay the celebration of 'reflection and choice' " (134) for writers on both sides of the ratification debate.

These ostensibly ancillary concerns with "literary character," then, actually stand at the heart of the representational dilemmas with which these eighteenth-century texts attempt to come to terms. In part because the realm of the "literary" encompasses for Publius and his peers the category of all written knowledge, his concern with "literary character" marks not some marginal concern about "form" (as opposed to a more substantial "content"), but instead the fundamental claims these essays might stake as veritable (in the older sense of authentic) and verifiable, rather than fictional or imaginative, representations. This attention to "form" is repeatedly thematized into "content," a supplemental concern only stabilized as it is carried in from the "margins" to explicate, and so confound, a text's ostensibly central concern with the political.

When Publius writes in No. 6 of a "summary of what has taken place in other countries, whose situations have borne the nearest resemblance to our own" (6: 108), he is once again invoking this diction of political mimesis, the way in which notions of textual representation, and in particular of mirroring, dominate the rhetorics of representation within these texts. Tellingly, Patrick Henry in his ardent condemnation of the proposed Constitution attacks Publius's premises—but not the overriding language of those premises—when he asks (however rhetorically), "Shall we *imitate* the example of those nations who have gone from a simple to a splendid Government? Are those nations more worthy of our imitation?" (F/A 122, emphasis added). Indeed one could summarize the whole of the debate over ratification as a contest about imitation and mimesis, of whether and how the simple, direct representation of a mirror is variously put at risk by the attractions of the "splendid" and the possibilities of interest. "Under the confusion of names," Publius writes, "it has been an easy task to transfer to a republic observations applicable to a democracy only . . ." (14: 141). But even if the reasons for these misnomers are innocent—and Publius calls them "accidental" (14: 141)—it does not keep him from vilifying their effect in the strongest possible terms. "I submit to you, my fellow-citizens," he writes,

> these considerations, in full confidence that the good sense which has so often marked your decisions will allow them their due weight and effect; and that you will never suffer difficulties . . . to drive you into the gloomy and perilous scene into which the advocates for disunion would conduct you. Hearken not to the unnatural voice which tells you that the people of America, knit together as they are by so many cords of affection, can no longer . . . be fellow-citizens of one great, respectable, and flourishing empire. Hearken not to the voice which petulantly tells you that the form of government recommended for your adoption is a novelty in the political world; that it has never yet had a place in the theories of the wildest projectors; that it rashly attempts what it is impossible to accomplish. No, my countrymen, shut your ears against this unhallowed language. Shut your hearts against the poison which it conveys. . . . (14: 144)

In this extended excerpt Publius the clear-headed rhetorician and legal expert switches roles in an instant to a fire-and-brimstone politico-preacher invoking the chaos of Babel ("the confusion of names") for whom different plans for the national government are not merely political options but rather moral choices ("unnatural voice," "unhallowed language"). The movement at the end of the passage into this highly charged language—a kind of reverse jeremiad, fearing a future Fall rather than lamenting one that has already occurred—contradicts Publius's repeated insistence that he will appeal only to his readers' "good sense" and reason. It also furnishes an important caveat for our reading of Christopher Looby's thesis about orality in *Voicing America,* in which he posits that "*voice* embodied a certain legitimating charisma" (4), a claim that recurs in his "Coda: The Voice of Patrick Henry." Writing of William Wirt's grail-like quest in the opening decades of the nineteenth century to recover Henry's "bold spirit and overpowering eloquence" (quoted on 266), Looby notes "Wirt's reduction of this discordant vocal mass [of the Founding] to a single charismatic originary voice" (278). But considered in relation to Publius's slippage into this fiery and *charismatic* language of hell-fire, it is clear that charisma was also perceived to carry great danger during these debates. If a charismatic speaker to redeem the garbled and imprecise demands of a "discordant vocal mass" was desirable, it was also fearful, for in the siren tones of the impassioned voice of a would-be Deliverer, period listeners heard as well the possibility of deception or of irrational appeals that would foil the best-laid plans of the revolutionary generation.

How then to make sense of Publius's lapse into the impassioned tones he presumably wants least to imitate? An insight Eric Havelock offers about the banishment of the poets from Plato's Republic may be of use. In his *Preface to Plato*, Havelock begins with a question about Plato's use of the word "mimesis": "Why should Plato, not content with applying the same word [*mimesis*] both to the creation and to the performance of the poem, also apply it to the learning act achieved by a pupil? Why in fact are the situations of artist, of actor and of pupil confused?" (24). The answer, Havelock argues, grows out of the fundamental assumption that in Platonic terms, true knowledge "is of the Forms and the Forms alone" (25), from which it follows that poets and artists are trebly removed from this true and absolute knowledge, insofar as they lack both "the precise knowledge that a craftsman . . . can apply to his trade" and "the precise aims and goals which guide the skilled educator in his training of the intellect" (25). The problem, then, is that poetry and poets indulge "in constant illusionism, confusion and irrationality," a "shadow-show of phantoms, like those images seen in the darkness on the wall of the cave" (25). If for Plato "reality is rational, scientific and logical," then poetry, "far from disclosing the true relations of things," merely disguises and distorts reality "by appealing to the shallowest of our sensibilities" (25–26). Here we come to the nub for our account of Publius.

Poets, like the sophists Publius so fears will pollute the debate over the Constitution, can play no part in the ideal polis, or in Publius's ideal debate, because *mimesis* is precisely the enemy of the rationalized world toward which Plato and Publius aspire.[56] Like early critics of the novel in the United States, Plato and Publius fear the artist's "power to make his audience identify almost pathologically, and certainly sympathetically with the content of what he is saying" (Havelock 45). This ability of poets in Greece to work themselves and their audiences into an utter identification with the characters in their epics stands in the way of the scientific rationalism of the kind that Plato—and

Publius after him—want to underwrite their ideal political system. The "un-hallowed language" Publius decries is a tempting language—an impassioned language that bypasses reason on a direct route to identification, or in Plato's time, memorization. It is precisely the attraction of the charismatic—Looby notwithstanding—Publius most wants his readers to avoid.

Or rather, it is, as always, a certain kind of charisma, a charisma in the service of the wrong ends—like a reading of history or of established authorities in the service of the wrong goals—that Publius decries, and so he enacts just what he would warn his readers against. This is the double-edgedness of the period's interests in oratory and the persuasive uses of tone, modulation, and vocal forms to close "the problematic gulf between intention and statement" (Fliegelman, Introduction xxxi). This is why charisma in the service of the right goals—the Constitution, for example—is a different matter. Publius's slip into the impassioned, charismatic rhetoric—into the markedly "literary character of the performance"—goes to the very heart of the representational quandary Publius and his compatriots face as they contest ratification: for if the charisma of the novel or the poet is persuasive, and one wants to be persuasive, then what is one—*generically speaking*—to do? Far from idle fears, these concerns reflect the highly charged nature of the public sphere within which these characterizations and arguments are taking place. (The passage of the Alien and Sedition Acts at the end of the decade is in this sense the precise culmination to the Constitutional episode, representing the profound distrust of a pervasive and popular political vernacular published in broadsides and newspapers by a wide range of citizens proclaiming their own "self-evident" truths rather than adhering to the truths articulated by the Founders. And as Nicholas Rombes notes, the Acts proscribed writing, printing, *and* uttering, "nearly the entire range of human expression," in its frenzied efforts to defend "the people," who, "because of their lack of civic virtue, . . . must be protected from the people themselves" [15–17].)[57]

Excursus: Poetic Federalism

> Emerson, for his part, addresses residues of the problem of charisma decades later by abolishing the partiality (read: subjectivity) on which it stands. The poet in Emerson's scheme transcribes poetry from a source that always and necessarily precedes and exceeds his limited temporal being:

> For poetry was all written before time was, and whenever we
> are so finely organized that we can penetrate into that region
> where the air is music, we hear those primal warblings, and
> attempt to write them down, but we lose ever and anon a
> word, or a verse, and substitute something of our own, and
> thus miswrite the poem. The men of more delicate ear write
> down these cadences more faithfully, and these transcripts,
> though imperfect, become the songs of the nations. ("The
> Poet" LAE 449)

In this manner, Emerson solves the problem of origins; poetry pre-
exists all poets, and if its perfected form is only ever approached
asymptotically—well, at least that is better than the pure contingency
of Publius's scheme, for Emerson has removed its origins in the vexing
limits of either individual or factional perspective. Thus Emerson's
Romanticism doesn't so much offer an individually invested alternative to the consensual style as address the problems inherited from an
earlier, eighteenth-century system in which the possibility of right
representation seems everywhere potentially thwarted.

Having "solved" this part of the writer/reader equation, Emerson
turns his attention to reception, and removes contingency from that as
well:

> Every one has some interest in the advent of the poet, and no
> one knows how much it may concern him. . . . All that we
> call sacred history attests that the birth of a poet is the princi-
> pal event in chronology. Man, never so often deceived, still
> watches for the arrival of a brother who can hold him steady
> to a truth, until he has made it his own. With what joy I begin
> to read a poem, which I confide in as an inspiration! And
> now my chains are to be broken. . . . (LAE 451)

In this scenario reading animates dimensions of a universal responsiveness always already present, and to that extent (when the
system is working properly) there is only One Proper response and
One Poet's Poetry that incites it. Out of many poets and poems,
one true transcription, one true voice. Publius's vision of filtration
perfected.

Disclaiming Interests

Two excerpts from *The Federalist* graphically illustrate how the fault lines around mimesis have in the 1780s opened up. In the first, Publius writes near the conclusion of his extended project:

> Thus have I, fellow-citizens, executed the task I had assigned to myself; with what success your conduct must determine. . . . I have addressed myself purely to your judgments, and have studiously avoided those asperities which are too apt to disgrace political disputants of all parties and which have been not a little provoked by the language and conduct of the opponents of the Constitution. The charge of a conspiracy against the liberties of the people which has been indiscriminately brought against the advocates of the plan has something in it too wanton and too malignant not to excite the indignation of every man who feels in his own bosom a refutation of the calumny. . . . The unwarrantable concealments and *misrepresentations* which have been in various ways practiced to keep the truth from the public eye have been of a nature to demand the reprobation of all honest men. It is not impossible that these circumstances may have occasionally betrayed me into intemperances of expression which I did not intend; it is certain that I have frequently felt a struggle between sensibility and moderation; and if the former has in some instances prevailed, it must be my excuse that it has been neither often nor much. (85: 482–83, emphasis added)

Publius's apology for those occasions in which he has lapsed into what he calls "asperities"—as in the "unhallowed language" passage—could hardly partake more fully of passive constructions: he depicts himself as no less the victim of his own verbal ingenuity (he has been "betrayed" into "intemperance") than of the "calumnies" of the class-baiting Anti-Federalists. First and last what concerns Publius is the truthfulness of his arguments, and so, not surprisingly, he finds entirely on the other side "unwarrantable concealments and misrepresentations."

Still, Publius's use of the word "misrepresentation" in this context is hardly coincidental, as Mark R. Patterson suggests: "What unites political and literary representation is the ease with which, in America at any rate, they can become misrepresentations" (*Authority* 50).[58] It is not, then, simply the case that Publius plays misrepresentation off against notions of truth-telling and appeals to his readers' "judgments"; rather, debates about the validity of various competing accounts of the Constitution's appropriateness or legality implicate themselves in the central substantive topic of those discussions—whether or not the government, and in particular, the legislative branch specified by the Constitution, is itself a "misrepresentation." What precisely constitutes "misrepresentation" is thus the topic of these Federalist and Anti-Federalist writings at a number of different levels, because they are invested not only in presenting their own arguments as "disinterested" but also in characterizing what it is that constitutes an interested argument in the first place. In a manner that should have profound consequences for our narratives about the development of literary representation in the United States, Federalists and Anti-Federalists agree that more than any other particular characteristic, an untrustworthy representation will reveal what they repeatedly refer to as "artfulness."

Thus Publius denounces "the little arts of little politicians" (11: 131), the "various arts and endeavors" (2: 93) deployed to produce a people's distrust in their leaders, and "the little arts of popularity" (68: 395) through which the unqualified gain important offices. His diminutive adjectives reinforce the contempt in which he holds these misguided and misguiding propagandists. Likewise Anti-Federalist writers have little patience for "the artful and ever active aristocracy" (F/A 34) and the "artful advocates" (F/A 98) of the new Constitution, who, they say, "are wilfully endeavouring [sic] to deceive" (F/A 43) in order to gain support for the convention's plan.

It is important to note that this skepticism about "art" and "artfulness" competes in the period against what seems to be their antonyms: a notion of "art" in the sense of the "artisanal" and referring to the useful occupations like printing, shoemaking, and the building trades. But these two discursive registers—one approbational, and one skeptical—are more harmonious than we might at first think. In part this is because artisanal skills are necessarily skills *about* something in particular, and, as Sean Wilentz and others have shown, these particular artisanal skills bring with them a corresponding concern with, and, especially over the course of the nineteenth century, a growing militancy in support of, particular interests. The federalizing distrust of the particular in favor of the common—a distrust, that is, of the direct in favor of the virtual, of the interested in favor of the disinterested—renders the seemingly approving cultural apprehension of the useful arts closer to the distrusted artfulness that is scorned.[59] Laura Rigal remarks on just this correspondence:

> In contrast to local assemblies and the federal House of Representatives, it was the federal Senate that was, in theory, less likely to become the "tool" of any particular interest or "mechanical" influence. By virtue of sheer distance, the Senate's view was to be relatively untainted by locale and particularity; it was expected to maintain an "elevated" view of the public or common good, while remaining dynamically balanced by the negative pull of local attachments. . . . Like federal poets, then, federal senators epitomized the principle of distanced and virtual, as opposed to actual, representation. . . . (32–33)[60]

Even where a discourse of art may not seem to carry the negative consequences of artfulness on which Publius and his Anti-Federalist counterparts endlessly declaim, the slippage of the one into the other is a possibility that is always available, and that further complicates the inheritances in the nineteenth century of these central paradigms. Within this logic, what others write are to Publius "the incoherent dreams of a delirious jealousy, or the misjudged exaggerations of a counterfeit zeal" rather than "sober apprehensions" (46: 301); the additional qualification of "counterfeit zeal" recalls the catalytic contest in these debates that inexorably pits copies of all kinds—political copies and literary copies, legislative copies as well as argumentative ones—against originals. (Indeed so untrustworthy are the Anti-Federalists that even their "zeal" is "counterfeit," a copy.) Publius's claims that he is providing for readers of *The Federalist* a "faithful copy" of the principle truths of the Constitution stand in particularly ironic counterpoint to his political recommendations for these same reasonable readers: a system of indirect, filtered representation that he insists is in their best interest.

Generic Anxiety

Nowhere is the example of the conflation between rhetorical and political representation more telling than when Publius loses touch with his prohibitions against "artful" representation and participates in the very kind of rhetoric he so forcefully renounces. The following passage begins plainly enough as one of the numerous strategies Publius employs to discredit the opposition:

> The moment we launch into conjectures about the usurpations of the federal government, we get into an unfathomable abyss and fairly put ourselves out of the reach of all reasoning. Imagination may range at

pleasure till it gets bewildered amidst the labyrinths of an enchanted castle, and knows not on which side to turn to escape from the apparitions which itself has raised. Whatever may be the limits or modifications of the powers of the Union, it is easy to imagine an endless train of possible dangers; and by indulging an excess of jealousy and timidity, we may bring ourselves to a state of absolute skepticism and irresolution. (31: 219)

For Publius any deliberation about "the usurpations of the federal government" leads inevitably to "an unfathomable abyss," even though, from one perspective, such a topic permits *only* hypothetical contemplation, there being quite literally no precedent (elsewhere one of Publius's chief argumentative undergirdings) on which to draw.[61] Publius distrusts any work of the imagination—what he calls "conjectures" and "ravings"; it is precisely this intolerance that makes all the more interesting Publius's expansion of the image of the abyss into "the labyrinths" of a castle. The elaboration of the metaphor points up a space (an abyss?) between form and content, between Publius's argument about the dangers of the imagination and his argumentative strategy for conveying these dangers. The disjunction grows especially visible in No. 29 when Publius's "imagination" seems to "range at pleasure" once again:

> In reading many of the publications against the Constitution, a man is apt to imagine that he is perusing some ill-written tale or romance, which, instead of natural and agreeable images, exhibits to the mind nothing but frightful and distorted shapes—
> "Gorgons, Hydras, and Chimeras dire";
> discoloring and disfiguring whatever it represents, and transforming everything it touches into a monster. (29: 211)

These lines not only make the expected argument that the authors of tracts against the Constitution are composing "some ill-written tale or romance"; Publius also suggests that it is *the reader* and his imagination that are responsible for the creation of these tales.[62] (In this respect his critique borrows from criticism against the eighteenth-century novel and its predominantly female readers.)

Publius also presents in these lines a nascent theory of genre, for it is not only the (presumably ill-tempered) reader who is responsible for these misguided effects, but also the genres of "ill-written tale[s] or romance[s]" that "discolor and disfigure whatever [they] represent." It should not be surprising that castles and labyrinths—in a word, the familiar framework of the gothic novel—find their way into Publius's argument. After all, in Cathy Davidson's succinct formulation, "the Gothic in particular questioned the rules of rationalism that, for those in power, conveniently ordered their interest and their status" (237). Even the passage's interpolated line—though from Milton's epic description of Hell in *Paradise Lost* (2.628)—replicates the horror of the gothic already present in the passage as a whole, while simultaneously aligning the gothic with the imaginative, the satanic, and (not least) the literary.[63]

Publius disavows the gothic, then, as the first step in his programmatic attempt to distance his writings from genres that place imagination, rather than moderation and rationalism, at their center.[64] In the next essay, he returns to the subject of genre:

> Reflections of this kind may have trifling weight with men who hope to see realized in America the halcyon scenes of the poetic or fabulous age; but to those who believe we are likely to experience a common portion of the vicissitudes and calamities which have fallen to the lot of other nations, they must appear entitled to serious attention. Such men must behold *the actual situation* of their country with painful solicitude, and deprecate the evils which ambition or revenge might, with too much facility, inflict upon it. (30: 216, emphasis added)

If the gothic as a mode of writing and, by extension, a metaphor for governmental intrigue have both been cast away as unreasonable (in a sense, unreadable, or perhaps, fearfully, *too* readable), this passage rejects the possibility of the poetic-pastoral and its "halcyon scenes." Publius insists to the end that representations provide apprehension of, and access to, "the actual situation." In centering his explication at the point of moderation and on a mode of representation that claims transparency—representation that is not really representation at all (and so cannot be charged with "virtuality")—Publius delimits some of the modes of the "literary" with which the nineteenth century and Romanticism will become invested. His profound distrust of the broad rubrics of artfulness will, with the advent of Romanticism, eventually come to be aligned with the valorized status of high art and high literary production. By the mid-nineteenth century, literary writing comes in part to be categorized and evaluated on the scheme of attributes that Publius here undermines in constructing his arguments in favor of the Constitution. "Artfulness" and "ravings" will, less and more, come to be the categories that mark the "artistic" value and achievements of those called "artists."

If the Constitution laid the groundwork for facing up to the virtuality—the built-in partiality—that is representation, then, looked at one way, the story of American literature in the United States is the story of gradually, over the course of the nineteenth century, making this virtuality into a "literary" virtue. What Publius tries to erase from the realm of the political—its interested, factional identity—eventually trickles down, unevenly, into the domain of the literary. Something of this development and its stakes are visible in Charles Brockden Brown's elaborate apology/"Advertisement" at the opening of *Wieland* (1798), in which he insists that the book corresponds to "the known principles of human nature" (3), even as the novel repeatedly characterizes Carwin, the biloquist and narrative prime mover whose appearance brings murder and incest, as an "Author."[65] As late as the Renaissance, some of Matthiessen's canonical figures evince a palpable discomfort with the "individuality" or the manifest "partiality" that virtuality imparts to all written representations. Thus Hawthorne's "Custom-House" narrator vouches for "the authenticity of the outline." Into the nineteenth-century—Matthiessen and his heirs notwithstanding—"Americans . . . think of linguistic performances as collective experiences imparting instruction" (Gilmore, "Literature" 546)—what Hawthorne calls, in the preface to *The House of the Seven Gables* (1851), a demonstration of the "truth of the human heart" (1).[66]

This chapter's examination of the place of representational virtuality in the Constitutional debates challenges American literary history to reflect more accurately the gradual emergence of the recognizably "literary," and to account more fully for the political consequences in relation to which such an emergence occurs. As Gilmore explains, "an individualized regimen in social and economic relations was the necessary complement to the rise of Romantic art in the United States" ("Literature" 555). But this process is variegated, and the legacies of an older, communal form persists alongside a tremendous skepticism about the artful and the interestedness of the individual's perspective. How two nineteenth-century writers play out some of these inheritances is the subject of the next three chapters.

Michael Warner has found in the eighteenth century a tension between two ways of conceptualizing print, roughly configured along a chasm between a public realm of civic virtue, and a less-sanctioned and morally suspect realm of private consumption.[67] In a related way, Cathy Davidson discusses the wholesale attacks on the novel by a wide range of political, cultural, and religious leaders who were reluctant to approve of writings associated with the much-maligned category of the privately pleasurable.[68] I would take these arguments a step further to say that the vision of America offered by *The Federalist* leaves almost no room for the kinds of imaginary projections and fantastic representations—in a word, the noninstrumentality—that, from a later perspective, have come to be associated with much that is valuable in literature and the literary arts. For Publius and his Anti-Federalist compatriots, there is little permissible space for the contrary-to-fact, for the irrational, for the novel(s)— or rather, little space before imagination reverts to the labyrinthine alleys of a castle from which there may be no escape. In the end, the consensual must have its day, and "literary production"—including the literature of political praxis, like *The Federalist*—remains what Ferguson has called "profoundly social" (*Enlightenment* 164). To the extent that the artful isolates the art of the individual apart, to that precise extent it is suspect. There are no American Adams in *The Federalist*.

Of course it is also a question whether there are any American Adams in the American Renaissance, and from this perspective we do well to reevaluate the writings of Ralph Waldo Emerson and Walt Whitman, especially to the extent that our canonical understanding of these two figures have been rooted in a presumed clarity of post-Romantic assumptions: about the distinction between the realms of the literary and the political, about the inherent value of Art. The conclusions I have drawn from this chapter's reading of the debates over the Constitution might well be taken as a provocation to approach Emerson and Whitman (along with the other writers of Matthiessen's Renaissance) from the other historical end, as it were, considering their writings as extensions of eighteenth-century textual and publishing practices rather than primarily as exemplars of Romantic and post-Romantic dicta.

Federalists and Anti-Federalists are best seen as participants in a larger debate—both in the sense that, as this book will demonstrate in subsequent chapters, the determination of the meanings of America and the Constitution did not end with ratification, and in the sense that the ostensibly "political" arguments in these documents meld repeatedly with the concerns that a later period will separate out as "the literary." The debate over ratification was, among other things, a single significant way station in an ongoing cultural conversation about representation in its rhetorical and political valences, and on both of these issues the two authors with whom *Reconstituting the American Renaissance* is centrally concerned have much to tell us.

CHAPTER TWO

REREADING EMERSON/WHITMAN

I would write on the lintels of the door-post, *Whim*.
—EMERSON, "Self-Reliance" (1841)

Unscrew the locks from the doors!
Unscrew the doors themselves from their jambs!
—WHITMAN, *Leaves of Grass* (1855)

In the early spring of 1860, Ralph Waldo Emerson and Walt Whitman walked across the Boston Common and disagreed as to whether the projected "Enfans d'Adam" section for the third edition of *Leaves of Grass* was suitable for publication. Though Emerson left no account of the exchange, and Whitman left at least three separate ones, it seems certain that Emerson argued that for various reasons the poems would best be left out. According to Whitman, Emerson was concerned that these explicitly erotic poems might limit the book's readership and so also its influence; a preponderance of critical accounts suggests that Emerson was offended by the explicit sexuality of the poems.[1] In response, Whitman felt, as he later told Horace Traubel, "the clear and unmistakeable [*sic*] conviction to disobey all" (quoted in Kaplan 249), and within a few weeks he published the poems on schedule in the third edition.

I raise this incident of dissensus on the Common to open out a largely forgotten possibility for American literary history: that we might interrogate, rather than simply assume, the nature of the relation between Emerson and Whitman. For, at least since the publication of F. O. Matthiessen's *American Renaissance* in 1941, the question of the nature of this central literary relation has not been much of a question at all: Whitman has usually been seen as the writer most directly and extensively influenced by Emerson. When Matthiessen reiterates near the end of *American Renaissance* that "Whitman set out more deliberately than any of his contemporaries to create the kind of hero whom Emerson had foreshadowed in his varying guises of the Scholar and the Poet" (650), he is recapitulating his central axiom of the Emerson/Whitman relation as marked definitively by Emerson's precedence and primacy: Whitman follows Emerson's model for becoming a Poet. More recently, David Reynolds has said of Emerson's famous 1855 letter to Whitman (discussed at some length below) that it "was by far the most glowing and, in terms of Whitman's poetic aims, the most appropriate. . . . If Lincoln's Gettysburg Address remade America, . . . Emerson's letter came close to making Whitman" (*Whitman's America* 341–42). Certainly there is a great deal to say about the uses to which this letter has been put—both by Whitman and by others—as well as about the political/literary comparison on which Reynolds builds this analogy. But his contention here also recapitulates the long-standing critical view that Emerson did not simply make Whitman's reputation but also somehow made Whitman himself. Of course one source for this commonplace may be the well-known but, it must be said, highly ambiguous quotation in which Whitman asserts that he had been "simmering, simmering, simmering; Emerson brought me to a boil" (quoted in Trowbridge 166).[2] What does it signify to be "simmering?" Is "boiling" a metaphor for unanimity, as most commentators have assumed? And what is the significance of the exchange Trowbridge records having with Whitman, just before this famous quotation?: "I asked him if he thought he would have come to himself without that help. He said, 'Yes, but it would have taken longer' " (166).

As organic as the link between Emerson and Whitman now appears to be, however, a review of critical history demonstrates that Emerson has not always been seen as the obvious writer in relation to whom any serious appraisal of Whitman must begin. A century ago W. S. Kennedy considered Whitman's relation to Emerson a topic meriting little more than a passing comment: "It, after all, makes very little difference what Emerson thought of Whitman," Kennedy wrote, "since the latter *clearly* sweeps an orbit vaster than his own, and has in every respect a broader and more massive nature" (78, emphasis added). Kennedy attributes Emerson's failure fully to grasp Whitman's achievement a function of "that clerical ancestry (eight generations of it), that Boston respectability!" (78):

> It is with mortification that one remembers that during all the years of Emerson's life he never printed one word of allusion to—let alone admi-

ration of—Whitman. In one of his posthumously published letters to
Carlyle he alludes apologetically to the poems of "one, Walt Whitman, a
printer," which he sends him telling him he can light his pipe with the
volume if does not like it. This is all very pitiful. (78–79)

There will be occasion to return to this characterization of Whitman as "a
printer" below, but for now it is important to note how resolutely Kennedy
takes care of Emerson. Of the genesis of the famous 1855 letter, Kennedy explains that Emerson "had for once been startled out of his starched clerical
propriety into an enthusiastic impulsive action; but, as Mr. Traubel has said, 'he
was never discovered off guard again' with regard to Whitman'" (*Fight* 58).
There is no deliberate re-creation by Whitman of himself in Emerson's image in
this version, no discipleship except perhaps Kennedy's of Whitman (no mean
discipleship, granted).[3] Instead there is a good deal of misrecognition, and not
all of it to Emerson's credit.

Since Kennedy, Matthiessen's monumental influence has all but precluded
the possibility of viewing Whitman's writings as significantly dissimilar from
Emerson's—through the lens, for example, of the incident on the Common,
which foregrounds disagreement and separation rather than identification.
Harold Bloom's Oedipal amplification of a master/disciple paradigm has pro-
vided further critical undergirding for this common version of Emerson/
Whitman. In Bloom's view Emerson set Whitman not only "simmering" but
anxiously struggling with his belatedness in relation to Emerson his "Master."
These are the parameters of well-known Bloomian anxiety, and in *Poetry and
Repression* Bloom rereads the opening sections of "Song of Myself" for their
simultaneous "swerve away from Emerson, even as they appear to celebrate an
Emersonian realization of the self" (256). Tracing what he considers the disin-
genuous statements Whitman made over many years about his debts to Emerson, Bloom sees Emerson as the single most sublime American obstacle for any
American writer, even one as "gigantic" (256) as the Whitman who seeks to
carve out an original space and discourse of his own.

Consolidating this account in a pair of review essays published in the *New
York Review of Books*, Bloom insists even more strenuously that Whitman
cannot be properly read without a full reckoning of his Emersonian essence:

I give the last word here . . . to Emerson, who wrote the first words about
Whitman in his celebrated 1855 letter to the poet, words that remain true
nearly a hundred and thirty years further on in our literary culture:

I am not blind to the worth of the wonderful gift of *Leaves of Grass*. I find it the most extraordinary piece of wit and wisdom that America has yet contributed. ("The Real Me" 7)

Bloom's giving the last word to Emerson makes sense insofar as his analysis begins with Emerson as well: "If Emerson founded the American literary religion, Whitman alone permanently holds the place most 'emblematic of the life of the spirit in America'" ("The Real Me" 4). Here we come face-to-face with the Whitman that Emerson creates (the Whitman created through Emerson), one who has abandoned the possibilities of the body in favor of the claims of "the spirit."

Indeed, Bloom insists that the corporeal constitutes no significant part of Whitman's "Real Me," a phrase that he uses as his title for the 1984 essay on Whitman that originally appears in a significant passage from *Poetry and Repression*:

The "real me" or "me myself" in Whitman could not bear to be touched, ever, except by the maternal trinity of night, death, and the sea, while Walt Whitman, one of the roughs, learned from Emerson to cry: "Contact!" There is a sublime pathos in Whitman making his Epicurean *clinamen* away from Emerson by overproclaiming the body. Emerson had nothing to say about two subjects and two subjects only, sex and death, because he was too healthy-minded to believe that there was much to say about either. Emerson had no sexual problems, and was a Stoic about death. (257)

In Bloom's account, Whitman's attachment and attention to the body generates two possibilities, though we would not want to pursue these without noticing first how his premises recapitulate a classically American equation between sex and sickness that has led Michael Warner lately to declare the United States the "land of sexual shame" (*Trouble* 21). For Bloom, Whitman's attention to the corporeal, to sex and to death, allows for two equally problematic alternatives: on the one hand, it is a mere stratagem by Whitman to distance himself from an omnipotent Emerson, a gesture that only betrays the repressed fact of true discipleship; on the other hand, such attention to sex and the body announces Whitman's sickness. These are difficult and reductive options.

Now without doubt Emerson does seem to crave "contact" in a way Bloom suggests: one thinks immediately of the lamentation in the essay "Experience" for the "evanescence and lubricity of all objects" that make Waldo's death frustratingly, grievously "caducous" and elicit the concomitant wish for a "rough rasping friction" (*LAE* 472–73). Chapter 4 below traces in detail the complex cultural frames through which both Emerson and Whitman engage and refract questions of materiality and the body's physicality, paying particular attention to the role that representations of slavery play in these dynamics. But it is the task of this chapter to demonstrate in detail that the "contact" Whitman endorses and strives after, as well as his relations to materiality more broadly, must come to be understood in fundamental terms as a great deal more than a mere (Bloomian) ploy to obscure a foundational, anxiogenic Emersonian origin.

Whitman offered at least three different accounts of his disagreement on the Boston Common with Emerson. Each account competes against the other similarly "authorized" versions, and in each Whitman is respectful of Emerson: in one version Emerson's position is called "unanswerable"; in another, Whitman describes him as "calm, equable, agreeable," "too wholesome, too well-balanced, to be moved by the small-fry moralities, the miniature vices," by which Whitman presumably means the charges against Whitman that he advocated free love and that Emerson might as a consequence be seen as guilty by association (quoted in Baker 417–18; also see 574n).[4]

In a third account, Whitman emphasizes the role of corporeality and begins with an assertion of Emerson's right-mindedness:

> Emerson's objections to the outcast passages in *Leaves of Grass* . . . were neither moral nor literary, but were given with an eye to my worldly success. He believed the book would sell—said that the American people should know the book: yes, would know it but for its sex handicap: and he thought he saw the way by which to accomplish what he called "the desirable end." He did not say I should drop a single line—he did not put it that way at all: he asked whether I could consent to eliminate certain popularly objectionable poems and passages. Emerson's position has been misunderstood: he offered absolutely no spiritual argument against the book exactly as it stood. Give it a chance to be seen, give the people a chance to want to see it—that was the gist of his contention. (20 April 1888; *WWWC* 1: 50–51; see also Baker 417–18)

Speaking to his own Boswell, Horace Traubel, who stands in for a group of similarly devoted disciples, the Whitman narrating here is at last himself the "Master"—to cite the complex word he used in the salutation of his 1856 reply to Emerson, his "Friend and Master." He can at last afford to be generous, which has of course very little to do with being either reliable or accurate. Thus to say that Emerson had no "spiritual argument against the book" is to say that Emerson had the good sense, from Whitman's (and Traubel's) perspective, to recognize the book's merits over and against a more generalized readership who paid very little attention to any of the first three editions of *Leaves of Grass*.

While it seeks to correct what Whitman apparently sees as a mistaken impression about Emerson, the passage nonetheless hinges on a distinction without a difference. Whitman clarifies that Emerson insisted on no excisions—"He did not say I should drop a single line"—though an instant later it seems Emerson would "eliminate certain popularly objectionable poems and passages," apparently to secure for the book the attention he (Emerson) felt it deserved. What Whitman gives with one hand—an Emerson who would leave the *Leaves* unchanged, an Emerson who understood what was central to the book's mission—is taken away in a broadened portrait of an Emerson who, Whitman tacitly suggests, utterly missed the point:

> If there was any weakness in [Emerson's] position, it was in his idea that the particular poems could be dropped and the *Leaves* remain the *Leaves* still: he did not see the significance of the sex element as I had put it into the book and resolutely there stuck to it—he did not see that if I had cut sex out I might just have well cut everything out—the full scheme would no longer exist—it would have been violated in its most sensitive spot. (*WWWC* 1: 51)

Emerson had no "spiritual argument against the book," but these lines reveal that he did demonstrate a "corporeal" argument against it, and that this is, Whitman makes clear, a nearly fatal failure of appreciation, however generous Emerson's overall appraisal may be.

Some months later, Whitman discussed with Traubel how he had treated Emerson over the course of his long life, and regrets, he says, that he wrongly, or ill-advisedly, or unfairly "used to charge Emerson (it was the one single charge I ever had to make against him) with culture—submitting too many things to the literary measurements." Already these terms invite analysis, for what is it to charge someone with "culture" but to invoke and to indict a deeply and complexly sedimented system of class assumptions that inform an individual's relations to the larger world? These social-class associations only become better synthesized in the sentence's remaining reference to "literary measurements."

"But nowadays," Whitman tells Traubel, speaking of the charges he has been prone to make against Emerson over the years, "I feel half inclined to retract it" (*wwwc* 4: 440). Whitman's most recent biographer discusses this exchange and asserts that "Whitman later regretted and rescinded the indictment." "Regretted" seems both possible and even likely as an interpretation of Whitman's discussion with Traubel; after all, if he did not regret it, why bring it up? But "rescinded" seems insufficiently nuanced as a summary for Whitman's claim that he feels "*half inclined* to retract" the criticism, because the verb "rescinded" leaves no space for this other "half."[5]

Beyond these local details of analysis, however, here arise the limitations of a strategy for reading Emerson/Whitman that relies heavily or solely on their own first-person accounts. This is the case not simply because of the complexity and even contradictions in these accounts, though Whitman's multiple versions of Emerson's response to the 1856 *Leaves* demonstrate this well enough. Rather, the genealogical approach to this relation begun in chapter 1 in the account of the Constitutional debates offers an alternative to the conflictual nature of these accounts, by proffering an alternative mode of interrogation concerned at its core, and quite literally, with where these two men are coming from—socially, ideologically, politically, culturally—at the time of the meetings these anecdotes variously narrate. To take Whitman's word as a methodological primer: "the other half" which remains when the anecdotal is "rescinded" permits interpretations that address evidence necessarily broader than the narrow circumstances of the moments when these two men's paths literally crossed. Displacing the local in this manner permits an encounter with the broader discourses that organize and pronounce Emerson's and Whitman's engagements not simply with each other, but with the world at large and the places of the word within it.

In this way Emerson's and Whitman's differences about the sexuality of the "Enfans d'Adam" cluster might be reimagined not as a mere conflict of "taste" or "literary measurements," but rather as a defining disagreement sufficient to undo the claims of a supposedly foundational Emersonianism in the first place. This would require acknowledging, for example, the corporeally and scatalogically inflected language that redoubles the central dispute when Whitman narrates Emerson's reaction to the "Children of Adam" cluster in the passages considered above. The primary issue is, of course, one of elimination; put simply: Emerson and Whitman disagree about what precisely counts as a "desirable end." This is not to say that Whitman does not wish to have the readers

Emerson apparently wants him to have; indeed, quite the contrary is apparently the case, and Emerson plays, as we shall see, an important role in Whitman's efforts to attract just such a readership. But Whitman also makes clear that Emerson's "spiritual" appreciation of the book fails to reckon how Whitman has "resolutely" "stuck to" the "sex element,"[6] and he explicitly describes Emerson's proposed deletions in corporeal terms: "if I had cut sex out I might just have well cut everything out" (WWWC 1: 51).

Following these analogies of editing-as-surgery from the poet who had, by the time of these narrations, seen his share of the horrors of amputation, the rhetoric concludes by reinscribing the anal erotics of Whitman's "desirable end" and the "weakness" of Emerson's position: excising these "popularly objectionable" materials would leave a book "violated in its most sensitive spot"— a thinly disguised allegory of bowdlerization and editing as rape. "Who touches this [book], touches a man." The story as Whitman narrates it suggests not only that Emerson missed the ultimate import of Whitman's writing, but that he also betrayed his own principles as set down in so seminal an essay as "Self-Reliance."[7] Asking Whitman to accede to the demands of the populace, Emerson violates the principle with which he was most closely associated: that any market-driven compromise is the first step down the slippery slope toward individual and cultural mediocrity. This is a point Whitman doesn't fail to make in (re-)writing the meeting on the Common.

One might take away from Whitman's narration the possibility that, when he chooses, Whitman can, in classically Bloomian style, out-Emerson Emerson; by refusing to remove the poems or edit the volume, he shows himself more self-reliant than the "Master." Bloom exemplifies this aspect of the paradigm's logic, calling Emerson "the inescapable theorist of all subsequent American writing" ("Mr. America" 19), while having earlier noted that "Whitman wishes to originate his own mode, but he cannot do so without some discontinuity with Emerson, a prophet of discontinuity, and how do you cast off an influence that itself denounces all influence?" (Poetry 256).

To challenge this paradigm, one must ask competing questions: how can a critic at this historical distance know when a "fundamental" difference in Emerson/Whitman is emerging—around, say, the site of the body and its "desirable ends"—and when one is facing instead what Bloom calls a "mere reaction-formation"? On what assumptions do even these distinctions depend? From what perspectives do they emerge? For it is possible to imagine that such distinctions might, over the course of a century and more's readings and misreadings, evaporate or even reverse themselves, one era's "fundamental" distinction—like Kennedy's "broader and more massive nature"—becoming another's quaintest critical delusion. To put this another way: Emerson is inescapable only within a hermetically sealed model of largely canon-driven literary history, one rooted at its core in a post-Romantic model of individual authorship that focuses on the achievements of particular writers whose influences on each other occur within some hyperbaric chamber of literary insight, independent of other aspects of culture, history, and experience. (Thus Bloom: "Indeed, 'Lilacs' echoes Tennyson, while 'As I Ebb'd' echoes Shelley and 'Crossing Brooklyn Ferry' invokes *King Lear*" ["Real Me" 6].)

But there must be innumerable influences that can be labeled an "origin" for any text, and more specifically, countless extra-Emersonian, pre-Emersonian, and non-Emersonian cultural sites and discourses in varied relation to which Whitman may have articulated what Kenneth Price calls "his version of manliness, his social outlook, and his attitude toward foreign inheritance" (45). These are precisely the sources and discourses that this book seeks to revisit, in part by insisting on the Constitutional episode as an ineffaceable precursor for the nineteenth century's Renaissance. To do so opens up these canonical relations and multiplies the historical sources and discursive contexts for reading and situating such textual artifacts.

In the particular case of Emerson/Whitman, for example, Emerson's rejection of the display of the body may have its discursive analogues in the disembodied virtuality of the Philadelphia plan, in which the embodied particularity of "the people" conveniently dissolves through the mechanism of representative filtration. Suddenly, what seemed to be "simply" a local dispute about a poetic cluster in the third edition of *Leaves of Grass* between these two representatives of the High canon occupies a new and vital historically situated plane. The problem of the body for Emerson and Whitman resonates with the problems of material particularity examined earlier in Publius's models for the abstracted constitution of a legislative body. In a similar manner the revolutionary aspirations of some toward a more equable distribution of material resources (Daniel Shays, among them) is replaced by the Founders with what some saw as a merely tepid redistribution of political power; recall James Wilson's refutation of the Constitution's privileging of stability over participation, its favoring the civil rights of property over the political rights of wide, democratic suffrage.

All of which is a way of saying that the body is never only about the body, that there is no pure apprehension of the corporeal, and that the fact of materiality is itself not simply the site of a Whitmanian swerve, but of a full-throated, however complicated, Whitmanian difference: his insistence that—"healthy minded" or not—the mundane facts of the physical universe, including the physical and sexual aspects of the human body, be incorporated into poetry on an *equal* footing with the "facts" of the spiritual universe. This chapter begins the present book's efforts to replace the standard version of Emerson/Whitman by investigating their relation within the broader frames of the materialist and macropolitical discourses put into play in chapter 1. Considered this way, what has looked like Whitman's resistance to Emerson may come to look instead like the persistence of contested differences within a genealogical chain that traces back (at least) to the moment of American constitution; their differences may newly register as the marks of Althusserian interpellative processes that are more capacious than the relation between these two men and that exceed the relatively local details of their letters, visits, and memories.

"Rereading Emerson/Whitman" investigates how the incident on the Common might usefully be deployed in a revaluation of Emerson/Whitman. My title attempts to map out quite specifically the parameters of this revision, for I seek not simply to repudiate Emerson/Whitman (the linkage often understood as influence-discipleship-resistance), but instead to reconsider a series of binarized terms through which American criticism routinely explains the writings Whitman produced both before and after the 1855 publication of *Leaves of Grass,* and which are commonly read in relation to Emerson. I am centrally interested in the "representative" status of the standard story of these writings derived from Matthiessen, and the documents (like the Emerson/Whitman correspondence) that are routinely invoked to authorize it. Do only *these* documents yield "representative" stories? Do these documents yield *only* this story? Where is the space in the standard view for Whitman's publication of the "Children of Adam" poems, for Emerson's willingness to excise "the sex element"? This chapter, then, is about estranging Emerson/Whitman, their relation to each other, and their relation to the stories we tell about the "literary" nineteenth century.

Intersection

One bit of evidence important for the disciple model in Whitman studies is a two-paragraph review of Emerson's lecture on "The Poet" taken from the

7 March 1842 issue of the *New York Aurora*, a paper which Whitman served as editor and for which he frequently wrote. The review has become important because it seems to answer a need in Whitman criticism to uncover what is repeatedly depicted as the mystery of Whitman's emergence. One of the most widely disseminated versions of this story appears in Malcolm Cowley's 1959 introduction to the Penguin reprint of the 1855 *Leaves of Grass*, an essay that has accompanied at least twenty-nine reprints of this oft-required classroom edition, and that declares the answer to the mystery of Whitman's emergence as "a mystical experience in the proper sense of the term . . . on a June morning in 1853 or 1854" (xii). Cowley utilizes a somewhat less specific version of the same model in his significantly titled "Walt Whitman: The Miracle": "There was a miracle in Whitman's life; we can find no other word for it. In his thirty-seventh year, the local politician and printer and failed editor suddenly became a world poet. No long apprenticeship; no process of growth that we can trace . . . ; not even much early promise: the poet materializes like a shape from the depths" (385). In Jerome Loving's coincident view, Whitman's attendance at Emerson's 1842 lecture in New York is the origin for his poetic development, his "drift away from the Actual toward the Real" while "in the meantime he was forced to continue as a journalist" (*Muse* 22).

Turning to the *Aurora* review, however, it does not seem that Whitman shares with either Emerson or the dictates of the transcendentalized literary history derived from him a predilection toward idealized abstraction and "the Real"; neither does it seem that he is pursuing journalism under duress. The review, on the contrary, treats Emerson's lecture as another good-natured opportunity for social observation and spends at least half its space delighting in the spectacle of "a very full house":

> There were a few beautiful maids—but more ugly women . . . ; several interesting young men with Byron collars, doctors, and parsons; Grahamites and abolitionists; sage editors, a few of whom were taking notes; and all the other species of literati. [Horace] Greeley was in ecstacies whenever anything particularly good was said . . . —he would flounce about like a fish out of water, or a tickled girl—look around, to see those behind him and at his side. . . . (*WWA* 105)[8]

Though the review is unsigned (as are so many of the editorial writings attributed to Whitman during this period, an issue examined below), it might be possible to identify precisely this excerpt's enumeration as a defining feature that links this review with other writings by Whitman, including the characteristic catalogs of *Leaves of Grass*. However, in the Emersonian model, as exemplified by Cowley, Loving, and others, the point is not continuity but rather a radical discontinuity that might be summarized in the binary "journalism/poetry": the process of "becoming" a poet is not artisanal, in the model of apprenticeship, but rather discontinuous and epiphanic. It is worth noting that the discontinuity of this model undermines the very term *foreground* as it appears in Emerson's welcoming letter ("I greet you at the beginning of a great career, which yet must have had a long foreground somewhere . . ."), and as it is often utilized in this school of criticism. For in a model that refuses or discounts a role for Whitman's journalism, the ground before, or in front of, Whitman-as-poet only *begins* with Emerson. What of the foreground prior to this Emersonian formation of the foreground, a foreground the very articulation of which in Emerson's letter seems to signal its unrecognizability?

Paul Zweig usefully shifts these origination studies in the direction of the material and the quotidian when he suggestively calls Whitman's compositional habits "journalistic . . . [and] formed by the professional habit of composing newspaper pages for all the jarring and ill-fitting tidbits of a day's news" (163). To read the evidence of Whitman's copious journalism in this way emphasizes a *continuity* between Whitman's early and later writings forged from the rough-and-tumble partisan politics of nineteenth-century newspapers, which were frequently financed by political parties. Indeed, it was a political quarrel with his boss that cost Whitman his job at the *Brooklyn Daily Eagle*. Imagining such continuities is in keeping with a version of the story Whitman provided in "A Backward Glance O'er Travel'd Roads" (1889):

> . . . I found myself remaining possess'd, at the age of thirty-one to thirty-three, with a special desire and conviction . . . to articulate and faithfully express in literary or poetic form, and uncompromisingly, my own physical, emotional, moral, intellectual, and aesthetic Personality, in the midst of, and tallying, the momentous spirit and facts of its immediate days, and of current America. . . . (LAW 657–58)

If the genre of *Leaves* has shifted toward "literary or poetic form," there is also a decided sense in which Whitman's mission in the poetry aligns with the modes and functions of his years spent as a newspaper editor. The attempt to chronicle "the . . . spirit and facts of . . . current America" and to align such a documentary function with the biographical intentions imbedded in that difficult word

"Personality" may usefully be seen as a version of the mixture of fact and fiction, of objective analysis and partisan, quasi-biographical speculation routinely offered up by nineteenth-century newspapers. As Lasch has explained, only in the late nineteenth century did newspapers begin to call themselves "objective" in the sense routinely in use today, and this process was by no means complete (if ever) in Whitman's early career.

Moreover, as Michael Gilmore explains, throughout the first half of the nineteenth century, "the Republic was not yet the definitively print society it became. . . . Print is usually thought of as a modernizing technology and a destroyer of oral culture, but the two media were not always distinct at this time . . ." ("Literature" 546). To remark these links between orality and print is to return to the ratification pamphlets and newspaper columns examined in chapter 1, and to highlight once more the continuities at sites where critical history has tended to see only discontinuity and rupture. The voice that is so resonant in Whitman's poetry reverberates the accents of pseudonymous authors like "Federal Farmer" in the eighteenth-century debating the Constitution and countless other civic matters. Indeed, Whitman's practice also recapitulates some of the tensions in these earlier texts, as when the common-man plain-spokenness resounding in an essay about taxation turns out to be a strategic fiction deployed by a member of the landed gentry.[9] Which is to say that noting the links between Whitman's practice and eighteenth-century analogues does not absolve literary historians from the hard work of adjudicating the standards of the "representative," though it does go some way toward answering the persistent strand in Whitman studies insisting that the Poet of Democracy arose "like a shape from the depths."

It has become a critical commonplace to assert as one of Whitman's most significant "literary" achievements his adoption of common language to the purposes of poetry, but this should not distract from the practices within which Whitman first "came to voice": more locally, newspapers, editorials, and the hustle of antebellum commercial print culture; more genealogically, the history of oralized print culture instrumentally present at least since the Revolution. *Leaves of Grass* represents from this perspective an *extension* of much that is found in Whitman's work as printer, editor, and all-around journalistic factotum. This "voice"—like Emerson's, as we shall see—is a complex hybrid.

The *Aurora* review of Emerson's lecture provides evidence of some qualitative, epistemological break only at the expense of its own colloquial texture and good-natured humor:

> This lecture was on the "Poetry of the Times." He said that the first
> man who called another an ass was a poet. Because the business of the
> poet is expression—the giving utterance to the emotions and sentiments
> of the soul; and metaphors. (*wwa* 105)

Whatever the diminution effect of these seemingly intentionally simple sentences, the fact is that the little Whitman does relate about the lecture—that the
poet gives voice to the stirrings of the soul—is knowledge anyone even remotely
aware of a movement called Transcendentalism might have carried into the
lecture. Indeed, a week before, the *Aurora* had offered a one-column explanation of the tenets of transcendentalism that Whitman is as likely to have written
as this review.[10] The review's ending lapses into extravagant platitudes—"it
would do the lecturer great injustice to attempt anything like a sketch of his
ideas"—alongside seemingly excessive, but probably equally common, hyperbole: "the lecture was one of the richest and most beautiful . . . ever heard
anywhere, at any time" (*wwa* 105). Was the reviewer—whether Whitman or
someone else—paying close enough attention to the speaker to offer anything
beyond these extravagant assertions? (It is a question students sometimes ask of
Emerson's letter to Whitman: did he even read *Leaves* before writing?) Whether
this reviewer listened to the lecture or not, he certainly seems to have recorded
well enough this cross-section of America listening.[11]

Pronominally Speaking: I/We

How a little-known newspaper editor and printer became "a uniquely important presence in the poetry of the twentieth century" (Ellmann and O'Clair 19)
is a central issue in Whitman studies. While this chapter presumes that much of
the "mystery" disappears when considered in the light of the continuities between the political and the literary as these functioned in the eighteenth and
nineteenth centuries, it nevertheless behooves us to interrogate more closely the
assumptions about the relation between journalism and poetry that may moti-
vate this question in the first place. These are distinctions that emerge as consequences of the larger genealogies this book addresses, and they bespeak a
tradition in literary studies that splits off the "emergence" of what becomes
the "literary" in the nineteenth century from the modes and genres of textual
circulation and linguistic performance that precede it in the eighteenth. The
handling of Whitman's early writings in relation to his "emergence" into the

poetic and the literary becomes within this analytical frame a microcosm within a single century for larger, macrocosmic trends at work across them.

The introductory materials to *The Gathering of the Forces*, a 1920 collection edited by Cleveland Rodgers and John Black that reprints Whitman's *Brooklyn Daily Eagle* writings, is a useful place to see these analytical mandates at work. The title of this collection is doubly significant: it places these editorials within a developmental scheme suggesting a gradual movement into full poetic battle dress, even as it separates out these writings from the truly literary achievements of the poetry. "In a peculiar sense," write the editors in their introduction,

> Whitman was The Eagle and The Eagle was Whitman. He made but slight use of the editorial "we" to give the appearance of anonymity to his writing, and quite frequently used the personal pronoun, unconsciously at times, as in his editorial on the monument to Lawrence: "I have a foolish weakness, when anything thrills me deeply, which in spite of all I can do, moistens my eyes." Such a human and Whitmanesque confession could never have come from an intriguing editorial "we." It is clear that Whitman often felt hampered by anonymity and the Whitman-Eagle duality produced some unique expressions. . . . (GF 1: xxxix)

The primary difficulty with this formulation is that, statistically, the evidence of the editorials themselves does not bear out the assertion that Whitman rarely employed the editorial "we." Quite to the contrary, most of these editorials display the standard nineteenth-century formula in which the first person plural forges a link between the editor and his usually partisan audience. But if it is difficult to understand the insistence that just the opposite is the case, it may be less difficult to speculate on the pressures that inform the compilers' decision to editorialize the evidence as they do.

One reason lies in that curiously mixed adjectival clause, "human and Whitmanesque," which works to combine Whitman's universal appeal with the particular artistry of the emerging poet. The editors of *Gathering* are in the peculiar position of having to argue both sides of the journalism/poetry binary at the same time: these editorials are mere preludes to the stronger, poetic efforts that will follow; at the same time, they are more than "common" editorials for having been written by Whitman. This oscillation surfaces in the difference between the first and last sentences in the excerpt just quoted. There, Whitman is at once perfectly matched to his medium—he is *The Eagle* and it is he—while at the same time (in the final sentence) he is artistically squelched by the newspaper's inherent limitations, the most significant of which is the convention of the plural pronoun. Indeed, that last sentence reverses itself yet again: Whitman is squelched by the pronoun conventions, but even this squelching results in "some unique expressions."

The specific problem of distinguishing the texture of Whitman's voice as original—and not, therefore, a generic and discursive hybrid—recurs in another edition of his early writings. In the prefatory materials to the volume of Whitman's articles from the *New York Aurora*, Professor W. L. Werner admits that "almost all these articles are unsigned," but then reassures us that Whitman wrote " 'most of the copy' " for the *Aurora* during his two months as editor. Werner writes that the greatest care in determining authorship has been taken by the editors: "Without attempting to establish every one of these items as Whitman's, Professors Rubin and Brown [the volume editors] have presented abundant internal evidence of Whitman's authorship by annotating later appearances of the same material and convincing parallels in style" (wwa vii).

Six pages later, though, Rubin and Brown do not sound nearly as certain. In a discussion of the relation between some competitor papers and the *Aurora* in the years before Whitman became editor, the editors cite the testimony of Thomas Nichols, who writes that, during his tenure at the *Herald* under the editorship of a Mr. Bennett, his (Nichols's) contributions to that paper were "so much in Mr. Bennett's style, in thought and expression, impudence and egotism, that my paragraphs were copied and credited to him about as often as his own" (wwa 1). Taken together these two accounts of the relation between individual voice and composite style betray an unease regarding authorial attribution: one side insists on the integrity of verbal parallels as a method for establishing authorship, while the other's notion of a "house style" makes apparent just how easy it might be to misattribute a text because so-called individuated styles can overlap. Put differently, the former of these positions insists on the determination of an author's individual style symbolized by the first person singular pronoun, while the latter calls that proposition into question by emphasizing the "we" of composite style implicitly behind (or within) the "I" (and here we might recall that the review of Emerson's lecture in the *Aurora* is unsigned).

Of course, one might argue that for Whitman just the opposite is the case, that the plural pronoun is actually his "characteristic," or "individualistic," mode of address across both the journalism *and* the poetry. This is evident not only in the exhortations in the poetry, its recurrent gestures toward "you and I," but even in the most "private" moments of the intensely "personal" "As I Ebb'd with the Ocean of Life," which, for all its self-examination, culminates in the speaker's splitting into component parts:

> We, capricious, brought hither we know not whence, spread out before
>   you,
> You up there walking or sitting,
> Whoever you are, we too lie in drifts at your feet.
>
> (*LG* 256)

These lines demonstrate a tendency even in Whitman's most seemingly private poetic moments to reach out toward some semblance of collectivity. Indeed, the movement from "I" to "we," the self as an always pluralizing "drift," may be one of the most insistent rhetorical moves in his entire corpus, as well as an extension of the insistently plural address and addressees of the newspaper. As Warner argues, "the public of print discourse was an abstract public *never localizable in any relation between persons*" (*Letters* 61, his emphasis).[12] Whitman's conceptions of writing, audience, and selfhood function within, and sometimes play against, a print-based notion of anonymity, and the consequences of these indistinctions for literary history is a much less clear account of the relations among (so-called) "literary" and "extra-literary" genres and texts in his corpus.[13]

The fact of a "house style" carries further repercussions beyond the relatively delimited question of whether the review in the *Aurora* can rightly be read as evidence of the historical intersection between Emerson and Whitman at a New York City lecture hall in 1842. Within the traditional conceptions of literary history, there are high stakes involved in asserting Whitman's individual poetic voice, figured metonymically as writing performed under the sign of the articulate and singular first person pronoun "I." The canonization of Whitman's poetic voice *as* original depends on an interpretation of these early writings that privileges singularity. Yet historically speaking, the distinction between authorial collaboration and individual authorship was itself a subject of contention when these writings were produced. Jay Fliegelman chronicles the consequences in the early nineteenth century of Jefferson's claim to be the sole "author" of the Declaration of Independence:

> The attacks on Jefferson all explicitly, in a new mode, identified author-
> ship with originality and the novelty of thought rather than with the act

of harmonizing—identified it, that is, with the articulation of one's individual personality rather than one's social nature. No longer was the ideal
of expression rooted in the authority of representativeness, the general
will, and historical precedent; it appeared, rather, in the articulation of a
sincere particular will, in a self-assertion that stigmatized the dissemina-
tion of traditional thought as but mechanical duplication. (*Declaring* 165)

Thinking historically about authorship's emergence complicates any account
about the usages and effects of the first person singular or plural pronouns as
these might be deployed in Whitman's (and/or Emerson's) writings. What may
look natural from our post-Romantic perspective—a perspective that Emerson
the prophet of self-reliance has had, in literary-historical terms, everything to
do with naturalizing—needs instead to be carefully placed within the traditions
of newspaper and printing practices, and of the period's writing conventions
more generally. Thus it makes sense to posit during these years an unrationalized coexistence of multiple modes of authorship associated with many varied
styles of pronominal use, the broadly consensualist mode described by Robert
Ferguson in chapter 1 shifting unevenly toward the assumptions about authorial individuality Fliegelman identifies. Looked at this way, it seems possible to
locate across Whitman's corpus a similarly unrationalized coexistence of modes
of the broadly collective and the uniquely individual: not a definite shift from
the "we" of the press to the "I" of the poems marking ("at last") artistic matu-
rity, but a fluid and fluent interchange between the two modes over the course
of many years that itself might productively be made the object of literary-
historical inquiry. Thus, too, Whitman's emergence after a singular identification with Emerson's "Poet" must be reconsidered as well.

Nominally Speaking

Few documents have more completely entered the mythology of American
literary history than the famous letter of 21 July 1855, which Emerson sent to
Whitman on receiving his complimentary copy of the first edition of *Leaves of
Grass*, a copy that may itself represent Whitman's intervention in what he knew
to be an insufficient system of marketing and promotion under which, as William Charvat noted, American authors often languished (*Profession* 46). The
letter is the best-known document in the "paper trail" of their relation, and yet
for precisely this reason—for being always so well-known—the letter is rarely

read at all. Yet only by examining the letter closely will a crucial fact about it emerge: neither the word "poet" nor the word "poetry" appears a single time in the 1855 congratulatory letter that has ostensibly marked the beginning of a great *poetic* career.[14] It is a realization of some consequence, given that the Emerson/Whitman relation is said so often to depend on precisely their conjunction at the central, still point of poetry—what it is, who makes it, how it works.

What Emerson writes, and what in fact frames his compliments, is a curious rhetoric of illusion and rebuttal. Beginning with its opening phrase—"I am not blind to the worth of the wonderful gift of 'Leaves of Grass,' " an assertion that begins, curiously, in negation—the letter recapitulates in at least two other places this emphasis on obscured vision and illusion. Moreover, grammatically speaking, Emerson's praise in this sentence goes to the "wonderful gift" and not to *Leaves of Grass* itself, imbedded as is Whitman's volume within the series of prepositional phrases. What we have discovered about this letter bears repeating, then: Emerson calls *Leaves of Grass* "the most extraordinary piece of *wit & wisdom* that America has yet contributed," and he applauds its "large perception." He declares it "free" and "brave," and sings its author's "courage"—but no variant of the word "poet" appears. If his latter correspondence is any sign, this seems an oversight of commission rather than omission; around this same time Emerson warns Carlyle that he may find *Leaves of Grass* "only an auctioneer's inventory of a warehouse" when sending him a copy, and he tells Caroline Sturgis it is "the best piece of *American philosophy* that any one has had the strength to write, American to the bone" (quoted in Loving, *Song* 221–22, emphasis added). "Wit," "inventory," "warehouse," "philosophy": the issue is not whether Emerson "liked" the book, or whether his letter to Whitman is "sincere," but what relation these other names for *Leaves of Grass* bear to the honorific title "Poetry," which occupies a position at the very heart of Emerson's epistemology.

Emerson's rhetoric of illusion notably recurs just after the most famous sentence in the letter:

> I greet you at the beginning of a great career, which yet must have had a long foreground somewhere, for such a start. I rubbed my eyes a little, to see if this sunbeam were no illusion; but the solid sense of the book is a sober certainty. (*1856 LG* 345)

Attention to the specifics of this rhetoric provides an equally solid sense that more than simply Emerson's vision is strained by the book he has in front of him. The notion of "foreground" that has catalyzed much Whitman scholarship signifies in the letter Emerson's attempt to recover a meaningful genealogy for the book, his effort to position it someplace within a range of publications or modes of writing. The emphasis, then, in this oft-quoted sentence could be on the "must," not the "foreground," where it has usually been placed. The prose then returns to its near-default image of blindness, of an inability to grasp; the metaphor of the "sunbeam"—"I rubbed my eyes a little, to see if this sunbeam were no illusion"—makes Whitman's book seem both delightful in its organicism and somehow threatening: it possesses a brilliance that almost makes its reader "blind." This rhetoric of the letter might be taken to record Emerson's surprise or disbelief at the discovery of something that is as alien and yet as familiar as Whitman's book may have seemed—a book that makes Emersonian claims to grandeur but that importantly changes the framework, language, and form of those claims. "It has the best merits, namely, of fortifying & encouraging," Emerson ends the paragraph, but he does not, significantly, tell who or what is being fortified and encouraged.[15] The book is powerful, but in an unfamiliar, ungraspable way—and the absence of grammatical objects at this end of the letter (as opposed to the sequence of prepositional objects at the beginning) bespeaks Emerson's difficulty of apprehension, or perhaps even his evasiveness.[16]

The possibility of illusion returns a final time in the letter's penultimate sentence: "I did not know until I, last night, saw the book advertised in a newspaper, that I could trust the name as real & available for a post-office." Of course it is clear what Emerson must mean: he seeks to verify the author's name, since it did not appear on the title page, and it takes two different forms where it does occur in the 1855 volume.[17] Nevertheless the form of this admission augments the undercurrents of disbelief or unbelief that wash through Emerson's response as a whole. This undercurrent rises to the surface nearly twenty years later when Emerson can find no place for the writer of *Leaves of Grass* in his 1874 *Parnassus* collection of American poetry (Monteiro 7). Within Emerson's canon of poetry in 1874, Whitman's name remains unreal, or at least unavailable.

Poetic Correspondences

Reading closely Emerson's letter, a different version of Emerson/Whitman begins to take shape, in part because instead of unequivocal praise or an announcement of the advent of the poet for whom Emerson had been looking,[18] the letter chronicles an Emerson who seems to be straining to account for the unusual object presented to him. Nonetheless Emerson's letter gains some of its deepest resonances in relation to the specific material context in which the names Emerson and Whitman very likely circulated together for the first time. For while Whitman released Emerson's letter to the *New York Tribune* for publication, and also printed copies of the letter which he specified at the top of each page were "for the convenience of private reading only" (Kaplan 205–6), the first published context in which Emerson and Whitman's names appeared together for at least some nineteenth-century readers would have been the 1856, second edition of *Leaves of Grass,* and, more precisely, the section of reviews reprinted just behind Emerson's letter in the appendix called "Leaves-Droppings."[19] Clearing our own vision of what it is we "know" to be true about Emerson's letter means clearing our vision as well of what we may surmise Whitman wants his readers most to notice about it. He, it seems safe to say, would have readers focus quite literally on Emerson's best-known endorsement—"I greet you at the beginning of a Great Career," which he embossed in gold on the second edition's spine (see figure 1). But it will also be the case that—however much Whitman might wish differently—one cannot judge the 1856 edition only by its cover.[20]

Placing our focus on the actual material characteristics of Emerson's words as they appear on the spine of the 1856 edition, it becomes clear that the quotation is actually much smaller than the critical history sometimes makes it seem. The volume was about six and one-half inches tall, and the quotation and its attribution—

I Greet You at the

Beginning of A

Great Career

R W Emerson

—take up approximately three-quarters of an inch of the book's spine. This should be compared to "Leaves of Grass" and "Walt Whitman," which also appear on the spine, and which, measured along with the leaf ornaments, occupy about two inches each. Whitman's own name is the most prominent information on the spine, at least if "prominence" is defined as proportion; moreover, this is the first edition of *Leaves of Grass* to announce an author's name anywhere on the cover or spine. Of course "prominence" might also be

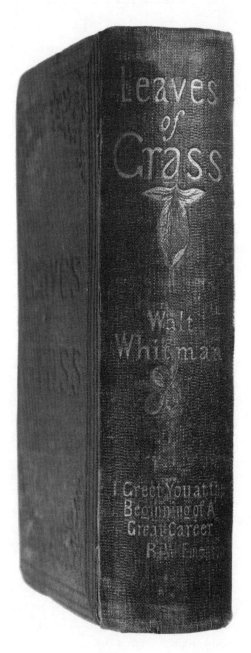

FIGURE 1. The spine of the second edition of *Leaves of Grass* (1856), including what will become Emerson's most famous sentence. Courtesy Special Collections, Northwestern University Library.

defined differently: as name recognition, for example, in which case Emerson is in 1856 probably better known within certain readerships, although Whitman's name was familiar in and around Brooklyn, and at the shop of Fowlers and Wells, where the edition was sold. Richard Teichgraeber, in tracing Emerson's growing national reputation, suggests that by the 1850s, and thanks to "a steadily growing number of excerpts and partial reprintings that appeared in anthologies, gift books, literary magazines, and newspapers," Emerson became a personage about whom "it became mandatory, despite the modest sales of the first American editions of his books, for educated Americans to establish where they stood in relation to his ideas and writings" (364). The question of the relative degree of overlap between these "educated Americans" and those who may have been patrons of Fowlers' phrenological bookstore nevertheless remains. More than anything, however, it may be the simple fact of these three lines of golden text in a position usually reserved for a publisher's name that most matters, since the second edition's use of the quotation on the spine in this manner seems quite unusual among nineteenth-century published books.

Indeed, I have been unable to find another example of a blurb used on a binding of a contemporaneous nineteenth-century book in the manner of the 1856 *Leaves*. Various practices of Fowlers and Wells may nevertheless give us a clue about Whitman's design. For example, bound volumes of their *American Phrenological Journal* show an embossed phrenological bust, in gold, at the same position on the spine that Whitman later placed the Emerson quotation (see figure 2). Likewise it seems Fowlers and Wells were fairly adept at tracking down accolades for phrenology wherever they could find them, and then reproducing them in the *Journal*. Madeleine Stern notes that "one of Emerson's half-praises of [phrenology] was picked up by the Fowlers who quoted a line or two from it as an endorsement of universal amateur phrenology" ("Emerson" 216). They would have had to choose their phrases carefully, since Emerson was a fairly skeptical commentator on this pseudoscience; the blurb was probably utilized in the 1860s or 1870s (see Stern, *Heads* 212).

For the few browsers who actually glanced at the spine of the 1856 edition in the shop of Fowlers and Wells at 308 Broadway in Manhattan, the "you" greeted by "R W Emerson" may have seemed initially to refer to themselves *as readers*, with Emerson a kind of publisher of the volume—a public(k)er, that is, which is precisely what Whitman makes sure he is. "I greet you [the reader] at the beginning of a great reading opportunity." "I greet you at the beginning of the great career of this writer." Leafing through the pages of poems these readers

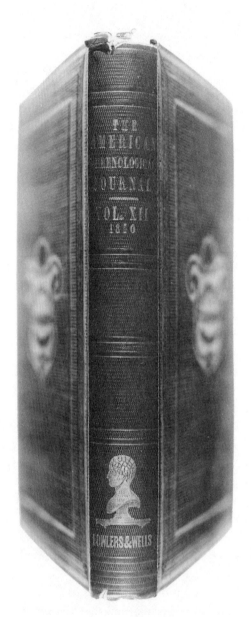

FIGURE 2. The spine of the 1850
volume of Fowlers and Wells's
American Phrenological Journal,
from which Whitman may have
learned some of the publicity and
design possibilities of the embossed
spine. Courtesy The Newberry
Library.

might have noticed that the pronouns function in a manner decidedly similar to that of the words on the spine, because in both places this casual reader would have found him or herself directly addressed, and similarly greeted, by the imprinted words:

> Listener up there! here you! what have you to confide to me?
> Look in my face while I snuff the sidle of evening,
> Talk honestly, no one else hears you, and I stay only a minute longer.
>
> (99)
>
> . . .
>
> Mon enfant! I give you my hand!
> I give you my love, more precious than money,
> I give you myself, before preaching or law;
> Will you give me yourself? Will you come travel with me?
>
> (239)

Whitman has appropriated Emerson's words and made them function as his own—and, to anticipate my argument, this is a paradigm that recurs wherever Emerson's name appears in the edition. Far from disappearing into the frame of its Emersonian endorsement, the 1856 edition integrates Emerson's words to a degree that may be difficult to reconstruct, in part because we read with a knowledge that a priori delimits the meaning of the quotation on the spine. We, for example, always already know who Emerson is, and, given the predominance of the discipleship model, we also already understand the significance of Whitman's gesture in light of what we perceive to be the overall movement of his career.

The prominence of Emerson's words on the spine, when viewed from within our canonical sensibilities, may also obscure certain other significant details about the 1856 edition: in particular, the latter edition's overall continuity with the first edition published the year before. For example, the steel engraving of the bearded Whitman that faces the title page in 1855 recurs in the second edition, where it faces a title page very similar to that of the original (see figure 4 in ch. 4). The widely divergent dimensions of the two books notwithstanding, there are in fact relatively few substantive changes between the two editions as far as the reader's entrance into the volume is concerned: the type for the word "Leaves" now appears in something like cursive in 1856—making it a bit more elegant—and the typeface of both the place ("Brooklyn, New York") and date of publication (obviously changed from 1855 to 1856) has been altered. Overall the

title page and its facing portrait in 1856 are similar to the earlier version, a continuity that may usefully be seen as Whitman's attempt to link the two editions,
and, perhaps, to attract a steady, or even returning, readership. So concerned
has literary history been with the obvious *differences* between the two editions—
Emerson's name on the spine, his letter reproduced in full at the back—that it
may have failed to appreciate the significance of these overarching similarities.[21]

William Charvat's argument that popular poetry "does not challenge the
reader on grounds where he does not wish to be met" (*Profession* 105) helps to
explain the second edition's curious mixture of revision and resemblance. The
latter volume is, as already noted, more modestly sized than the 1855 edition and
consequently easier to hold in one's hands. Likewise the second edition's table
of contents makes the book considerably more "user-friendly." Though, as
Charvat notes, selling poetry in the nineteenth century was a highly dubious
enterprise, the 1856 edition seeks not simply to capture sales but to train a
committed readership, and the table of contents accomplishes this in two
ways.[22] First, it provides titles for the poems that announce their subjects for
ease of reading and comprehension: "Poem of The Propositions of Nakedness,"
"Poem of A Few Greatnesses," "Poem of Faces," and "Poem of Walt Whitman,
an American" eventually titled (in 1881) "Song of Myself." Second, the word
"poem" appears in every single title in the 1856 edition, and in twenty-three of
them, "poem" is the first word. From a perspective in which the category
"poetry" is contested rather than "given," this repetition operates as a friendly
but no less resolute interpellation of readers, Whitman's insisting perfor-
matively on a valid "poetic" status for these unfamiliar and distinctly *un*poetic
writings, by any conventional understanding of poetry, to a possibly puzzled
and resistant audience that may have expected rhyme, fixed meter, and deco-
rous subjects.

The second edition is in these ways distinct from the first edition, which
contained no explanatory or descriptive table of contents and no titles to offset
the unfamiliar, rhymeless groups of lines. The print between the covers of the
1855 *Leaves of Grass* may not have seemed like poetry, and would thus not have
been "consumable" or "purchasable" for the reason Fredric Jameson clarifies
when he notes that literary genres may best be seen as "social contracts . . .
[that] specify the proper use of a particular cultural artifact" (106).[23] The 1856
edition, by contrast, attempts to live up *in part* to some conventional aspects of
the "poetry" contract (a table of contents, helpful "poetic" titles, a more handy
book shape and size), but without renouncing its radical thematic and formal

projects. In fact, in terms of its commercial mission—to sell copies, to train and to win readers—these are not concessions at all. Instead of conventionalizing either his meter or the topics he discusses in his poetry, Whitman redoubles in the 1856 edition his efforts to shape an appropriate audience for the unusual features of his writing. He appropriates the culture's privileged category "poetry" and applies it directly to his text by framing it with an apparatus designed to ease the reader into largely the same universe as 1855.[24] Though its lines failed to rhyme or demonstrate fixed meter and often extended virtually from one edge of the page to the other, and though its poems dealt with overtly political and sometimes sexually explicit subjects, the 1856 edition of *Leaves of Grass* insists that it rightly deserves to be included in the generic category "poetry"— despite Emerson's exclusion of the word. This is an assertion that carries important consequences for what has been called "The Continuity of American Poetry."

Rather than bespeaking Whitman's uncomplicated admiration or simple indebtedness, Emerson's name in the 1856 edition functions at the text's margins (on the spine, and in the supplemental "Leaves-Droppings") as a figure shown to be *both* useful for, *and* opposed to, the goals and prospects of Whitmanian poetics. In this way, "Emerson" fits into the edition's search for a readership as one element in a multifaceted advertising scheme.

What Is a Poet?

Indeed, some of Whitman's earliest extant notebooks, which date from between 1847 and the early 1850s, describe the work of the poet in ways so different from anything found in Emerson's writings as to shed profound doubts on the notion of "continuity" almost before the traditional story of modern American poetry has begun. These notebook pages show Whitman working out a conception of the poet intimately linked to two, and sometimes three, unexpected occupations—nurse, priest, and soldier. Emerson, it will pay to recall, portrays the poet as fundamentally a prophet of language and of abstracted Truth:

> The poet is the sayer, the namer, and represents beauty. He is a sovereign, and stands on the centre. For the world is not painted, or adorned, but is from the beginning beautiful; and God has not made some beautiful things, but Beauty is the creator of the universe. Therefore the poet is not any permissive potentate, but is emperor in his own right. . . . The poet

does not wait for the hero or the sage, but, as they act and think primarily, so he writes primarily what will and must be spoken. . . . (*LAE* 449)

By contrast, Whitman's notebook entries on the poet's role foreground physicality:

> I am the poet of Strength
> > and Hope
> Where is the house of
> > any one dying?
> Thither I speed and
> > turn the knob of the door.
> (Let) The physician and the
> > priest truly withdraw
> That I seize on the "ghastly" man
> > and raise him with
> > resistless will.
> Here is my arm,
> > press your whole
> > weight upon me

In these lines the poet's tasks merge with those of the physician and the priest—recalling the prophecy in the 1855 "Preface" that "There will soon be no more priests"—and he rushes to the aid of the dying person in need of his heroic nurturing attentions.

Subsequent pages in the notebook, written around 1850, confirm this poet's role:

> I dilate you with tremendous
> > breath,
> I buoy you up,
> Every room of your house do
> > I fill with armed men
> Lovers of me, bafflers of hell.
> Sleep! for I and they stand
> > guard this night
> Not doubt, not fear, not
> > Death shall lay finger
> > upon you

~~God and~~ I have embraced you, and
     henceforth possess you
     all to {our/my} selves,
And when you rise in the
     morning you shall find it
     is so.—[25]

As a gauge of this speaker's profound powers, the speaker's shunting God aside, by crossing him out on the original manuscript page, has left the passage grammatically incorrect, though perhaps appropriately so: the "I" who embraces the dying possesses multiple "selves," instead of a singular "myself." It is perhaps a logical error, one that registers something of the complex connection between this powerful poetic self and the others whom he attends. The passage, some of which makes its way into the 1855 *Leaves* (45), is everywhere about resuscitation, about the speaker's healing powers, dilating the dying with "tremendous breath," a dilation through written poetry and through the audible rushings of voice. Thus *dilation* is a particularly polyvalent word for describing the full range of this poet's task in raising the nearly dead to new life, and differently from the "utterer," "beholder," and "transcriber" of truths Emerson depicts.[26] Were we to search for a single term to describe the difference, we could do worse than to settle on the word "embodied"—just as the account of the disagreement on the Boston Common prepared us to conclude.

Whitmen

The first thing to note about Whitman's long printed reply to Emerson in the 1856 volume is the fact that the "letter," despite its appearance in the "Correspondence" subsection of the appendix called "Leaves-Droppings," is not, as Kenneth Price notes, really a letter at all—at least not within the standard definition of the term. Reproduced in "several thousand copies" because, Whitman writes, he could not "satisfy myself with sending any usual acknowledgment" of Emerson's letter, the reply marks another of the generic mixtures on which the 1856 edition is built, here redefining not poetry, but the presumed privacy and exclusivity of the letter in terms that collapse its differences from the publicity and anonymity of the print sphere. Which is to say that there is more than a little pamphleteering going on in Whitman's 1856 reply to Emerson—to borrow that term from the circulation traditions of the eighteenth-century ratification debates observed in chapter 1, and the whole range of published "letters" through which these debates were carried out. (Crèvecoeur's *Letters from an American Farmer* of 1783 may be the best-known example of this publication strategy.) The 1856 edition attempts to install a fiction that the various "editorial" writings that follow the poems are merely afterthoughts that could well have been left out entirely. Instead these appendices, when viewed in light of the marketing strategies deployed elsewhere in the edition, help specify the various references to Emerson as part of a network designed to convert readers to the project of the *Leaves*. Hardly "dropped," that is to say, this section exposes some of the most integral instrumental effects of the 1856 edition as a whole.[27]

Another way to approach this intersection of marketing strategies and the commercial with the literary would be to recall that around the time he was writing the early editions of *Leaves* Whitman was also writing lecture notes that were first issued as *An American Primer* about a decade after his death. One of the central motivating concerns for Whitman in these notes had become, in his executor Horace Traubel's words, "How am I to deliver my goods?" (vii). Despite having two, or possibly three editions of poetry in print or in process, Whitman (according to Traubel) was not yet fully committed to pursuing the path of *Leaves of Grass* as such:

> Whitman wrote at this Primer in the early fifties. . . . The most of the manuscript notes are scribbled on sheets of various tints improvised from the paper covers used on the unbound copies of the 1855 edition. There is later paper and later handwriting. But the notes were largely written in the rather exciting five years before the war. . . . After he found the book [*Leaves of Grass*] surviving into the 1856 and 1860 editions, some of his old plans, this lecture scheme among them, were abandoned. (vii–viii)

To read literally the correspondence between the remnant pages of the 1855 edition and these lecture notes foregrounds a possibility that Traubel hints at: namely, that Whitman is in this period at a crossroads in deciding how to get his message out. Indeed, Traubel's syntax reinforces this possibility when he writes Whitman as a kind of "spectator"—instead of an intentioned author— who "*found* the book surviving into the 1856 and 1860 editions."

In fact, one gets a considerably broadened view of Whitman's reaction to the simple marketing potential of Emerson's letter by recalling that he was also at this time continuing work as a newspaper editor, as an excerpt from the 1858

Brooklyn Daily Times shows. Here is Whitman at his playful, jokester, but no less self-promoting, best:

> Among the Supervisors elect of Westchester County, we notice the name of our friend William Cauldwell of Morisania. We cannot say, as R. W. Emerson did to the author of Leaves of Grass, "We greet thee on the threshold of a great career"; but we do say, with all our heart, full as it is, at the moment, of ancient reminiscences of many halcyon days passed with our friend Cauldwell, when we were both wont to read the Declaration of Independence on our cotton pocket handkerchiefs, All hail! brother Cauldwell. . . . (*I Sit* 173)

As expected, the editors of these early writings are quick to isolate this moment as Whitman's "only reference in the *Times* to his poetic work" (*I Sit* 231 n.21), but even if they are correct, it is also true that the passage cannot help but interrogate the canonical, high literary presumptions that have largely governed the reading of Emerson's letter and Whitman's reply. Moreover, it is hard to fail to notice that Whitman misquotes the line of Emerson's that has in American literary history come to assume so much importance. Or perhaps this is again Whitman appropriating Emerson: does Whitman see himself on a threshold—between what?—rather than at a beginning?

All of which is a way of saying that at the time of the second edition, there were a number of routes that must have presented themselves. Whereas from our perspective the 1856 edition is the second in a series that is Whitman's continuous life project, Traubel's notes force us to forfeit what Milton in quite another context called "foreknowledge absolute" in order to recognize that Whitman could not have known in 1856 what would be the success, or at least the duration, of the plans he had just begun to set in motion. Indeed there is no better material/textual fact to rid ourselves of the recurring critical notion that there occurred some singular, miraculous shift in Whitman's life around 1855, or 1842, than to consider what Traubel presents: a Whitman who is "recycling" as early as 1855, writing lecture notes on the discarded and unbound printed sheets of his "literary" debut, and unsure as to what is the best medium for his "goods." As Traubel writes in another passage from his introduction to *An American Primer*, "Whitman was undoubtedly convinced that he had a mission. This conviction never assumed fanatic forms" (vi). As the evidence about Whitman's multiple occupations and intertwined genres in this period attests, Whitman was not "fanatic" about the particular "form" of his "mission"—that is, about the particular *generic* forms that would best accommodate his inter-meshed political/literary ends. More important, it seems, was his concern that the "goods" get out. Would it be lectures, the polemic of "The Eighteenth Presidency!" or the restyled poetry he was calling *Leaves of Grass*? That the poetic form often understood as the most significant innovation by one of the founders of modern American poetry may have been—to him—beside the point (a medium rather than the message?) is, to say the least, an interesting possibility to contemplate.

Emersons

Turning in the 1856 edition of *Leaves* to the subsection in "Leaves-Droppings" labeled "Opinions 1855–6," a reader would have read this opinion quoted from the *London Weekly Dispatch*: "What Emerson has pronounced to be good must not be lightly treated . . . " (359). This straightforward assessment is the zenith for Emerson's "stock" in the 1856 edition's sampling of "Opinions." In the remainder of the extracts, references to Emerson and his writings are simply absent, or—more surprisingly—when they do appear, they function as an invitation to the reader to embrace *Leaves of Grass* specifically for its *counter-*Emersonian dynamics.

The *Examiner* of London's review, for example, draws on Emerson's 1855 letter; the critic wonders sardonically whether an ordinary list of items to be put up for sale at an auction "does not transcend in wisdom and in wit 'the most extraordinary piece of wit and wisdom that' (according to Mr. Emerson) 'America has yet contributed'" (381). The echoes in this London review would seem to demonstrate something of Whitman's success in circulating Emerson's letter far and wide. Nevertheless there seems no other way to account for this review's presence in the extracts section except as a calculated effort to capitalize on anti-Emersonian sentiment wherever it may occur. Where, that is to say, is one to locate Whitman's identification with Emerson if this "opinion" can be found in the same edition in which a line from Emerson's letter is embossed in gold on the binding, and in which Emerson is addressed as "Friend and Master"? These complications also speak against an approach that unduly homogenizes the notion of readership, since the 1856 edition seems designed to appeal to a range of readers: at the very least, it is aimed at both Emersonians and anti-Emersonians.

Melville's roughly contemporaneous *The Confidence-Man* (1857) suggests that there was a recognizably anti-Emersonian audience whom Whitman might have attempted to attract, though the keynote in many of the other included opinions is their decidedly class-based rhetoric. The first of these, from the *Boston Intelligencer*, faces the advertisement at the back of the 1856 edition and its listing of agents nationwide from whom a reader may order a copy of *Leaves*; the juxtaposition of the review and this most obvious mechanism of the market is particularly ironic: "This book," says the review,

> should find no place where humanity urges any claim to respect, and the author should be kicked from all decent society as below the level of the brute. There is neither wit nor method in his disjointed babbling, and it seems to us he must be some escaped lunatic, raving in pitiable delirium.
> (384)

A first response to this review may be simply to recall that, for the poet who would "sound [his] barbaric yawp over the roofs of the world," being "kicked from all decent society" may be very high praise indeed.[28] Still, the word "wit" reiterates Emerson's phrase in the 1855 letter, and, as I hope to show, the connection is not a spurious one. This review is founded on the same logic that underwrites Emerson's 1855 letter, in which Emerson praises Whitman's book but withholds from it the privileged name "poetry." Emerson's calling Whitman's book a "piece of wit and wisdom"—a phrase that makes *Leaves of Grass* sound like a nineteenth-century version of, say, *Poor Richard's Almanac*—shares with this review an inability, or unwillingness, to see Whitman's writings as the work of a "poet." The review takes the next logical step by identifying Whitman's writing as "neither wit nor method" and as "disjointed babbling," descriptions that deny the formal possibilities of the writing as poetry, even as they reject the content as representationally nonsensical. Still, Whitman chose to reprint both the review and Emerson's letter in the edition, which raises a now obvious but perhaps previously unexpected possibility: that Whitman reads and deploys Emerson's letter not simply as an endorsement, but as a negative review, like the one just quoted.

The 1856 edition wants to have it both ways—at least: to marshal the full marketing potential of Emerson's "endorsement," or simple acknowledgment, even while marking its differences from Emerson and from "traditional" poetry more generally. Rather than signaling discipleship, then, Whitman's foregrounding Emerson's letter, when reconsidered within the larger context of the other reviews reprinted in the 1856 edition, helps to restage their relation within a much broader and more complex range of concerns, having to do especially with the contested meanings of poetry. To say as much recalls the generic anxieties considered in chapter 1 and yields the renewed insight that—far from clear and established categories—the "proper" configuration of literary genres and the distinctions between them remains a subject of contestation into the period of the Renaissance, and beyond. What's more, these issues encompass not merely linguistic strategies restricted to some separate realm of "the literary" but are connected to shifting norms of (literary) propriety as well.

The generic slippage—poetry is not the unitary genre it has in literary history sometimes been said to be—opens out the possibility of other kinds of slippages that are kept in check by the generic category. Suddenly, Emerson's writing to Whitman is not only the extraordinary event that it has seemed to be. Though it is that, it can also now be fruitfully seen as another facet in the nineteenth century's ongoing conversation about poetry, and the reviews printed at the back of the second edition of *Leaves of Grass* along with Emerson's letter become pieces of the rich evidence we possess about the competing agendas of these debates. What are these distinctions between mere wit and poetry? Who decides in nineteenth-century America what qualifies as poetry? How do such decisions intersect with configurations of social class? with the publishing exigencies of a vastly decentralized market? Returning to the material text restores the possibilities and possibly the dangers of the market and of circulation, and what appeared to be static and authenticated (in Matthiessen's words, "Whitman set out more deliberately than any of his contemporaries to create the kind of hero whom Emerson had foreshadowed") now appears dynamic and open to review.

Another extract from the "Opinions" further demonstrates what is at stake in recovering a counter-, or non-Emersonian presence in this second edition. This review originally appeared in the London *Critic* and concerns in part the well-known engraving of Whitman that faced the title pages in both the first and second editions of *Leaves of Grass*. The *Critic's* reviewer makes his point schematically: "This portrait expresses all the features of the hard democrat, and none of the flexile delicacy of the civilized poet" (374). This brief excerpt dismisses precisely the possibility of the kind of democratic poetics *Leaves of Grass* might be said to embody, by placing as incompatible the roles "democrat" on one side, and "poet" on the other. Indeed, the democrat and the poet align themselves along something very close to stereotypical nineteenth-century gender lines, with the masculine "democrat" sharply differentiated from the effeminized, "civilized" poet. It may be sufficient simply to note how disruptive to the (British?) generic contract is Whitman's gendered configuration of the poet as nurturing, "tenderest lover" and simultaneously as butch/working-class Everyman.

This review signals once more a telling split in the Emerson/Whitman relation, not only because of Emerson's own squeamishness at some of the "hard" topics Whitman insisted were suitable for display in his writing, but because of Emerson's resistance about explicitly calling Whitman's work "poetry," even when he is otherwise bestowing praise. Another passage from the *Critic* highlights these contradictions. "Can it be possible," the reviewer asks,

> that its author intended this as a portion of a poem? Is it not more reasonable to suppose that Walt Whitman has been learning to write, and that the compositor has got hold of his copy-book? The American critics are, in the main, pleased with this man because he is self-reliant, and because he assumes all the attributes of his country. If Walt Whitman has really assumed those attributes, America should hasten to repudiate them, be they what they may. (376)

The rhetoric in this quotation engages what is and what is not "poetry" by drawing liberally on an array of class-based assumptions about America. Not the least of these is a strict hierarchy between the composing poet and the processes that bring his works before the public, specifically the manual labors of a compositor. The description is in this context unintentionally apt, of course, because Whitman performed the full range of the roles associated with—but increasingly, over the course of the nineteenth century, separated out and hierarchized within—the mechanisms of the literary market. Whitman *was* the composing poet, but that is a Whitman privileged at the expense of the *other* Whitmans who took part in the production of *Leaves of Grass*: Whitman the composing compositor, the printer, the publisher, as well as the all-around promoter and reviewer for the texts he produced.

These job descriptions and the labors they represent provide the substantial and definitive *material* basis for the familiar trope in both Whitman's writings and in critical thinking about them: the conflation of Whitman with his text. The 1855 or 1856 editions of *Leaves*—like the broad sheets of the 1848 *Brooklyn Freeman*—that a contemporaneous reader of Whitman's might have picked up would at least some of the time have been ones Whitman had literally produced.[29] These texts are themselves evidence of the time before "manu-" has dropped off the word "manufactory" in the artisanal zone of the printing house; Whitman participated in the production of his texts in precisely the way the English reviewer in the *Critic* (and Emerson) cannot understand. To return to the review's diction, Whitman *has* been learning to "write"; the "compositors" are now themselves writing the poems. Whitman's diction in his 1856 letter—"I much enjoy making poems. . . . the work of my life is making poems" (*LG* 732–33)—records these distinctions between poetry as epiphanic, as a transcription of celestial music (as Emerson describes it in "The Poet"), and of poetry as a trade, a form of embodied labor explicitly tied to larger economies of publishing, newspapers, and the book market more generally.[30]

The locus of anti-Emersonian sentiment in the review, however, is the damning reference to self-reliance—"The American critics are, in the main, pleased with this man because he is self-reliant . . ."—and the suggestion that it be repudiated. While the OED assigns credit for the phrase "self-reliance" elsewhere,[31] for many readers in the United States, Emerson represented this doctrine's leading and most familiar theorist; his essay titled "Self-Reliance" was first published in the 1841 *Essays: First Series*, although Rusk shows that he drew on the theme in lyceum lectures he gave on "The Philosophy of History" as early as December 1836 (244–6).[32] Thus the energy in this review's denunciation directed against Whitman is a recognizable broad-shot at Emerson as well, an effect that the reviewer perhaps attempts to account for, or even to soften, with the highly ambiguous final phrase "be they what they may." The reviewer at one level of course simply means that any "attributes" responsible for such monstrous writing as Whitman's must immediately be denounced, but he may also be aware that one of these "attributes," and the only one explicitly mentioned, is associated closely with the much-revered Emerson. The complexity of the situation becomes only more palpable when one remembers that the text within which this damning reference to self-reliance has been reprinted is one in which, to a very great extent, the author *has been* self-reliant with respect to so many aspects of its production.

The 1856 edition expects at least some of its readers to recognize these anti-Emersonian "extracts" in the "Leaves-Droppings" section, although these are hardly the only infusions of Emersonian *dis*identification to be found in the edition. The more significant place in which Whitman differentiates his volume from his Emersonian "Master" is the reply letter to Emerson itself.[33] The letter possesses a number of important distinctions that Whitman makes between his practice and Emerson's, including the important one already raised: Whitman's perception of his literary practice in distinctly material terms, as "making," not "creating," not "transcribing."

At the same time the 1856 reply makes strictly Emersonian points onto which literary critics and historians have forcefully latched; there is, for example, a call to arms addressed to American writers and thinkers that could have derived from the pages of Emerson's 1837 address "The American Scholar":

> America, grandest of lands in the theory of its politics . . . where are any mental expressions from you, beyond what you have copied or stolen? Where the born throngs of poets, literats, orators, you promised? Will you but tag after other nations? (*1856 LG* 348)

But if, as William Charvat has written, Emerson's "American Scholar" address before the Phi Beta Kappa Society at Harvard might best be seen as "a plea to his own class to recapture cultural power" (*Profession* 65)—that is, if we need to take care not to reduce Emerson's talk into an "essence" apart from the particularities of its occasion and audience—we should be no less careful in considering Whitman's revisions of Emerson's "message."[34]

To put the issue differently, Whitman's is a particularly idiosyncratic redaction of Emerson's themes in "The American Scholar," one that renders it different from a mere variation on the elder's theme. For Whitman, the reasons that the United States must produce a unique literary heritage reside firmly in the substantial facts of printing press capacities and circulation figures, and so once more bear comparison with the disembodied utterances of Emerson's "The Poet":

> Of authors and editors I do not know how many there are in The States, but there are thousands. . . . Of the twenty-four modern mammoth two-double, three-double, and four-double cylinder presses now in the world, printing by steam, twenty-one of them are in These States. The twelve thousand large and small shops for dispensing books and newspapers . . . —the one-cent and two-cent journals—the political ones, no matter what side—the weeklies in the country—the sporting and pictorial papers—the monthly magazines, with plentiful imported feed—the sentimental novels, numberless copies of them . . . —all are prophetic; all waft rapidly on. (*1856 LG* 349)

Whitman sounds in this emblematic passage like a proleptic William Charvat, explaining the development of a native literature by demonstrating the material conditions and publishing networks that render such development inevitable;

indeed, he shows it to be already underway. If Emerson takes heart at the beginning of "The American Scholar" that there remains in America a predictably ethereal "indestructible instinct" which he calls "the love of letters" (*LAE* 53), Whitman is bolstered by the fact that more than eighty-five percent of the most modern printing presses operate in American print-shops; there is in the distinction—the different foundations on which each man's observations are constructed—a world of representative difference. And this is importantly a distinction about materiality, which in the nineteenth century (as today) carries important connotations of social class, gender, and race. To recover the material basis, grounding, and instrumentality of what are often said to be Whitman's revisions of mainline transcendental Emersonianism is to change that Emersonianism in such a way, and to such a degree, as to render it in the end distinct from its very self.

Foregrounding the body as a prime site of Whitman's and Emerson's material differences, other divergences in the letter emerge as well. The most well-known is the issue of the representation (the representability) of sex in literature, and we return in conclusion to a debate we began by considering: Emerson trying to dissuade Whitman in 1860 from publishing "Children of Adam" while the two walked on Boston Common. Whitman's "promulging" of sex is a central tenet of the 1856 letter:

> To the lack of an avowed, empowered, unabashed development of sex, (the only salvation for the same,) and to the fact of speakers and writers fraudulently assuming as always dead what every one knows to be always alive, is attributable the remarkable non-personality and indistinctness of modern productions in books, art, talk. . . . By silence or obedience the pens of savans, poets, historians, biographers, and the rest, have long connived at the filthy law, and books enslaved to it, that what makes the manhood of a man, that sex, womanhood, maternity, desires, lusty animations, organs, acts, are unmentionable and to be ashamed of, to be driven to skulk out of literature with whatever belongs to them. This filthy law has to be repealed—it stands in the way of great reforms. (*1856 LG* 355)

This passage, among its other effects, turns the bourgeois order upside down by assigning the adjective "filthy" to what others might call discretion or decency. As Kenneth Price makes clear, Whitman's "early poems emphasize what Emerson dismissed from importance: the soul's medium is the body" (47).

Whitman establishes as the precondition for the development of literature in America this new sexual openness. "If it comes to a question," he writes, "it is whether they [American bards] shall celebrate in poems the eternal decency of the amativeness of Nature, . . . or whether they shall be the bards of the fashionable delusion of the inherent nastiness of sex, and of the feeble and querulous modesty of deprivation" (*1856 LG* 356).[35] And close on the heels of his emphasis on the necessity of articulating sex in literature, Whitman answers Emerson's doubts about the development of an American national literature. "Of course, we shall have a national character, an identity," he tells Emerson, and, not accidentally, everyone else who is reading: "As it ought to be, and as soon as it ought to be, it will be" (*1856 LG* 357). The assured, even complacent, tone—and its mixture of not a little teacherly, good-humored condescension— has the effect of undoing precisely the teacher/student hierarchy on which the letter in its opening salutation stakes out its origin: just who is "Master," and who the disciple, by this point in a correspondence articulated through, and articulating, noncorrespondence?

The end of the 1856 letter founders on precisely this sort of ambiguity. After Whitman has significantly rewritten Emerson's concerns as his own specific project for American literature, after he has projected independently a new American future—

> . . . that new moral American continent without which, *I see*, the physi-
> cal continent remained incomplete, may-be a carcass, a bloat . . . (*1856*
> *LG* 357–58, emphasis added)

—he is perfectly willing once more to invoke the name of his self-appointed patron, in order to close the circle that began with the letter's salutation, and indeed, with the binding of the book:

> These shores you found. I say you have led The States there—have led Me
> there. I say that none has ever done, or ever can do, a greater deed for The
> States, than your deed. . . .
>
> Receive, dear Master, these statements and assurances through me, for
> all the young men, and for an earnest that we know none before you, but
> the best following you; and that we demand to take your name into our
> keeping, and that we understand what you have indicated, and find the
> same indicated in ourselves. . . . (*1856 LG* 358)

This peroration may resonate with some of the hyperbole in the *Aurora* review of Emerson's lecture. The capitalized "Me" (vs. the lowercase "you") in the first paragraph just quoted is the initial sign that Whitman as composer-compositor may be less than willing to pass along *all* the credit and the reverence to Emerson. More clearly, its ambiguity circulates around the two uses of "indicate," neither of which offers definite antecedents for the two objects ("what" or "same"). Of course, in some sense the antecedent in both cases is the whole of the preceding letter—long-winded and complicated as it is, and by no means a simple redaction or recapitulation of a strictly Emersonian line.

The notion of discipleship, however, grows utterly more complicated at the moment that Whitman, speaking for *his* followers, "demand[s] to take your name into our keeping." In the first place, "keeping" itself brings with it the sense of preservation, of something antiquated and removed for security, perhaps even of taking Emerson, crucially, out of circulation. Moreover such a "demand" effectively reverses at its initial utterance the power relations presumably inscribed in the letter's first sentence: "Here are thirty-two Poems, which I send you, dear Friend and Master . . ." (*1856 LG* 346): indeed, it may now be apparent that the very terms of this salutation (Friend/Master) are contradictory, if in a classically antebellum American way.[36] Whitman's demand, in the voice of a plural "we," might also usefully be taken as an epigrammatic summary for the whole of this analysis of the 1856 edition, for that volume is a grand gesture in "taking" Emerson's name, absorbing it, "keeping" it, and binding it—in short, trading on it—as one in an array of devices employed, ultimately, to secure readers for *Leaves of Grass*. "No one," W. S. Kennedy wrote, "has denied that Whitman was not aware of the slowly rising fame of Emerson, and that he had not read notices and reviews of his books in the journals. In fact he knew just enough about him to think it worth while to send him a cheap paper-covered copy of the book" (*Fight* 80).

Whitman's use of Emerson's letter as endorsement for a book filled with additional poems that, as Justin Kaplan notes, "Emerson could not possibly have seen" (207) may actually serve as a microcosm of the different conceptions of literary property and social propriety—not to say poetry—that the two men bring to their newly begun relation in 1856. Indeed, it does sometimes seem as if the whole of the relations I have been attempting to sketch out returns again to those two cognates: property and propriety. What is the proper subject matter of poetry and what the proper use of a private letter? How does a former newspaper editor and editorialist, accustomed to writing always in the first person plural, read, or deploy in print, the singular, first person pronoun of Emerson's congratulatory letter?

To ask these questions is only to hint at the manifold ways in which the 1856 *Leaves of Grass* articulates, contravenes, ventriloquizes, disputes, refuses, and relies on a range of printing, phrenological, publishing, poetic, periodical, and political discourses of nineteenth-century Manhattan and the United States. I have in this chapter attempted to intervene in our received American literary history, in part to demonstrate the necessity of imagining Whitman's work (and Emerson's, for that matter) as originating in, and reflective of, a much more capacious discursive context than the singularity of an author-driven canonical history permits. The following two chapters also address these larger discursive and material contexts, while focusing on a range of texts associated with the names "Emerson" and "Whitman," in order to demonstrate further both the persistence of the nation's founding compromises and the insistent presence of its political contests within a realm increasingly understood to constitute the literary.

CHAPTER THREE

CLASS ACTIONS

∾

"Now, you can . . . say, 'Ah, but he wasn't thinking of any of that stuff.' Well, of course, he wasn't. But to say that he wasn't doing it is something else."
—GREIL MARCUS, on Elvis Presley

The substantial function of literature is to *secure consent.*
—FRANCO MORETTI, *Signs Taken for Wonders*

Among the 154 journals, notebooks, account books, and pocket diaries compiled and published in the standard edition of Emerson's *Journals and Miscellaneous Notebooks* (*JMN*), four stand out as peculiar textual artifacts, not so much for what is written inside them as for their form.[1] In each of these four notebooks, Ralph Waldo Emerson made space for his own compositions or daily entries by first excising writings by his father—sometimes simply by crossing out or writing over extant lines, but usually also by tearing out pages or whole quires and the old spine and then rebinding a "new" volume within the covers used first by William Emerson.[2] Because his techniques were anything but uniform, these notebooks are veritable palimpsests, containing not only various compositions by Ralph Waldo Emerson but traces of writing by William Emerson, by a number of Ralph's brothers,[3] and by his son (Edward Waldo Emerson, the editor of the first collected *Journals*)—not to mention other early collaborating editors (like James Eliot Cabot, who worked with Edward on the first edition), and the editors of *JMN*.[4]

Interpolation

At the very least, the presence of multiple hands in these texts complicates the authorcentric model imposed on them by the editors of *JMN*, but I aim with this comment not to devalue their very significant labors; no scholar who has perused Emerson's often illegible handwriting, fading marginalia, partial erasures, and insistent interlineations can come away with anything but the utmost respect for the efforts of the editorial team that produced over the course of a quarter-century this latest edition of the journals. Quite to the contrary, I mean to emphasize the extent to which the original source texts actively oppose even the most arduous attempts at accurate and complete transcription of what Emerson wrote, as this passage from the editorial guidelines of JMN suggests:

> The text, while partially emended, comes as close to a *literatim* transcription into print as is feasible. It represents what Emerson wrote, in the way he wrote it, including cancellations, revisions, and variants. Omitted silently are Emerson's miscellaneous markings, practice penmanship, false starts at words, isolated words or letters, and other trivia, if in each instance there is maximum certainty that the element omitted has neither meaning nor significance. (JMN 1: xxxviii)

Such are the strict discriminations needed to "tame" the manuscripts and make them conform to the parameters and assumptions governing the reproduction of "what Emerson wrote, in the way he wrote it." And this is not yet to mention the elaborate array of symbols and abbreviations the editors utilize to signal penmanship styles, ink types, and text positions, as well as the copious footnotes filled with translations and annotations that variously make accessible aspects of the text in the shift from manuscript to print.[5] On any single page in JMN, these textual mechanisms police the perimeters of the author's sanctioned work, while brackets alert the reader to the infiltrations of the writing of others, and footnotes literally underwrite the productions attributed to the author—not to say, the production of the Author. In a word, the editorial project in JMN epitomizes what Foucault has observed, the author-function performing at its most orthodox as the "principle of thrift" delimiting "the proliferation of meaning" ("Author?" 118). Having set for themselves a standard to include everything except those elements that they are certain possess neither "meaning nor significance," at once an extremely ambitious and ambiguous goal, requires nothing less than these multiple domesticating editorial procedures and translations. From what perspective can all possible "meaning and significance" be known? Where would one have to be standing to see such a definitive, and definitively limiting parameter? Despite their heroic labors, or perhaps because of them, this is not a question the editors are able to ask.

This chapter's investigation of the representational strategies and attendant class dynamics encoded in early writings by Emerson and Whitman opens by first reconsidering the authorial paradigm within which the editors produced *JMN*, and the mode of individualism with which it is aligned. To do so requires a more detailed consideration of a significant omission in the editors' transcription of one of the four palimpsestic texts I have begun to describe. Referring to the inside of the front cover of the text they have named "Sermons and Journal," the *JMN* editors specify that

> the page bears a partial index to "Vol. 39" of William Emerson's manuscript sermons. Besides writing by William Emerson, writing of other different styles appears. But there is no positive reason to suppose that except for a penciled note by Charles C. Emerson the writing is not Emerson's own at different times. (*JMN* 3: 120)

This index attributed to William Emerson and the lines by others do not appear anywhere in the transcription of "Sermons and Journal"—seemingly in accordance with the editorial intention to recover and reproduce only what Ralph Waldo Emerson wrote.

But this omission also excludes the lines Ralph Waldo Emerson drew through the entries in that index when he prepared what had been his father's notebook for his own writings. Not only are these expunging lines missing, however; also quite literally lost in the transcription is any sense of the way the younger Emerson interspersed his epigraphs to the journal (passages from Juvenal, Bacon, and Locke, among others) in the spaces *between* the entries in the index he had crossed out, even though such details would seem to go some way toward meeting the *JMN* editors' criterion for including "the way he wrote it." Additionally, the exclusion of the crossed-out lines of the index comes at the expense of the strongest metaphorical resonances of another passage on the page in Ralph Waldo Emerson's hand that the editors do reproduce:

> I Seid Abn Haer built this pyramid in six years. Let him that cometh after me & says he is equal to me pull ⟨it⟩ down the pyramid in ⟨3⟩ thirty. And yet it is easier to pluck down ⟨tree⟩ than to ⟨pull⟩ build up. (*JMN* 3: 120)[6]

Restored to its original context in the source journal that belonged to his father, the passage reflects somewhat ironically on the project Ralph Waldo Emerson has just completed—not only writing his own sermons in the remnants (the covers) of his father's book, but "pulling down" by tearing out the pages of William Emerson's sermons and the spine that bound them together. This reading is lost because neither the remnants of William Emerson's words nor the lines drawn through them are transcribed in *JMN*. Instead those words (or representations of them) are relegated to the footnotes. For a reader of only the transcribed journal, this summary leaves unanswered a number of details: what part of the page? how partial? in what form does the index appear?

My interest in these questions has less to do with the particular features of this specific text and more to do with the assumptions that guide the decisions: specifically, the notion of the individual author as it becomes implicated in the space between the edited version of this inside front cover, and that cover's prepublished form on the shelf in Harvard's Houghton Library. The actual journal offers a very different version of Emerson the author, one that foregrounds not his independence and isolated authority but rather his participation in various practices that are both culturally situated and historically specific. Most significantly, the text-as-palimpsest grounds these propositions in material forms and in a way that (as my punning title to this section suggests) usefully engages with Althusser's significant formulations about interpellation in his widely known essay "Ideology and Ideological State Apparatuses": that the ideological interpellation of the subject is imbedded in and carried out by particular material practices and rituals dispersed among a number of ideological state apparatuses, including the educational system and the church.

It may be useful before delving into these Althusserian paradigms to consider another example of Ralph Waldo Emerson's material inheritance: a notebook used by William Emerson as a copybook for prayers that his son recycled as a catalog for book titles between 1870 and 1877. In "Books Large" (the *JMN* title for this notebook, transcribed in volume 16), Emerson crossed out his father's table of contents on the inside front cover before flipping the whole book over and using its back cover as his front. But he also went to the trouble of tearing out—perhaps with the help of a straight edge—the pages his father had used, a process that has left for bibliographers stubs ranging from three-quarters of an inch to one- and one-half inches wide. Thus a book largely given over to a listing of classic texts in many disciplines across many centuries began with the excision of writings by his father that were themselves more than half a century old.[7] And the ineradicable fact of "Books Large" is the way, once more, that Ralph Waldo Emerson's book is literally bound within the remnants of the older text; moreover, in at least one place, the text records the younger Emerson's writing on a page his father had written on some sixty years earlier.

I want in the following pages to complicate the notions of authorship and literary production that underwrite the editorial praxis in *JMN* by incorporating a genealogical reading of Emerson and Whitman not simply as makers, but as at once "made" by, and re-makers of, discursive traditions that have their roots in the nation's constitutive representative dilemmas. Such an interpretation places at its core the Althusserian assumption that "all ideology hails or interpellates concrete individuals as concrete subjects" (173). The significance of this claim emerges when Althusser draws out of the humanist term "subject" not merely the notion of "a free subjectivity, . . . author of and responsible for its actions," but also "a subjected being, who submits to a higher authority, and is therefore stripped of all freedom except that of freely accepting his submission" (182). Within the practices that sustain ideological interpellation, the independent agency of subjects is primarily fictional, since "the subject acts insofar as he is acted by the . . . system" (170).

The goal in revolving this chapter around the fixed point of Althusser's hypotheses, however, is not to root a "definitive" meaning for Emerson's and Whitman's writings in some kind of overtly deterministic universe.[8] Rather, by invoking Althusser's formulations, I seek to shift our perspective sufficiently to examine the ways in which Emerson and Whitman might themselves be considered "representative" subjects, particularly with regard to the cultural institutions and practices of social class. In this way we may have occasion to revisit our investment in the unique literary generativity that these two men have come to represent, by considering their interpellated positions as subjects writing within—and so necessarily and variously constrained by—larger sociocultural frames. Such an approach may have the significant effect of balancing what has been the more usual approach to these writers and their texts, an approach evidenced in Matthiessen's *American Renaissance* (although not originating with him) when he explains that his "main subject has become the conceptions held by five of our major writers concerning the function and nature of literature, and the degree to which their practice bore out their theories" (vii); thus Matthiessen announces the governing interpretive tautology in *American Renaissance*, which treats the author as a singular, productive agent, not only of texts, but of the terms for the critique of those texts as well.

Rather than read Emerson's appropriation of his father's books and these scenes of unwriting and rewriting as the inscriptions of Oedipal conflict, I take as my point of departure the startling material *continuity* between the writings of this father and his son, whom Evelyn Barish rightly nominates a "scion of New England's oldest intellectual traditions" (248). William Emerson's writings *enable* those of his son, and the most straightforward assertion that might be derived from the bibliographical details just rehearsed might run this way: William Emerson quite literally left a place in which his son could take up a pen and begin to write. Ralph Waldo Emerson's writings bound within the covers of texts provided by his father thus reveal themselves a fitting emblem of the Althusserian binding(s)/boundaries of subjectivity. And in the pages that follow I seek by way of contrast to unfold the no less concrete inheritances that enable the writings of Whitman as well. If Matthiessen treats Emerson's and Whitman's works as if they emerged out of, and consequently filled, a vacuum—as quintessentially and equivalently "American" for having been written by Americans in an essentially classless America—this chapter reads an abundance of detail from these texts to reconceive not only the relationship of these two authors to the republic within which they both lived and wrote, but also (continuing the project of chapter 2) their relationship to one another. To examine the class-inflected dynamics present in the writings of these two men makes visible features of their relationship previously obscured, partly because the presumed generic equivalence between them at the site of poetry helps hold some of these other issues at bay. Here is further evidence for unmasking what chapter 2 began to suggest: an Emerson and a Whitman caught in 1856 midstep in a dance of mutual misrecognition.

"Good blood does not lie"

American criticism at least since Matthiessen has widely disseminated an Emerson who is a rebel and a democrat, but the Emerson who emerges from his early writings is not clearly either of these; he seems rather the spokesman of political axioms—like the current section heading (*JMN* 3: 356)—inherited from his father's social position in which "to be termed a 'democrat' was a reproach" (Barish 14). This is a younger Emerson who, at the age of seventeen, writes in his journal that the "privilege" of separating "the soul for sublime contemplation" "is denied altogether to three classes," which he goes on to identify as "the queer," "the downright," and "the ungainly."[9] These rather cryptic categories refer respectively to those who show a "lack of common sense," those who "do jobs," and an unspecified group who for one reason or another, Emerson writes, "shocked my nerves" (*JMN* 1: 33–34). The sentiments reiterate in many ways those his father had presented in a sermon delivered fifteen years earlier, in 1805, to commemorate the fifth anniversary of a charity called the Boston Female Asylum. On that occasion, William Emerson assured his audience of wealthy listeners that the girls in the asylum would be educated sufficiently that they might read their Bibles, but not so much that they might challenge the economic and social systems that, in his words, "destined" them to what he called a life of "service"—by which he intended the menial occupations the charity had trained them to perform (Barish 14–15).

Such examples help establish how the younger Emerson shares with his father a great deal more than simply the four books in which they both composed sermons or kept journal entries. In their affiliations with Boston's most significant Unitarian churches, and with Harvard College (both took degrees there, and both served as members of the Board of Overseers), father and son demonstrated their access to, and substantial status within, a Boston cultural aristocracy based in social standing as much as economics, and consisting of the families of prominent men in the church, politics, and the administration and faculty of Harvard College. Ronald Story helps explain these coincidences when he calls attention to the increasingly nepotistic tendencies of these Boston institutions over the course of the nineteenth century, "which tended to channel oncoming generations into given slots in an 'increasingly hierarchical structure'" (8). While Emerson's family came to know indigence in the years following William Emerson's early death in 1811, his family "was not invisible within the small society of Boston, . . . and the plight of . . . [the family] of the city's most fashionable minister recommended . . . charity" (Barish 56). Another word for "charity" in this case might be "connectedness": from the beginning, Ralph Waldo Emerson's future prospects depended to an important and sometimes overlooked degree on his inherited position within a religious and cultural elite affiliated with Harvard, overwhelmingly Federalist and Unitarian in their political and religious affiliations, and active in a wide range of civic, cultural, and commercial concerns (Story 7–8).

Significantly, then—and somewhat counterintuitively, given the teaching positions and other jobs he held to help his family make ends meet in the years following his father's death—Emerson's list of those excluded from the presumed benefits of spiritual contemplation includes those who "do jobs," common workers. To explain why this may be the case, Story argues that the years that overlap with Emerson's attendance at Harvard saw a gradual "process of exclusion" of students from less privileged or connected Boston backgrounds (90–94).[10] He also traces a gradual homogenization of student behavior and expression at Harvard that begins in this same period (ch. 7). Taken together, Emerson's exclusion of laborers and its concomitant negation of his own work may signal his socialization within the new demographic and social expectations at his undergraduate institution. Mary Cayton has described a "latent but important conflict between [Emerson's] ascribed social station and the material circumstances of his life" that has its roots in this period (*Emergence* 15), and it is important to note where Emerson's allegiance in both his public and private writings is repeatedly aligned.

There is a journal passage from 1823 in which Emerson, traveling in Connecticut, recounts meeting and talking with a miner; the tone of the account is not condescension so much as good-hearted amazement at how hard the man works: "In this part of the work he has 40 dollars for every foot he advances and it occupies him ten days to earn this" (*JMN* 2: 184).[11] In these early writings composed during and soon after his attendance at Harvard, Emerson's stance on the question of labor oscillates between, on the one hand, the wonder displayed in the passage about the miner, and, on the other, simple erasure, since most of the time, workers and work, per se, play no part in his schemes, except when he actively denies their participation.[12] George Kateb appropriately remarks how difficult it is "to believe that Emerson appreciates the typical activities of ordinary persons in the world" (*Self-Reliance* 25).

Very much the same pattern exhibits itself many years later, after Emerson has left the ministry and begun his lecturing career. In his address "The Uses Of Natural History"—presented in 1833 to the Boston Society of Natural History, an association of gentlemen, including Emerson's cousin, George B. Emerson, who helped him get the speaking engagement—his perspective on the issue still excludes manual laborers:

> The history of modern times has repeatedly shown that a single man devoted to science may carry forward the mechanic arts and multiply the products of commerce more than the united population of a country can accomplish in ages. . . . This is forcibly illustrated by the historical fact of the influence produced in France by the appointment of the celebrated Duhamel to the professorship of the School of Mines. (*EL* 1: 12)

Emerson goes on to quote approvingly the Secretary of the French Academy, who offers this summary after cataloguing a long list of the industrial benefits that have come about through Duhamel's appointment:

> "Doubtless it is not to a single man, nor to the appointment of a single professorship that all this may be attributed[,] but it is not the less true that this one man, this one professorship has been the primary cause of these advantages." (EL 1: 13)

One can easily understand why Emerson would incorporate such a quotation into his lecture, since the Secretary's remarks enunciate one of his recurring central themes: the power and influence of the single dedicated man. But it is no less true that, at one very significant level, Emerson (like the Secretary) fails to account for the actual "primary cause" of the benefits France has garnered, for nowhere in this rhetoric is there a position for the miners who actually enter the mines and through their labor permit France, in the Secretary's words, " 'to yield iron at the same price as in England' " (EL 1: 13). Indeed the verb "yield" makes it seem as if the earth voluntarily gives up the ore directly to an awaiting French marketplace. These lines are only a few logical steps away from the better-known formulation of a similar sentiment, from *Nature*: ". . . you cannot freely admire a noble landscape, if laborers are digging in the field hard by" (LAE 42).

This exclusion of labor and the laborer is a recurring Emersonian blind spot, as when he muses about "Progress" in an early notebook: "The plough displaces the spade, the bridge the watermen, the press the scrivener" (JMN 4: 253).[13] The passage is revealing precisely because it treats as (rhetorically) parallel what are two importantly different modes of "progress": one marked by improved mechanical implements (from spade to plow), but the other including human laborers who nevertheless stand in equivalent grammatical positions to those implements in the last two clauses (from watermen to bridge, from scrivener to press). As Christopher Beach has compellingly explained, relying in part on Bourdieu's notion of "bodily hexis," and in part on Charley Shively's groundbreaking work on Whitman's "Working-Class Camerados,"[14] Whitman is in many ways precisely the type of working-class individual whom Emerson's rhetoric routinely excludes; indeed chapter 2 shows his insistent self-depiction of his work as a poet in the specific terms of labor and craft—or, more resonantly, "pressman" and "scrivener": "I much enjoy making poems."[15]

This distinction becomes strikingly clear when viewed in the light of a syllogism from Emerson's 1836 lecture on "Art" given at the Masonic Temple in Boston:

> What is it that gives force to the blow of the axe or crowbar? Is it the muscles of the laborer's arm, or is it the attraction of the whole globe below it, on the axe or bar? In short, in all our operations we seek not to use our own, but to bring a quite infinite force to bear. (EL 2: 45)

Here the rhetorical movement is sharp and smooth, at the expense of erasing the laborer and his effort: by the time of the second question, he who wields the tool has all but disappeared, replaced in Emerson's answer by a universalized "we." Whitman's "Broad-Axe Poem," first published in 1856, provides in relation to this passage a pointed study in contrasts that lingers with more than incidental attention on various aspects of workers' laboring bodies: "The blows of mallets and hammers, the attitudes of the men, their curv'd limbs, / Bending, standing, astride the beams, driving in pins, holding on by posts and braces, / The hook'd arm over the plate, the other arm wielding the axe . . ." (LG 186).[16]

Emerson's attitudes toward labor complement another rhetorical strand that recurs in the early journals and lectures: an emphasis on the concept of inheritance, which, oddly, he names one of the most substantial achievements of America's new order. To precisely these contingencies Emerson dedicates "Wide World 7," an 1822 journal, in a tribute to "The Spirit of America":

> If the nations of Europe can find anything to idolize in their ruinous & enslaved institutions, we are content, though we are astonished at their satisfaction. But let them not ignorantly mock at the pride of an American, as if it were misplaced or unfounded. . . . He [the American] points to his native land as the only one where freedom has not degenerated to licentiousness; . . [.] in whose well ordered districts education & intelligence dwell with good morals; whose rich estates peacefully descend from sire to son, without the shadow of an interference from private violence or public tyranny. . . . (JMN 2: 4)

The passage discounts an "enslaved" Europe, but its praise for America's "free" institutions insistently returns to modes of predictability and constraint: thus freedom is not too free, the districts are "well ordered," and primogeniture is in place.[17] In this respect as well, Emerson echoes the words of his father, who warned in the course of his Fourth of July oration in 1802 that the American Revolution had been fought to defend property as well as to protect liberty, and that dire consequences would ensue if America chose to follow France's lead into a revolution marred by atheism and corruption (Barish 14).[18] The younger Emerson's writings and their relation to his father's reveal the wide range of sometimes contradictory positions that need to be included in order to make any sense of Matthiessen's claim that all the writers of the Renaissance shared a common belief in what he called "the possibilities of democracy" (ix). It seems certain from passages such as these that it would be at least as true to say that "democracy" in the first half of the nineteenth century had as many definitions as it had definers. And as this book's opening chapter has described, these definitions of a democracy that is not too democratic emerge out of distinctions drawn at the Founding, decisions made in the Constitutional episode that privilege the rights of property over the expansion of political rights. As will become apparent, Whitman along with Emerson is shaped by these founding limitations on democratic expansion, though in a way that is inflected differently.

We/The People

Inheritance marks not only a subject of the young Emerson's ruminations but also a useful way of characterizing the material forms of at least some of the journals within which he considered the topic, and the ideological assumptions that inform his opinions about it. On occasion, and in a way reminiscent of his father's 1802 Independence Day sermon, Emerson seems less assured about America's orderly rules for inheritance than panicked by their potential disruption.

> It is a matter of great doubt to me whether or not the *populace* of all ages is essentially the same in character. I am not a competent judge to decide if inconsistent institutions will affect & alter the prominent features of the moral character. . . . Will vulgar blood always rebel and rail and against honourable, virtuous, and opulent members of the same society? Will the good always be in peril from the misdeeds & menaces of the bad? (*JMN* 1: 117–18)

Emerson answers these concluding questions—with their relatively easy alignment of economic categories with discriminations of virtue—in the affirmative. Another passage in which Emerson comments widely on human history brings together the earlier validation of order and calm with the last excerpt's distinctions of social class:

> Speculative men are prone to remark that the world presents no variety; that this age beholds the same characters & the same scenes from which the elder moralists deduced ominous or pleasing conclusions; that while modes & forms change, the principle remains substantially the same. . . . There is another view of human affairs which . . . fiercely admonishes them that while they murmur at this weary calm they ought to be thankful that the storm is not loosed and this uniform peace broken up by the dreadful activity of the unchained elements. (*JMN* 1: 124)

These lines open out an alliance between cogitation and economics by foregrounding with the very first word what Gillian Brown usefully calls "the cohabitation of the individual with the economic," the way in which "material conditions and mental states accordingly coalesce" (9–10). As Richard Poirier has suggested about similar diction in *The Conduct of Life*, it is hard not to read Emerson's "speculative men" in this passage as *speculating* men, worried whether "unchained elements" will be loosed on their fortunes and bring disaster in ways reminiscent of Antonio's fears at the opening of *The Merchant of Venice*.[19]

The passage offers further proof of the necessary contexts within which even philosophical speculation occurs; Emerson's sweeping vision draws on his era's great symbol of chaos, since these elements are "unchained" and figuratively representative of the omnipresent white fear of slave rebellion: here is the alignment (indeed, equation) of the disruptive forces of social class and race in the single image of "the unchained." Years later, in explaining the course of the 1848 revolutions convulsing Europe, Emerson will return to some of the foundational assumptions that govern his reading of the world in these passages written in some cases a quarter-century before.[20]

The early Emerson is at times equally uncertain about the relative advantages of the democratic government that variously empowers the common people he sees around him. In 1822, musing on the decline of the Roman Empire, Emerson decides that the restoration of "the responsibility and powers of the senate as far as an old and free aristocracy" would have been one "obvious" way of "retarding the footsteps of fate" (*JMN* 1: 70). He suggests further that "the modern inventions of perfect representation" would also perhaps have saved Rome since a body of men to whom is committed the correction of political mistakes may completely and safely revolutionize the government[. . . . It] is to be recalled that it is in fact a refinement upon democracy [when] the wisdom of the people is brought to the senate house purged of their ignorance and local bigotries. (*JMN* 1: 70–71)[21]

Here Emerson sounds like no one so much as Publius in *The Federalist*: he, like Publius, consistently seeks out improvements on "the people"; he, like Publius, looks to "safely revolutionize the government" (a striking, if not simply oxymoronic phrase) by restoring power to the hands of a "purged" senate.

Foregrounding passages such as these furthers the project begun in this book's first chapter: to find in the writings of Emerson and Whitman traces of the debates over representative governance that the eighteenth century stages but does not by any means put conclusively to rest. In this specific instance Emerson's meditations on the history of republics affords a conspicuous opportunity to examine the political affiliations that underwrite his early compositions. To do so requires revisiting one of the central issues about this period in American history: its status as the Jacksonian Age of the Common Man, which has in recent years been seriously undermined in the view of many, perhaps most, historians.[22] For our purposes, however, what is essential is not so much the "truth" of the period as revisionist historians have come to project it, but rather the perceptions that were held by people living and writing through it—perceptions that, true or illusory, founded or unfounded, nevertheless evinced consequences. I am therefore interested in the way discourses having to do with the "Common Man" make their appearance in the writings of Emerson and Whitman, as well as the way their representational styles and modes of publication demonstrate their participation (whether imagined as voluntary or involuntary) within certain of these political and social "truths."

A poster from the campaign of 1828 provides a good example of what is at stake in taking this broadened discursive approach to the period of Jackson's first presidential attempt and the "age" that eventually took his name. According to this poster—a cultural document at once constituted by, and constitutive of, certain political beliefs in circulation—the general who had defeated the British at New Orleans during the War of 1812 was "The Man of the People! / HE WHO COULD NOT BARTER NOR BARGAIN FOR THE / PRESIDENCY / . . . BECAUSE / It should be derived from the PEOPLE!" (quoted in Blum 210). The poster refers to the widely held belief that John Quincy Adams had duplicitously negotiated for Henry Clay's supporters in order to assure his election when he failed to secure sufficient electoral votes to win the presidency outright in 1824. When Adams followed up his victory in the House of Representatives by making Clay secretary of state—a position many believed to be all but an assured next step to the presidency—the cries of foul play were so widespread that the campaign of '28 began virtually simultaneously with the victorious Adams's oath of office. All of which is to say that, whatever the "truth" of the period—however the actual distribution of wealth or of political power seems to have been apportioned or exchanged—the battle lines in the 1820s between those perceived to stand with the people and those who stood against them were firmly and securely drawn. (Here it might be useful to recall that Jackson won the popular vote in 1824 by nearly half again as much as Adams.)[23]

If historians have most recently come to side against Whitman and his man, Jackson—that is, if they have come to see that the possibility of upward mobility that had long been held to signify "The Age of the Common Man" cannot be borne out by statistics—there is nevertheless a value in recognizing the often diametrically opposed idioms through which Whitman and Emerson considered the prospects and the legacies of these Jacksonian years. To stifle or to overlook those differences because, from our perspective, certain "truths" about the period have emerged, would be the worst sort of anachronism.[24] One might notice as well that the poster's rhetoric, about the presidency being "derived" from the people—though perhaps intended as a stark confirmation of the common people's power—may nevertheless echo the filtration model that wins out with the Constitution's adoption, since a rhetoric of "derivation" implies as well a whole host of synonyms suggested by Federalist notions of distillation and deferral.

Two textual sites in the collected journals stand out as markers of the political assumptions within and through which Emerson comes to voice in this pre-Renaissance period. The first of these appears as an admittedly minor manuscript detail: in an extended "Catalogue of Books read from the date December 1819" that Emerson compiled while at Harvard, the single title that appears completely capitalized is "FEDERALIST"—this in a list that covers a period of about five years and contains more than one hundred titles (*JMN* 1: 397).

But this manuscript curiosity gains increased significance when placed beside a meeting Emerson's journal records for February 1825, which he seems to have considered anything but minor: "Today I went to Quincy to see its Patriarch. The old President sat in a large stuffed arm chair. . . . " The visit is, of course, to former President John Adams, and the occasion is the election of his son, John Quincy Adams, to the presidency; the incident was important enough to Emerson that he twice indicated the page number of this entry on the spine, some time after he rebound for his own use the notebook that had been his father's thirteenth volume of sermons.[25] In Emerson's words, he went to see Adams in order "to join our Congratulations to those of the nation on the happiness of his house" (*JMN* 2: 333); this projected unanimity, in which Emerson joins with "the nation," is worthy of attention, if for no other reason than the fact that Adams's 1824 election was anything but uncontested. Emerson may here be enunciating a typical Massachusetts/New England bias when he unconsciously equates his home state's happiness at the election of one of its ("our") sons with the much less uniform contentment of the nation as a whole.

The meeting, however, much more than a mere courtesy call, is a play of deference, a material practice that substitutes for countless others named and unnamed through which Emerson's interpellated subjectivity within these Federalist estates is forged. As such, "Patriarch" may well be the precise word for what Adams and his son represent: both were invested in the rule of the "best men" in leading the nation, both were Federalists or defenders of the Federalist legacy, and both were members of the family that most closely resembled in early American politics a European aristocratic dynasty, or, as Emerson puts it above, "house."[26] It is hard not to see Emerson's meeting with Adams— although they had never met before—as a homecoming. Indeed, a passage written three years before the meeting with Adams suggests Emerson was already home: ". . . a levelling [*sic*] democracy of intellect without leaders and without stings of ambition would produce a pigmy republic of insipid triflers. Away with the scheme; it is the vanity of vanities" (*JMN* 2: 70). Of course the subject here is not government, per se: this passage is part of a longer meditation on the nature of intellectual progress and the history of ideas. But its language clearly intersects with early-nineteenth-century discourses about government, and the demeaning use of the word "democracy" is unmistakably Adamsian in its resonances. It is not, however, a matter simply of denouncing Emerson's conservatism so much as it is a need to recognize the Federalist imperatives that Emerson's rhetoric in these "private" journals and "public" lectures repeatedly ventriloquizes.[27]

Thus in Emerson's "The American Scholar," the specific, identifiable antecedents for the first person plural pronouns in the peroration merit comment, though they have traditionally been read in terms of a supposed universal applicability:

> Patience,—patience;—with the shades of all the good and great for company; and for solace, the perspective of your own infinite life; and for work, the study and the communication of principles, the making those instincts prevalent, the conversion of the world. Is it not the chief disgrace in the world, not to be an unit;—not to be reckoned one character;—not to yield that peculiar fruit which each man was created to bear, but to be reckoned in the gross, in the hundred, or the thousand, of the party, the section, to which we belong; and our opinion predicted geographically, as the north, or the south? Not so, brothers and friends,—please God, ours shall not be so. We will walk on our own feet; we will work with our own hands; we will speak our own minds. (LAE 70–71)

In keeping with the occasion for the address—the Phi Beta Kappa assembly at Harvard on 31 August 1837, the day after Commencement—Emerson's invocations of "we" and "our" are addressed most directly to the tightly knit and largely closed circle of the Harvard-affiliated cultural elite in attendance at Brattle Street Church. The quoted lines depict precisely the dilemma of this exclusivity, professing at once an aversion to any sense of collectivity or of collective accountability ("Is it not the chief disgrace in the world . . . to be reckoned in the gross, in the hundred, or the thousand"), at the same time that they invoke (indeed, produce) precisely such a distinct community ("Not so, brothers and friends . . . *ours* shall not be so. *We* will walk . . . "). Even the speaker of the best-known comments on Emerson's address—Oliver Wendell Holmes's appraisal of it as "our intellectual Declaration of Independence"— reinforces with his use of the plural pronoun precisely the same effect.[28] Such a reading may also make more obvious the significance of the address's title— "The American *Scholar*"—then as now a fairly specialized category of employment with educational requirements by no means open to the broadest spectrum of citizens to whom the address has nevertheless often been said to be directed.[29] Examining passages such as these with an eye toward their political or social class underpinnings demonstrates that writings by Emerson and Whitman—far from sharing some homogenized appreciation about "democracy"—reflect instead significant, long-standing, and deeply wrought divisions about social order and cultural hierarchy in the United States.

It is instructive, for just this reason, to consider their contrasting views on the election of Andrew Jackson in 1828 as John Quincy Adams's successor, an event around which many of these issues coalesce. Emerson imagines the probable outcome of the election in these terms:

> It is said public opinion will not bear it. Really? Public opinion, I am sorry to say, will bear a great deal of nonsense. There is scarce any absurdity so gross whether in religion, politics, science, or manners, which it will not bear. . . . It will bear Andrew Jackson for President. (*JMN* 3: 100)

"Gross" in this passage, as in the previous excerpt from "American Scholar," surely carries the widest range that the OED provides for operative meanings in the period: not simply "uncultivated," "rude," and "ignorant," but "flagrant," and "monstrous," as well as the more particularized and deeply resonant senses of "generalized" (as opposed to "particular") and "coarse" (as opposed to "spiritual"). Four years later, neither Emerson's contempt nor the alignments between political choices and dirt/disease has been diminished: "Yet seemeth it to me that we shall all feel dirty if Jackson is reëlected" (*JMN* 4: 57). Even this sentence's diction, including its reversion to an archaic verb form ("seemeth"), imparts a proper, refined air and so carries the charge of Emerson's animosity. And on those occasions when Emerson can find something generous to say of the Jacksonian legacy, it occurs in largely the same derogatory terms, as when he attempts in 1834 to take the long view:

> Good is promoted by the worst. Don't despise even the . . . Andrew Jacksons. In the great cycle they find their place & like the insect that fertilizes the soil . . . they perform a beneficence they know not of, & cannot hinder if they would. (*JMN* 4: 281)[30]

Emerson in this passage denies the capacity for any sort of advantage from the efforts of "insects" like Jackson, who is reduced to something like manure ("fertilizer"). The best that the Jacksonians can accomplish is a kind of serendipitous purgation of the tired forms Emerson desires to be abandoned.[31]

Whitman exactly reverses the poles of Emerson's reflections; while he recalls in the pages of the *Brooklyn Daily Eagle* in 1846 "that gloomy period, the administration of the older Adams," the anniversary of the Battle of New Orleans allows him in the pages of the same newspaper to expound the glorious achievements of Andrew Jackson, "sage and hero":

We are, in this hurrying and busy land, not very apt, or else forget, to trace events back to their beginnings; otherwise we should give the credit of some of the greatest Democratic reforms, even of a late date, to President Jackson. . . . Andrew Jackson was a *Man of the People*, worth more than hundreds of political leaders—worth, indeed, more than all the selfish ones that ever lived. His example, his stern honesty and love of the truth, are fitting themes for both the present and future. . . . (GF 2: 180)

As effective in expounding the grounds of Whitman's own political investments is a piece he wrote for the *New Orleans Crescent* in 1848, titled "The People and John Quincy Adams." Whitman takes as his point of departure "the generous testimonials [about Adams] which have been offered from all quarters":

If the remarks had merely been confined to a superlative laudation of Mr. Adams, there would be no present need of response, even from those who do not concur in such excessive praise. But when the mass of the people are brought up as before a tribunal, and treated with a sort of cynical sarcasm, because they did not attach themselves more closely to the Ex-President, there is full propriety, it seems to us, in a few thoughts like the following:

John Quincy Adams was a virtuous man—a learned man—and had singularly enlarged diplomatic knowledge; but he was not a man of the People. Never, at any time, did he heartily espouse the side of any of those hot struggles for the rights of men, as opposed to wealth and conservatism, which the last [late ?] years of the last century, and all the hitherto years of the present one, show so many of. Is it wonderful, then, that he never was a popular man? O, the people know well enough who stand by them.[32]

Beyond noting the almost phrenological appraisal of Adams and his "singularly enlarged diplomatic knowledge," it is crucial to take away from this extract Whitman's insistence that the people are capable of recognizing their own defenders. The passage may in this way recall Whitman's own ideological interpellation and how different it must have been from Emerson's: not only his fabled childhood encounter in Brooklyn with the French hero of the American Revolution, General Lafayette, but the way the names of his own brothers—

George Washington Whitman, Thomas Jefferson Whitman, and Andrew Jackson Whitman—represent a kind of familial mnemonic, at once public and private emblems of the Whitman family's investment in a version of the republic's history and the patriots who were said always to have stood on the side of the people in defense of popular liberty.[33] From within this context that defined to a significant extent his own position as one of the people, Whitman claims his ties to Jackson the People's Defender.

Conversely, Emerson sees and writes from the significantly different perspective that he has gained in Boston, the scene of what Mary Cayton calls his "Education in Federalism,"[34] with the consequence that, even when he seems determined to justify the potential of ordinary Americans against the claims of an elite, he is unable to do so without revealing the tensions that arise with such effort. Take this example from the journals written in July 1828, while Emerson was studying at Harvard Divinity School:

> I am always made uneasy when the conversation turns in my presence upon popular ignorance & the duty of adapting our public harangues & writings to the minds of the people. 'Tis all pedantry & ignorance. The people know as much & reason as well as we do. None so quick as they to discern brilliant genius or solid parts. And I observe that all those who use this cant most, are such as do not rise above mediocrity of understanding. (*JMN* 3: 136)

At one level the passage aims at a defense of the people not unlike Whitman's when he argues that "the people know well enough who stand by them." But rather than any concern about aspersions cast in the direction of "popular ignorance" or the common folk, what sparks Emerson's ire in this passage is the possibility (someone's suggestion) that he may need to adapt his speaking style or his lectures to the needs and concerns of an audience. In response, he is more than willing (with the last sentence quoted) to denounce as inferior those who make the recommendation. Far from leveling "the people" with the "we," the passage chronicles the construction of additional hierarchies, the maneuverings of an "I" insistent on staying apart and above. Even at the expense of contradictions about the capacities of the people, this speaker implies that "they [will] discern [his] brilliant genius." Concerning the complex nature of these interactions between speaker and audience, however—including the alignment between those social roles and categories considered earlier (common/proper, many/one)—there remains a great deal more to say.

Who Touches This Book?

To an extent that has gone largely unremarked in literary criticism of the Renaissance, the writings of Emerson and Whitman encode dramatically different dynamics between the writer and the reader that both reflect and reproduce contrasting antebellum conceptions about the relations between the many and the few, between the representative man and the constituencies to whom and for whom he speaks. From a perspective of post-1980s identity politics, although not only from this perspective, it might be tempting to ask: how could this help but be the case? Interpellated by their widely different cultural and educational milieus—their lived lives in Cambridge, Concord, Brooklyn, and Manhattan—into quite distinct notions of the relations between leaders and followers, Emerson and Whitman come into the supposedly homogenized period of Matthiessen's Renaissance with very different conceptions of the functions and class associations of the (poetic) word in the world.[35]

As a means of detailing some of the distinctions in the presentational modes encoded in texts by Emerson and Whitman, it is useful to begin by exploring some of Emerson's earliest journal entries that register a fascination with the powerful man standing alone. Not surprisingly, coming from as many successive generations of churchmen as did Emerson, these leaders as often as not appear in a pulpit:

> . . . let us suppose a pulpit Orator to whom the path of his profession is yet untried but whose talents are good & feelings strong & his independence as a man in opinion and action is established[;] let him ascend the pulpit for the first time not to please or displease the multitude but to expound to them the words of the book & to waft their minds & devotions to heaven. Let him come to them in solemnity & strength & when he speaks he will chain attention with an interesting figure & an interested face. (*JMN* 1: 7–8)

Central to this passage is the "ascension" of the speaker over (and against) "the multitude," a hierarchizing image that becomes particularly prominent in relation to the "chain" that recalls the "unchained elements" considered earlier; slavery once again reveals itself to be a dominant imaginative presence as the discussion reaches after a characterization of verbal mastery and control.

Emerson dedicates his 1823 journal, "Wide World 10," in similarly "masterful" terms:

> Then [God] gave [man] an articulate voice. He gave him an organ ex-
> quisitely endowed, which was independent of his grosser parts,—but the
> minister of his mind & the interpreter of its thoughts. It was designed
> moreover as a Sceptre of irresistible command, by whose force, the great
> & wise should still the tumult of the vulgar million, & direct their blind
> energies to a right operation. (*JMN* 2: 104–05)

If we can read past the phallic excess (though it is not by any means unrelated),
this passage echoes the familiar exhortation from Genesis giving man dominion
over the earth, but rewrites its mandate explicitly in the terms of social class,
making "an articulate voice" the divinely endorsed means employed by "the
great & wise" for controlling not simply animals but "the vulgar million." Such a
depiction of the power of the orator would seem to leave little room for either
compromise or exchange, not even of the sort that Melville's Father Mapple exhibits, praying and preaching from his ship-pulpit high above, but nonetheless
adapting the story and speaking a language the "vulgar" sailors can understand:

> "Shipmates, this book, containing only four chapters—four yarns—is one
> of the smallest strands in the mighty cable of the Scriptures. Yet what
> depths of the soul does Jonah's deep sea-line sound!"[36]

Emerson's vision, on the contrary, is that of the inspired man of knowledge, an
affecting and effective prophet, but standing and speaking apart.

The hierarchized ambitions figured in these passages about the orator align
themselves on one side of a fault line considered in some detail in chapter 1, for
Emerson rehearses here essential aspects of the Federalist arguments in favor of
filtered representation. In this regard Emerson seems to have reversed the
pattern of his father's career, which started when William Emerson became a
minister in the small village of Harvard, Massachusetts, where he gained a
reputation as something of an innovator, making suggestions for changes in
church policy that the community repeatedly and forcefully rejected time after
time. When the call came from Boston offering William Emerson the pulpit of
the First Church, it "must have seemed a precious opportunity to which he
must assiduously fit himself" (Barish 12), and by all accounts that is precisely
what William Emerson did.[37] But Ralph Waldo Emerson proceeded in the
opposite direction, beginning as a spokesman of orthodoxy and then splitting
away from organized faith after 1832 on the grounds of his own leanings and
spiritual truths—what has often been called his antinomianism.

Nevertheless these journal passages reveal an unshakable assumption that Emerson inherited from his father's orthodox years in Boston, and that appears very much the leading characteristic of his ruminations on the role of the orator. Virtually unchanging in Emerson's depiction of the relationship between a speaker and the public is the same dynamic that surfaces when he elsewhere turns his attention to more strictly "political" questions and writes (echoing the older Adams) that "The great & wise are the representative governors of the mass of men" (JMN 2: 401). Emerson invests this natural aristocracy with an authority that corresponds to the belief of Adams and the Founders that mechanisms must be devised in order to bypass the rasher judgments of an uneducated (uneducable?) public. The speaker's power is irresistible, and that common men "surrender" to it is all to the good. The point to be drawn from this carries broad ramifications: even when he actively turned away from his role as spokesman for the Church, or rejected what he called in a passage quoted earlier "the hollow dilettantism" exhibited by some with whom he nevertheless shared social prominence, Emerson retained a foundational belief in his own elevated status as truth-giver to the masses, like one of Shelley's "unacknowledged legislators of the world." To precisely that extent, he remained both his father's son, as well as a true Federalist heir.[38]

Emerson's journals are filled with references that reinforce this notion of a nearly unbridgeable distance between author-orators and the public.

> The man of talents who brings his poetry & eloquence to the market is like the hawk which I have seen wheeling up to heaven in the face of noon—& all to have a better view of mice & moles & chickens. (JMN 5: 191)

Emerson's disdain for the "market" and mass culture—inscribed here in a version of Dickinson's "Publication is the Auction of the Mind"—does not fully account for the contempt for the audience that is a virtual keynote of this budding orator's meditations. The resolution once again calls for perspective from above:

> I acknowledge that as far back as I can see the winding procession of humanity the marchers are lame & blind & deaf; but, to the soul, that whole past is but the finite series in its infinite scope. . . . Let me begin anew. Let me teach the finite to know its Master. Let me ascend above my fate and work down upon my world. (JMN 5: 332)

We are used to reading Emerson's optimism in a passage like this, his clear vision that challenges us to look beyond materiality toward its more significant spiritual analogues. But from within this chapter's interpretive matrix, it may be once again difficult to read past the passage's introduction of the deeply resonant diction of "Masters," which has its corollaries in Emerson's lyceum lectures in which the possibilities of democratic debate are pushed aside in favor of an older, authoritarian version of the single leader dispensing Truth to an appropriately spellbound public.

In a series of lectures from the mid-1830s, Emerson's language repeatedly returns to notions of tyranny and autocratic control, especially when he discusses the workings of Spiritual Law. In a discussion of the grandeur of Shakespeare's sonnets, for example, Emerson says he does not know "where in English or in foreign poetry more remarkable examples can be found of the tyranny of the imagination or the perfect control assumed of all nature by the poet" (EL 1: 293). In a broader lecture titled "Art" given about a year later, Emerson speaks of the "despotism of eloquence" (EL 2: 42). As depicted in these lectures, the excellence of imagination and of eloquence in the orator participates in a familiar pattern, under the auspices of which the irrational mob is brought under the control of the Law. From this perspective, certain equivalences open out between terms that might not otherwise seem reconcilable: that is, considered from the point of view of the power relations they inscribe, "God," "Art," "Eloquence," the Senate, or alternately, the Lecturer—Emerson himself—all come to occupy similarly dominant positions.

A significant journal entry from 1834 demonstrates the way Emerson's approach to his lecturing is imbedded within these political contingencies, including those of the lyceums themselves, which, as Carl Bode has shown, were usually organized and run by men "of substance and standing in the community" as a "socially approved institution" (32):

> . . . when you come to write Lyceum lectures, remember that you are not to say, What must be said in a Lyceum? but[,] what discoveries or stimulating thoughts have I to impart to a thousand persons? not what they will expect to hear[,] but what is fit for me to say. (JMN 4: 372)

In a passage such as this Emerson's depiction of the orator's power as autocrat reiterates the model of the relations between leaders and citizens as explained by President John Quincy Adams in his first address to Congress in 1825:

While foreign nations . . . are advancing with gigantic strides in the career of public improvement, were we to slumber in indolence or fold up our arms and proclaim to the world that we are palsied by the will of our constituents, would it not be to cast away the bounties of Providence and doom ourselves to perpetual inferiority? (quoted in Mayfield 99–100)

As Charles Sellers summarizes the younger Adams exhibited in these lines, "No American notable was less qualified by experience, conviction, and temperament to cope with surging democracy." "While Adams acknowledged 'the will of the people' as the source of government 'and the happiness of the people [as its] end,' he insisted on a 'confederated representative democracy' in which gentlemen defined the public happiness," and in which those gentlemen were, in turn, defined by " 'talents and virtue alone' " (271).[39] Such analogizing—from Emerson's journal to Adams's address—may serve to remind us that, as Allen Grossman has argued, "an entailment of any style a person speaks is the structure of a social world that can receive it—a political formation and its kind of conscious life" (185). What then are the parameters and "political formations" of the social worlds Emerson's and Adams's writings entail?

In *The Emerson Effect*, Christopher Newfield emphasizes an Emerson who "defines freedom as individual movement and personal growth, but accompanies these with the pleasurable loss of self-governance" (13), a writer and theorist for whom "inequality is not simply overlooked but becomes a positive necessary component of the law that binds" (38). In other places, though, Newfield's Emerson cannot support even these limited negotiations between autonomy and the law: "Emerson's theory of language [Newfield writes] does not either succeed or fail adequately to imagine personal autonomy, for whatever its cultural reception has been, it does not seek autonomy in the first place" (45–46). Newfield is in part here remarking the subsumption of eloquence and the eloquent man in Emerson's scheme by the Universal Oversoul.

Likewise, for Kevin Van Anglen, Emerson speaks "a language of authority that simultaneously affirmed the autonomy and freedom of the self and yet fused that *concession* to antinomian claims with a more imperious and patriarchal conception of the writer's role than that ever envisaged by the critics of Unitarian Boston" (119, emphasis added). For our purposes, the task becomes how to reckon the differences between Emerson and Whitman around these central and representative issues, though it seems quite clear that Whitman, in his fierce 1856 polemic "The Eighteenth Presidency!"—to take but one salient example—is expressing his dissent:

> I expect to see the day when the like of the present personnel of the governments . . . will be looked upon with derision, and when qualified mechanics and young men will reach Congress and other official stations, sent in their working costumes, fresh from their benches and tools, and returning to them again with dignity. (LAW 1308)

It is useful first to notice how closely Whitman's rhetoric here follows Jackson's own language in describing his transformation of public administration: "the duties of all public officers are . . . ," Jackson wrote, "made so plain and simple that men of intelligence may readily qualify themselves for their performance; and I cannot but believe that more is lost by the continuance of men in office than is generally to be gained by their experience" (quoted in Morone 87).

But Whitman's refusal of virtual political representation is also noteworthy because it functions as a parallel gesture to the parataxis that structures verbal representation in *Leaves of Grass*, a logic Allen Grossman has described as "a taxonomy of which the sorting index is mere being-at-all," and which promises "the bestowal of presence across time" (188).

> Instead of a "poetic language" (always a mimetic version of the language of one class) Whitman has devised a universal "conjunctive principle" whose manifest structure is the sequence of end-stopped, nonequivalent, but equipollent lines. . . . The principle of the language . . . is the deletion . . . of centralizing hypotactic grammar. . . . What is obtained is an unprecedented trope of inclusion. . . . (193, 195)

This is inclusivity with high costs, to be sure: Grossman argues that it is in fact a "new slave culture" that Whitman creates, because "the Whitmanian voice, like the slave, is uncanny—a servant of persons" (195). But it is only from the outside that the Whitmanian voice looks or sounds this way, only if our gaze is directed lovingly and our ears tuned longingly toward our canonized poet, fearing that he shall be lost. Is it possible, however, that Whitman delights at these moments in exactly such absence, a distant corollary to the mood exhibited in "As I Ebb'd with the Ocean of Life": "Oppress'd with myself that I have dared to open my mouth . . . " (LG 254)? In the catalogs, Whitman's speaker stops speaking and closes his mouth—or at least hides that mouth from our hungry eyes and ears.

This is all by way of suggesting that it may be the wrong question to ask where Whitman's disappearance as uncanny slave would leave *us*, and that we should instead look toward Whitman in the text and in his times, the 1850s, before there was a canonical Whitman. In gazing at Whitman the other way—in striving ever and always for his canonical attentions—we are in fact looking at him as we would look at Emerson. Or we are seeing Whitman as Emerson has trained us to see the speaker-orator and public, self-reliant man. Allen Grossman, too, is somehow seeing Whitman this way—as Emerson sees—when he worries over the uncanniness of the nearly lost or just plain lost Whitmanian voice and vision of the catalogs.

How does Emerson see? The answer, assisted by Newfield, might be that he doesn't. Or rather, he sees beyond, not feelingly, but transparently, beyond to the *greater* inclusivity, the greater stakes in a different world of clarity.

But politically, Whitman's vision (and sometimes his other senses as well) may be staging in the catalogs a mode of virtual representation in which, by means of *his* virtual absence—that loss of presence about which Allen Grossman is worried—specificity and particularity—those working men in their costumes—is not lost.[40] In Emerson, on the other hand, specificity is always lost, or often lost. These processes may be visible in Emerson's poem "The Rhodora" (1834), which opens with the pointed observation of the single flower—"In May, when sea-winds pierced our solitudes, / I found the fresh Rhodora in the woods"—but slips by the end into a generalized diffidence that leaves the flower an all but entirely obscured catalyst and the speaker, at the very least, sharing the spotlight:

> Why thou wert there, O rival of the rose!
> I never thought to ask, I never knew:
> But, in my simple ignorance, suppose
> The self-same Power that brought me there brought you.
>
> (lines 13–16)

In fact, the point in Emerson may well be this loss of specificity, in favor of the transcendent, the universal. As Newfield writes, "Emerson imagines not those contemporaries who are extraordinary for their independence, originality, or freedom, but those who submit like children to the highest authority" (23).

Emerson—unlike the Whitman of the catalogs—supervises these actions; he is present in the mediated apprehension of the rhodora (and "The Rhodora"), and his interrogation largely fills out the substance of the poem after the opening lines.[41]

One finds a similar version of the catalogic virtuality of Whitman's speaker even in those places—such as the opening lines of "Song of Myself"—in which something like an authoritarian power play seems to be one of the text's multiple agendas. For when the speaker asserts "And what I assume you shall assume," the autocratic tendencies that grow out of his heightened awareness and insight are coupled with what is rarely found in the Emersonian version: an acknowledgment of the reader as a distinct entity, invited to *participate* in a dynamic that is at once highly structured but also shared (or, as the last line of the first poem in 1855 puts it: "I stop somewhere waiting for you").[42] It depends, as it so often does, on an imbedded ambiguity: shall we read "shall" ("you shall assume") as future tense or as an imperative? This space of negotiation, this dynamic of interchange, however, functions just as the logic of parataxis might require, since the representational dynamics of the Whitmanian line at the very least impede—and it may do a great deal more—the movement toward some universalized or totalized claims, toward the claims of the virtual, except the virtuality of Whitman's speaker himself. And that is a virtuality that Emerson first and last rejects (and one Whitman rejects sometimes, too, of course).[43]

The political valences of Emerson's representational dynamics thus become clearer when placed beside Whitman's, which from this perspective reveal their reliance on a broadly Jacksonian vision of the relationship between constituents and representatives, speakers and listeners, writers and readers that may very well have its origins (for Jackson, too) in the writings of Thomas Paine. Paine is a recurring topic in Whitman's discussions with Traubel at the end of his life, someone for whom he says he promised as a young man to "do public justice," and to bear "true witness where the great majority have borne false witness—in thick and thin, come what might to me" (*wwwc* 2: 206). Fulfilling this promise, Whitman spoke at Paine's 140th birthday commemoration in Philadelphia in 1877. He seems to imagine Paine as a similarly long-suffering and big-hearted democratic version of himself. But this lifelong support of Paine has another logic, for his beliefs and Whitman's read as virtual versions of each other: in Eric Foner's summary, "a belief in natural rights and human perfectibility," a resistance against "artificial privilege," and an anticlericalism that was Paine's undoing and that dates back in Whitman's writings at least to the preface to the first edition: "There will soon be no more priests" (*Tom Paine* 264).

Chapter 2 brought many of the differences between Emerson and Whitman to the foreground in its extended discussion of the implications of the first person plural pronoun (we/our) that is the regular form of address in Whitman's editorials and newspaper writings, as well as the way in which Whitman's poetry consistently invites the reader to share in the making of meaning.[44] To put these practices into perspective requires following out the logic of one of Kerry Larson's very provocative suggestions, that Whitman's is a poetics that "externalizes the achievement of assent as an active and indeed central feature of its drama" (6).

Recalling how the roots of this poetic praxis are present in the early writings of Whitman-the-newspaperman, it becomes apparent that Larson's formulation about the dynamics of assent in Whitman's poetry functions analogically as a description of the rhetoric and praxis of political participation in the Age of Jackson—the period's gradual, uneven movement toward an acknowledgment of the ordinary citizen's stake and role in the nation's governance. This is a dynamic partially glimpsed in Jackson's 1832 veto of the National Bank's charter, which addressed what Harry L. Watson calls "a great popular majority instead of a single social class" (147). (Moreover, Jackson believed the 1832 election to be the people's referendum on the same issue: Jackson and No Bank vs. Clay and the Bank).[45] While "direct popular democracy . . . was never a reality in Jacksonian America, 'Jacksonian democracy' did liberate ordinary white men from many of the deferential constraints of eighteenth-century political culture, and it gave their feelings and opinions a new respect in the public sphere" (Watson 13).[46] I want to locate Whitman's formal innovations within these arenas of Jacksonian political expression. Staging participation in all its contradictions is a key to Whitmanian poetics, and it lies as well at the heart of the class-based revisions of literature that Whitman's poetics simultaneously enact. That is, not merely Whitman's theory but his practice—the encodings in his writings of the relationship between reader and writer—often refuses the monologic and hierarchized relation on which Emerson's writings depend.

No sooner, however, do we note the Jacksonian resonances in Whitman's poetics than we confront the limitations in Whitman's revisions of these modes of representative address, as well as the eighteenth-century origins of antebellum American writing. In this regard it is instructive to return to Larson's

deeply perceptive account of Emerson/Whitman in his chapter resonantly titled "Lessons of the Master." Larson finds in Emerson and Whitman "two
competing models of consensus": Whitman's quest for "a speech of unbounded
inclusiveness capable of uniting the many and the one without dependence on a
pre-established hierarchy of sacrifice and exclusion," which, Larson argues,
ends up repeatedly and perhaps inevitably in "a vivid oscillation between the
two extremes." On the other hand, according to Larson, Emerson is aware that
"inclusion and exclusion are not simply the risks any representative speech
must run but are in principle inevitable to it" (31). Thus Larson concludes that
Emerson's "stance toward all forms of exchange, whether political, literary, or
cultural, was ironic: liberation produces its own enslavements, which in turn
engender the need for further liberation, which produces further enslavement" (31).

It is precisely this notion of the ironic that can ground a new, revisionist
account of Emerson/Whitman. For what marks most prominently the stance
of the ironist is distance, which is precisely the position Whitman was not
permitted, or only rarely permitted himself, in relation to the central political
problems of his time. Put differently, irony is itself an emblem of hierarchy, and
consequentially it is not a position Whitman's socioeconomic position permits:
his concerns about free white labor that distort into polemic his views on the
enslavement of Africans and African Americans in America nevertheless pronounce Whitman's own concerns as, himself, a free white laborer. This does
not, quite obviously, excuse the sometimes devouring racism of these attitudes,
whether or not one believes that this racism may be partly mitigated in passages
like that of the runaway slave, as many commentators have noted. But it does go
some way toward explaining his willingness to, as he writes in "The Eighteenth
Presidency!" "Circulate and reprint this Voice of mine for the workingmen's
sake. I hereby permit and invite any rich person, anywhere, to stereotype it, or
re-produce it in any form . . . . I am not afraid to say that among [the working-
men] I seek to initiate my name, Walt Whitman, and that I shall in future have
much to say to them" (LAW 1323). In his participation in these central debates
in the antebellum period, Whitman displays none of the distance that keeps
Emerson for so long out of the fray.[47] As Cornel West suggests, Emerson's class
status permits him the distance from the social that he enunciates in these
lectures: "at the end of the line of [Emerson's] fervid moral voluntarism lies a
vague yet comforting mysticism that discourages an engaged political activism"
(Evasion 25). To say as much is not to refute the powerful incursion many

people felt Emerson made into the field of antislavery protest, but rather to note the relative lateness and the position of relative safety from which Emerson heeds the call.

Many of Emerson's lectures and writings against slavery speak directly to the role the individual should assume in relation to the central political controversies of his age. "But whilst I insist on the doctrine of the independence and the inspiration of the individual," Emerson writes in his 1855 lecture on slavery, "I do not cripple but exalt the social action."

> Patriotism, public opinion, have a real meaning, though there is so much counterfeit rag money abroad under it, that the name is apt to disgust. A wise man delights in the powers of many people. Charles Fourier noting that each man had a different talent, computed that you must collect 1800 or 2000 souls to make one complete man. We shall need to call them all out. (*Antislavery Writings* 103)

This is indeed an important revision of the fear Emerson expressed in "American Scholar" that "the state of society is one in which the members have suffered amputation from the trunk, and strut about so many walking monsters,—a good finger, a neck, a stomach, an elbow, but never a man" (*LAE* 54). But the revision also maintains some of the earlier emphasis, particularly in the way the phrase "powers of many people" may identify not simply collective action but the independent and separate powers of distinct individuals joining forces. Emerson's emphasis remains on the individual, even when he speaks out in favor of—and, indeed, lends his own voice to—a collective. Of course the passage has foregrounded (once again) this solitary individual from the start: "A wise man. . . . "

The editors of *Emerson's Antislavery Writings*, in collecting these texts, seek to present an Emerson different from the "individual with a limited or tepid interest in matters of social reform" (lv) whom they say is usually represented in American literary scholarship. But the diffidence of this "old" Emerson regarding the promises of collectivity recurs even within the "new" Emerson's "exaltation" of the social:

> I approach the grave and bitter subject of American slavery with diffidence and pain. . . . I have not either the taste or the talent that is needed for the disposition of political questions, and I leave them to those who have. Still there is somewhat exceptional in this question, which seems to

require of every citizen at one time or other, to show his hand, and to cast
his suffrage in such manner as he uses. And, whilst I confide that heaven
too has a hand in these events, and will surely give the last shape to these
ends which we hew very roughly, yet I remember that our will and
obedience is one of its means. (91)

This call to arms presents an intervention as closely allied to quietism as one
could perhaps find, and for reasons that John Carlos Rowe has analyzed with
care. In *At Emerson's Tomb* he notes

the fundamental problem with Emerson's political writings from 1844 to
1863—the period of his most active commitment to the cause of abolition
as well as the period of his 1855 lecture, "Woman": Emerson either must
abandon the fundamentals of transcendentalism or the principles of political activism. (21)

Rowe locates this fundamental incompatibility "at the heart of . . . the intellectual schizophrenia of Emerson in these writings in this period" (21). Some of
this incongruity is visible in the excerpt above—in its return, for example, to
reluctance and resistance as a kind of refrain, from its opening "diffidence" to
the declared, and rehearsed, refusal to join on the grounds of "taste" and
"talent." Its last sentence is built on a distinction without a difference, shifting
from "whilst" to "yet," but confirming in both halves the same principle: that
"heaven" ultimately shapes both the outcome of these struggles and "our will
and obedience." This return to obedience echoes Newfield's reminder that for
Emerson, first and last, "the moment of freedom is constituted by the moment
of submission to superior, active power" (59). The passage may recall in the end
nothing so much as Hawthorne's famous characterization of slavery as "one of
those evils which divine Providence does not leave to be remedied by human
contrivances, but which, in its own good time, by some means impossible to be
anticipated, but of the simplest and easiest operation, when all its uses have
been fulfilled, it causes to vanish like a dream" (quoted in AR 317).

Of course Emerson's views against reform movements and reformists and in
favor of the empowered individual are well known, and there can be little doubt
that his lectures against the Fugitive Slave Law are powerful, stirring in-
dictments of a system corrupt at its core. "I do not often speak to public
questions," Emerson says in his address delivered in New York in March 1854.
"They are odious and hurtful, and it seems like meddling or leaving your work.

I have my own spirits in prison,—spirits in deeper prisons, whom no man visits, if I do not" (73). But faced with the Whitman at the crossroads discussed in chapter 2, a Whitman deciding on the proper and most powerful medium for his broad participation in the central questions of his day, it is hard to overlook Emerson's resistances, the separations he bequeaths to an American literary history that has become enthralled ever since with the notion of a space apart, whether described as an "optative mood," "an American Adam," "an Imperial self," or, perhaps most miraculously, because most incongruously, as the site where interracial male couples set out for the frontier on their own.[48] From within this tradition, Whitman's manifold engagements—prose and poetic, printed or published or imagined as the stuff for a lecture tour—and riddled as they are with ideological contradictions and racialism (if not simple racism), provide an alternative to this vision, even in those texts, such as "Calamus," when the poetry disavows any overt relation to "institutions" in the first place.[49]

"We are all Republicans, we are all Federalists"

To imagine Whitman as an alternative may really only be to say that he has inherited a differently weighted form of the Federalism Emerson has imbibed, because Federalism—with its emphasis on autocratic filtration, on top-down leadership—becomes, with the adoption of the Constitution, the governing trope with which writers of all political persuasions must come to terms: such is the intersection of the political and literary discourses of representation even to the brink of the Renaissance. Thus it is not possible to note Emerson's Federalist interpellation without seeing the ways in which Whitman's own autocratic tendencies are necessarily shaped in the same forge. From this perspective, the broad ecumenism visible in the line from Jefferson's First Inaugural, which I have chosen for this section's title, records not parity or compromise so much as a hard fact of political life, even for the ostensible opposition party, after the Constitution's ratification. That this is the case follows from Jennifer Nedelsky's reminder that the Federalists' winning vision was concerned first and last "with the way the structure as a whole would contain the dangers of democracy while providing the power necessary for effective national government" (10). Believing as Whitman does that the Constitution's "architects were some mighty prophets and gods"—the Constitution is "a perfect and entire thing," he writes in "The Eighteenth Presidency!" (*LAW* 1318)—it should perhaps not be surprising that he is unable to produce, or is able to produce only intermittently, a genuinely democratic alternative.

Against what has emerged as Emerson's submissive tendencies as analyzed by Newfield, there is nevertheless a utility in labeling Whitman, following the taxonomies of Anti-Federalist dissent in Saul Cornell's recent work, an "elite Anti-Federalist," a seemingly oxymoronic title that nevertheless captures the many gradations of populist and localist sentiment that ignited the opposition to ratification. In its attention to a political space where the prerogatives of the local and the federal clash (or exactly fail to clash), Whitman's "A Boston Ballad," as discussed in chapter 1, furnishes a correlative to the insistent localism of Whitman's catalogs. Cornell helpfully notes in this regard that "the version of the public sphere defended by elite Anti-Federalists was far more localist than that of the Federalists" (74).

These comparisons are well served by returning to Emerson's first "secular" publication after he resigns the pulpit: *Nature* in 1836. With no author's name on the cover, the small book inscribes a notion of anonymous circulation rather than the pseudonymity through which eighteenth-century gentlemen entered the political debates over Constitutional ratification. *Nature* is utterly above the fray, a statement—as its very title suggests—rather than some contingent or strategic proposition deployed within the field of a broader debate. It is a last word: "Undoubtedly we have no questions to ask which are unanswerable. . . . Whenever a true theory appears, it will be its own evidence. Its test is, that it will explain all phenomena" (*LAE* 7). And what is the truth *Nature* tells? It tells the unvarnished lessons of universal Federalism.

> It is not so pertinent to man to know all the individuals of the animal kingdom, as it is to know whence and whereto is this tyrannizing unity in his constitution, which evermore separates and classifies things, endeavoring to reduce the most diverse to one form. (*LAE* 43)

Whence indeed "this tyrannizing unity." Emersonian epistemology moves away from particulars and toward universals, as Newfield suggests. Genealogically speaking, it is in this way an extension of the eighteenth-century Federalist insistence that the clamoring particularity of the states or of interested parties more generally must somehow be rendered uniform, and so manageable. Here in this founding document of the American Renaissance Publius's filtration returns as a simple "fact" of man's "constitution," a perfect correspondence between the nature of men and the harmony embodied in the Federalist Union.

Nature provides a primer on the universal necessity of these federalizing principles: as Newfield writes, "the empirical mind lacks creative power and discovers truth only by reuniting with the timeless One who slumbers, already perfect, in the soul" (50–51). Of the certainty that "every natural process is a version of a moral sentence," *Nature*'s readers are assured that "herein is especially apprehended the unity of Nature,—the unity in variety,—which meets us everywhere. All the endless variety of things make an identical impression" (*LAE* 29).

In its echoes of "E pluribus unum," the nation's motto, these formulations offer Federalism writ large: an overriding harmony in which the axis of the federal plan and the axis of Nature's decrees are perfectly aligned: "all thought of multitude is lost in a tranquil sense of unity" (*LAE* 43).[50] Beauty itself concurs:

> The standard of beauty is the entire circuit of natural forms,—the totality of nature; which the Italians expressed by defining beauty "il più nell' uno." Nothing is quite beautiful alone: nothing but is beautiful in the whole. (*LAE* 18)

This is Nature's and *Nature*'s refrain: "The many in one," shorthand for a natural science and an epistemology founded on the principles of Federalist republicanism.[51] Or is it a defense of Federalist republicanism founded on the languages of a fully naturalized (and nationalized) epistemology?[52] Coming to Emerson's foundational "literary" text from within the genealogical investigations this book has emphasized, it is no longer quite clear in which order the relation should be configured.[53]

Writers and Readers

A passage from one of Whitman's notebooks further explicates this point. Under the heading "Style," and the subheading "A main requirement of any Lecture" appears this summary:

> . . . Does it embody and express fitted to popular apprehension without too much complication—and the accessories . . . all carefully kept down so that the *strong colors lights and lines* of the lecture mark that *one simple leading idea or theory*. . . . (*NUP* 1: 409 original emphases)

"Fitted to popular apprehension without too much complication": it would be difficult to find a conception of the role of the lecturer more different from Emerson's, insofar as Whitman's description of his mission "embodies" a negotiation between the one and the many. The "one simple leading idea or the-ory"—a phrase whose unanimity may recall the domination of the Emersonian orator—works instead in the service of participation, making of the lecture an expression of consensus, and even (figuratively speaking, perhaps, but not less consequential for being so), of dialogue.

Beach makes a useful argument in this regard by asking "who Whitman's intended reader is." Citing the more-than-rhetorical questions early in *Leaves of Grass*—"Have you practiced so long to learn to read? / Have you felt so proud to get at the meaning of poems?" (*1855 LG* 14)—Beach writes:

> Unlike the assumed readership of Emerson or the fireside poets, for whom reading books, or even reading and understanding poems, would have been considered a normal or expected accomplishment, Whitman's implied reader is a member of a class for whom reading is still difficult, for whom poetry is a challenge and perhaps a source of confusion or uncertainty. Thus when Whitman proposes to "belch" the words of his voice or to send his "barbaric yawps" over the rooftops, it is as much an attempt to send a reassuring message of physicality to his working-class brethren as to *épater le bourgeois*. (159)

This broadening of a potential readership foregrounds Whitman's interven-tions regarding literacy and access, as well as his challenges to inherited as-sumptions about the literary and the membership of his presumed audiences.

But Whitman's search for a single, leading idea is also a mode of filtration, and behind it lies the assumption that a lecture style must be adapted to the presumed limitations of his audience. In this regard, we are looking not at the Emerson who stands behind Whitman, but instead at the Federalism that stands behind both of them, and with it an assumption about the disinterested, knowing few leading an unenlightened many. The legacies of the Constitutional settlement made any unvarnished, uncomplicated invocation of, or investment in, "the people" difficult to sustain, even for a populist in the Paine mode as Whitman styled himself: the question of the proper place of the people per-sists. Thus Betsy Erkkila's important observation about Whitman's democratic praxis in another, related mode: "For all their poetic democracy, Whitman's catalogues could operate paradoxically as a kind of formal tyranny, muting the fact of inequality, race conflict, and radical difference within a rhetorical econ-omy of many and one" (*Political Poet* 102).

Barbara Packer has made a virtue out of the difficulty readers have historically felt in approaching Emerson's writings when she argues that "self-reliance is to [Emerson] first of all what it was to his Protestant ancestors: the liberty to interpret texts according to the Spirit" (7). But that liberty has never been absolute, and Packer's summation leaves out a significant dimension of the calculus of interpretation for Emerson's texts that this chapter has explored in detail: the way in which Emerson's stance as orator and as writer attempts rather to delimit (interpretive) space for only one truth—that of the speaker/writer. While it may be entirely true to say that once a text—any text—enters the marketplace, readers/listeners are indeed unconstrained to read into/out of it what they choose, Packer's view obscures an autocratic Emerson by constructing him as the proponent of an unfettered imaginative and interpretive free space.[54] She is closer to the target, I think, when she cites Stanley Cavell's appraisal of Emerson's prose—" 'It does not require us' " (7)—because, as we have seen, the reader/audience does indeed seem to be purely ancillary to the task of the truth-giver, and to the truth-giver himself, as that role is defined in Emerson's texts.[55]

It is in Whitman often a different dynamic that engages a reader with the writer/speaker. In the "Introductory" to his temperance novel *Franklin Evans* (1842), for example, Whitman offers the open-ended and collaborative alternative to Emerson's relative disinterest in the reader:

> And though, as before remarked, the writer has abstained from thrusting the moral upon the reader, by dry and abstract disquisitions—preferring the more pleasant and quite as profitable method of letting the reader draw it himself from the occurrences—it is hoped that the New and Popular reform now in the course of progress over the land, will find no trifling help from a TALE OF THE TIMES. (6)

These lines envision cooperation between reader and writer, while at the same time importantly aligning this collective practice with the specific end of furthering social and political reforms.

Even when Whitman did stand up in the guise of a lecturer before an audience, his performance seems to have lacked the authoritarian tenor uncovered in Emerson's writings on the subject. Instead, for his commemorative lectures on the assassination of Abraham Lincoln, Whitman made himself over into an embodiment of corporate memory, a representative, as in *Leaves of Grass*, figuratively encompassing the whole nation and offering a "ritual re-enactment of the Passion of Abraham Lincoln" (Kaplan 30). Most telling, perhaps, is the conclusion of the "ritual" that inevitably followed Whitman's description of the agonies of the war and of the night of Lincoln's assassination: the evening concluded with Whitman's "customary obligatory reading" (Kaplan 29) of "O Captain, My Captain." Whitman's reading this poem—ever his most popular, despite his own antipathies toward it[56]—reflects his willingness to bend to the popular taste at the expense of his own preferences or literary evaluations. This compromise between lecturer and audience gestures toward, and participates in, a competing version in the antebellum period of the relationship between a representative and his constituency, one in which the public's preferences play an active role in the decision-making, one in which the active desires of listeners are not simply filtered away, but instead may make a final determination against the "better judgment" of the man standing apart.

The forms of Emerson's and Whitman's writings, rather than coincident, apolitical "essences" speaking the representative consensus of their age, demonstrate instead the period's dynamism, its Revolutionary-era contentiousness about the meaning of the republic and the place of the many in relation to the few. This chapter taken as a whole offers a cross-section of the complicated answers Emerson and Whitman separately provide to Kerry Larson's provocative inquiry whether "there [is] a form of unanimity possible which would not be profaned or violated in the moment of its announcement" (41)?

Dispersal

I want to conclude by turning at last to the opening epigraph, Greil Marcus's provocative comment that deconstructs authorial intention at the same time that it endorses it. That is, what is significant about this rather offhand comment is its capacity to keep in balance the fact that an "author" undoubtedly possesses "intentions," although the meanings placed into circulation by a given work may range far beyond them. This has lessons for our ongoing efforts to restore the classic texts of American literature to the historical contexts within which they arise. The cultural work that a text performs in the world may ultimately stand at some remove from either the work its author thought it would do, or the work that author might have done.

Nowhere, perhaps, is this clearer than in the case of Emerson's *Nature*. Indeed, the central publication of an author who has emerged in his journals determined to disseminate his own special brand of truths seems to have been the object of at least two sets of responses that were anything but what its author intended. In the first instance, as Larry Reynolds has described, Emerson's work may have played a significant role in helping to spark the 1848 revolutionary activity in France, since his writings were held in high esteem by three lecturers at the College de France who used it to cultivate "revolutionary impulses in their students" (4);[57] here is a literalization of Emerson's calls for "an original relation to the universe," and a throwing off of the old forms that raises the question, as Reynolds suggests, of just how literal Emerson in his Concord garden wished such revolutions to be.

In this regard, Mary Cayton has examined the reception of some of Emerson's lectures and found a fairly ubiquitous problem, at least judging from newspaper accounts. Listeners at Emerson's lectures, it seems, rarely seemed to reach for, or to grasp, the spiritual level that we often take as Emerson's central message. Looking at printed responses to Emerson's lectures, Cayton finds that often, during his lecture tours through the Midwest in the 1850s,

> Emerson seemed to his listeners to be merely passing along practical advice on practical subjects—the epitome of self-culture. . . . If the audience was pleased by Emerson's "common sense," it was because his compelling images drawn from everyday life could be understood in a practical, materalist way as well as in the metaphorical, idealist sense in which Emerson probably intended them. ("Making" 89–90)[58]

It is, as Greil Marcus suggests, one thing to recognize intentions, and quite another to recognize the possibilities that printed or spoken language places into circulation.

With these observations in mind this chapter concludes with two "readings" Emerson's work received—one during his lifetime, and one at the beginning of the twentieth century—in order further to examine the versions of Emerson we have inherited, and some revisions that may be warranted.

Ocular Proof

Sometime after the publication of the first edition of *Nature* in 1836, Christopher Pearse Cranch produced line drawings of various passages from the small book that would become Ralph Waldo Emerson's best-known work. This was not the only time Emerson's writings provided inspiration for Cranch: in addition to passages from *Nature* he also illustrated lines from Emerson's "American Scholar": for example, for "Man thinking becomes a bookworm," Cranch drew exactly that: a worm with a human face reading an open book near other scattered piles of books.[59] For "I expand and live in the warm day like corn and melons" from *Nature*, Cranch's line drawing shows a large pumpkin with a face, arms, and legs, contentedly basking in the sun among fellow pumpkins in a patch.[60] In general these drawings have garnered little scholarly attention, and when critics have been concerned with them, it has usually been to determine whether Cranch's attempts at illustration should be understood as mocking or as an idiosyncratic tribute.

Cayton's discussion of the reception of Emerson's lectures provides an interesting angle for thinking about how we might read these drawings. It might be possible to assert that Cranch's sketch interpretations of Emerson, like those of the audiences Cayton discusses, share a similar resistance to apprehending the spiritual dimensions toward which Emerson was coaxing them, as a result of a specific failure to appreciate sufficiently the presumed metaphoricity of Emerson's language. Looked at this way, Cranch's drawings might be seen as concrete examples of the many Emerson listeners who clung to the literal meanings of his words. One biographer of Emerson follows out the logic of this suggestion when he takes Cranch's better-known illustration of Emerson's "transparent eye-ball" passage (see figure 3) as proof that the artist was an "unsympathetic reader" of Emerson's project in *Nature* who produced only "caricatures."[61]

While Cranch's intentions cannot be ascertained merely by looking at these illustrations, other materials by Cranch suggest he may have been among Emerson's most ardent admirers. These include a manuscript poem titled "Emerson" and signed "Christopher P. Cranch, May 1882"—that is, it seems to have been written within a month of Emerson's death on 27 April. The poem is a twenty-four stanza biographical ode, recalling the course of Emerson's long life as poet and prophet:

> For to his eye all objects and events
> 　　Revealed symbolic meanings, and his mind
> Pierced with the poet's vision through the dense
> 　　Dull surface to the larger truth behind.[62]

These lines, which celebrate Emerson's visionary acumen, suggest that Cranch was aware of Emerson's "deeper," underlying meanings, whatever his illustra-

FIGURE 3. Christopher Pearse Cranch's illustration of Emerson's "transparent Eye-ball," c. 1836. Courtesy Houghton Library, Harvard University.

tions seem to do. This stanza from the ode gains particular interest in relation to the illustration Cranch produced of the moment of epiphany described in the opening pages of *Nature*.

The central text Cranch chose to illustrate in this instance is probably the most remarked-on passage Emerson ever composed:

> Standing on the bare ground,—my head bathed by the blithe air, and uplifted into infinite space,—all mean egotism vanishes. I become a transparent eye-ball. (13)

The most salient element of this drawing is the towering character Cranch created as the representation of the Emersonian persona who experiences this spiritual epiphany. It is not quite human: its huge eyeball, including upper and lower lids and lashes, takes the place of a human head, and it has no arms or neck, but only very long legs and bare feet. There is a semblance of clouds at the top of the drawing, representing, perhaps, the "blithe air" into which this selfless self has evacuated personal identity and touched "infinite space." The personage is nearly three inches tall and towers over both the distant hills and the nearer church steeples and roofs of the town; for modern viewers, the scene may recall nothing so much as the standard moment in grade-B horror films when the colossal monster prowls the countryside, except Cranch's model seems to be at rest, and even leaning a bit, with "his" weight on "his" right foot. I say "his"—rather than "its"—because Cranch's figure is definitively male: he wears a hat (somewhat peculiarly on the top of his eye), a short-tailed coat, and a shirt with a high collar.

Though the figure is male, he is by no means generically so, because his clothing—particularly the long coat with tails and the shirt with high collar— functions within the cultural constructions of social class, making this representative of heightened awareness a male vision/ary of an equally elevated social standing. If clothes make the "man," then what Cranch has banished from the drawing is one of the oldest definitional strands for the adjective in Emerson's phrase "mean egotism": that is, Cranch's "man" is precisely not "inferior in rank or quality," or "of low degree." Or, put another way, Cranch has followed Emerson's lead by removing the sartorial indications of, again, "mean egotism," but what remains is quite as important, and this includes evidence of the socially elevated foundations on which (within which) identity ("egotism") is imagined. If the entire episode in *Nature* records a reduction of the self that is at the same time an infinite expansion, Cranch has captured the limitations beyond which the diminution of ego cannot conceivably proceed. What remains in Cranch's drawing is precisely *un-mean* egotism, the boundaries of a specifically classed "essential" self within these cultural contexts masquerading as essential or, to use Emerson's term, "transparent."[63] The trappings without which Cranch seems unable to imagine an experience that is at its very core, according to Emerson, defined by an eradication of all the outward trappings of egotism, and presumably the body itself, provide an example of the temporality of the ecstatic vision, its groundedness in history. We can look in a history of fashion to identify the coat and clothing and thus resituate this figure out-of-time back within history's insistent narratives.[64] Its position in a defensive Emersonian critical tradition notwithstanding, the image may in the end serve to remind us that Cranch was a particularly good reader of Emerson after all.

Subscribing to Harvard

Borrowing from Althusser's notion of interpellation, I have argued, in part, that a certain culturally privileged position within the Boston elite was "prepared" for Ralph Waldo Emerson by means of his father's standing as the city's most prominent Unitarian minister. Some twenty years after his death, a changed but no less recognizable Boston/Cambridge elite organized to secure—indeed monumentalize—Emerson's position by constructing a memorial on a site with particularly overt significance in relation to this elite's cultural prestige and control. The site of the edifice was Harvard Yard, and the building, completed in 1906, would be called Emerson Hall.

Ronald Story writes about a growing exclusivity at Harvard over the course of the nineteenth century, a turn of events that should be seen as part of a more complex social dynamic changing the demographics of urban America as a whole, and that is represented well by an object as substantial as Emerson Hall itself: the enclosure of Harvard Yard within "brick walls and iron gates after 1870" (116). Nevertheless, this exclusivity, as well as the correspondence that details the fund-raising process that took place before the building was completed, corroborates this chapter's reading of Emerson's position within a decidedly Federalist version of republicanism.

For example, William James (then a member of Harvard's psychology department, and working closely with the committee organized to raise money for construction), in a letter dated 20 March 1903, answers a request for a list of possible subscribers to the project:

> . . . William Endicott Jr. of the Hovey Firm . . . might name some beings
> who have lately grown rapidly rich, outside of the brahminic circle, and
> who might like to enter into it as benefactors of Harvard. Pork men, grain
> men, automobile men, iron men, etc.[65]

James in this letter offers admission to "the brahminic circle" to any who can pay the entrance fee: a substantial donation to the Emerson Hall building fund. Within this arrangement, Emerson functions as a sort of stable placeholder: even if the "brahminic" class seems no longer to be self-perpetuating, those offering a contribution to the building fund in Emerson's honor are said to be "benefactors of Harvard." However good-humored, James seems to betray some uneasiness that the hereditary ranks of the Brahmins are no longer as formidable as they had once been. Nowhere challenged in the letter is an implicit equation between Emerson and Harvard.

This is an equation that may seem odd to us, since our view of Emerson and Harvard often emphasizes the Divinity School "Address" and Emerson's subsequent banishment but rarely recalls that Emerson returned to sit on Harvard's Board of Overseers, in 1867, as had his father decades earlier. For all the insubordination he may have accomplished in his youth, that is, Emerson was to a significant extent reincorporated within the bosom of the (alma) mater.[66] The hall named in his honor is, of course, the most significant emblem of their mutual allegiance.

Emerson's membership in Harvard's socially empowered networks is also exhibited by other documents concerning the fund-raising. Here is part of a newspaper account of the fund-raising efforts:

> The committee in charge of the Emerson Hall fund is anxious to have it
> fully realized by all that their desire is to make the memorial as widely
> representative as possible of popular interest in Emerson and popular
> regard for him, and that to this end all subscriptions, small as well as
> large, will be gratefully accepted.

To this announcement it pays to juxtapose Harvard President Charles Eliot's appraisal of the same situation in a letter to Charles W. Dorr, chairman of the building committee. The letter is dated 10 May 1903; it seems likely that the newspaper account just quoted appeared roughly at the same time.[67]

> I shall report to the Corporation tomorrow that the Emerson Hall sub-
> scription is sure to be completed and that it is for them . . . to go ahead.

> I am glad the committee is now to make a general appeal. It will be a
> satisfaction to the [Emerson] family if a considerable number of small
> subscriptions can be procured.[68]

Taking the two excerpts in reverse order, Eliot's letter gives the lie to the proclamation in the newspaper excerpt; that is, while the smaller subscriptions may
have been a boon to the esteem of the Emerson family, they were clearly seen by
Eliot as secondary. The majority of the funding for the building must already
have been secured by the time of the newspaper announcement, since if it were
not, Eliot would not have planned to present before the Corporation the very
next day. The newspaper account betrays something like this to be the case with
its passive syntax: "The committee in charge . . . is anxious to have it fully
realized by all . . ." (though this grammatical construction may be a consequence of the newspaper account being a report of an announcement).[69]

Another broadsheet in the Harvard Archives substantiates the idea that the
public donations were considered ancillary to the completion of the project,
and that the extension of the fund-raising appeal was the subject of some
"anxiety." This broadsheet looks to have been prepared for wide distribution
and, perhaps, posting and contains this explanation:

> The Visiting Committee of the Alumni in charge of raising funds for a
> memorial hall to Emerson at Harvard University desire to lay that project
> before all who value Emerson and all Harvard men, that all may have an
> opportunity to manifest their interest by contributions, large or small.

Emerson is manifestly ("representatively") a Harvard man in this sheet's formulations.[70] But the most significant fact about the poster is that it is dated,
beneath the list of committee members, "Boston, Mass., May 16th, 1903"—that
is, six days after Eliot has written to Dorr announcing the successful completion
of the fund-raising, and five days after he has presumably reported that fact to
the Corporation.

Taken as a whole these documents detail not simply Emerson's long-
standing affiliation with Harvard—he has been constructed virtually to embody the principles of the University at the time these fund-raising appeals are
propagated—but also how fitting is Emerson Hall as a monument brought to
fruition all but entirely by the Harvard elite. Emerson's relation to this elite is
reproduced in his writings, which reproduce at their heart, and even across
decades, some of the assumptions about politics, the place of the "best men,"

and the standing and claims of particularity that, as his birthright, he shared with the planners of this memorial to him.

Thus we might return to President Eliot's letter to Chairman Dorr, in which he also wrote that "The Hall will be a great thing for the College. It is the first of its buildings to be named for a Poet." Remembering Althusser, we might say that Emerson Hall installs a particular memory of Emerson—as a "Poet"—and we might at last hear in that word the resonance of all the categories, discriminations, and alliances on which such a naming depends, as well as the others it actively works to disavow.

CHAPTER FOUR

REPRESENTING MEN

The market square—that epitome of the "common place"—so definite and comforting in its phenomenological presence at the heart of the community, is only ever an *intersection*, a crossing of ways. . . . The marketplace gives the illusion of independent identity, of being a self-sustaining totality, and this illusion is one of separateness and enclosure. Thinking the marketplace is thus somewhat like thinking the body: adequate conception founders upon the problematic familiarity, the enfolding intimacy, of its domain. The tangibility of its boundaries implies a local closure and stability, even a unique sense of belonging, which obscure its structural dependence upon a "beyond" through which this "familiar" and "local" feeling is itself produced.—STALLYBRASS AND WHITE, *The Politics and Poetics of Transgression*

There's another rendering now; but still one text.
—MELVILLE, "The Doubloon," *Moby-Dick*

Near the end of the last chapter I sketched the ineradicable historicity of the classed body that Christopher Cranch's drawing of Emerson's "transparent eyeball" perhaps unwittingly places into circulation. This chapter treats another aspect of the historicity of both the body and of bodilessness in antebellum writings by examining the traces of slavery ubiquitous to the American literary cultures of transcendentalism of the kind Emerson and Whitman variously describe and represent. The present chapter explicates the various contexts within which these writings—no less than Cranch's drawing—occur, although in its exposition of contexts, the chapter repeatedly returns to the oscillation that word always already enacts in relation to the "texts" that lie within it. The chapter seeks to flesh out the fullest significance of the lines from *Nature* that immediately follow those Cranch illustrated: "The name of the nearest friend sounds then foreign and accidental: to be brothers, to be acquaintances,— master or servant, is then a trifle and a disturbance" (*LAE* 10). These lines figure not simply the idealized isolation of the transparent eye-ball, but do so by disclaiming what this chapter argues is one of the primary relations of the antebellum era, that between "master and servant." Just as Cranch has shown the boundaries of social class beyond which Emerson's version of an unencumbered self cannot venture, this chapter demonstrates the pervasiveness of the epistemology of the slave market as it infuses writings by Emerson and Whitman, among many others, and across a whole range of antebellum discourses.

In this reading slavery and the slave market occupy the cultural site of epistemic ground zero; writings produced under its dispensations reiterate the central paradigms of enslavement—of "master and servant"—quite apart from any particular political investment a text might demonstrate pertaining to slavery. That this is the case gives the lie to a strategy discussed in chapter 3, looking to Emerson's overt statement on slavery as a sure sign of his commitment in the central political debates of his time. In this chapter, such participation is refigured discursively, with the consequence that the notion of any author's intention comes to seem a sort of ruse; that is, texts across a spectrum of discourses speak the intertwined discourses of slavery in an antebellum American culture epistemologically saturated by its diction, its images, and its consequences. While neither "slavery" nor "abolition" appears in the index to Matthiessen's *American Renaissance*, this chapter restores the prominence of these terms to texts that have sometimes been said to offer a world apart. And while that claim has been disrupted from a number of different angles in the last few decades of American literary studies, this chapter shifts the terms of the critique once more by opening up the connection between the texts of Matthiessen's Renaissance and the eighteenth-century representations out of which the nation and these writings emerged. Like the Continental Congress's excision of Jefferson's violent passage from the draft of the Declaration of Independence, slavery has sometimes seemed to recur mostly as an absence in the literary history of the Renaissance. But it is there at the beginning—indeed, before the beginning—a national primal scene repudiated but never fully removed, and the traces of which are visible whenever we allow them to be read. This book's insistence on juxtaposing two centuries that have traditionally been divided in literary and political histories of the United States marks another strategy for restoring slavery and witnessing its effects on the familiar stories we think we know.

In keeping with the understanding of a market provided by Stallybrass and White in my first epigraph, this chapter examines both a "brick and mortar," "flesh and blood" market—the largest slave market in the country in New

Orleans, which Whitman saw while working at the *Daily Crescent* in 1848—as well as the market as a placeless, ubiquitous "intersection," a place of crossing for multiple discourses as slavery emerges into the 1850s as the dominant political issue facing the nation. Elsewhere Stallybrass and White remark on the market as simultaneously "the epitome of local identity . . . and the unsettling of that identity by the trade and traffic of goods from elsewhere. At the market centre of the polis we discover a commingling of categories usually kept separate and opposed: centre and periphery, inside and outside, . . . high and low" (27). This chapter centers on a correspondent "commingling" that slavery and its practices instantiate. It examines penny-press potboiler fiction like Whitman's *Franklin Evans* as a stand-in for a range of reformist tracts, and it links these to texts as disparate as presidential proclamations and Emerson's transcendentalist polemics. The discussion traces as well an incipient rhetoric of homoerotic desire at the site of the racialized body and its bourgeois management that the disciplinary and supervisory structures of the antebellum slave market bring into sometimes shocking relief.

Stallybrass and White's methodological insights provide an additional vocabulary for rethinking the relation between representations of the body and of slavery in transcendentalist writings of the antebellum period. While they have demonstrated convincingly the "transcoding" of the hierarchy of the bourgeois body onto the topographical hierarchies of the city, there is a similar dynamic at work with regard to the slavery/body connection. While Stallybrass and White presume "body and social formation are inseparable" (145), this chapter offers a complementary account to the discussion at the opening of chapter 2, which emphasized differences between Emerson and Whitman regarding the suitability of poetic, print representations of sex and of the female body in the "Children of Adam" cluster in the 1860 *Leaves*. Shifting the focus now toward race, this chapter examines at a number of different sites a single, central proposition: Emerson's and Whitman's shared reliance in their depictions of the human body on rhetorics associated with the practices of American slavery.

Reforming Bodies

To say that the physical bodies in relation to which the transcendental moments in Emerson and Whitman take their force derive from the practice of slavery is also to reinforce one of the assumptions behind the introduction of Althusserian interpellation in chapter 3. It is to insist once again on the participation of Emerson's and Whitman's writings in discourses within which they are "hailed" and consequently "brought to voice." Indeed, by focusing on the ways in which images of enslaved bodies appear in a range of writings by Emerson and Whitman, we can see these writers' relation to an even wider genre of largely forgotten antebellum writing become apparent: namely, their intersections with the period's pervasive reform literature. Whitman's participation in antebellum reform movements includes not only his temperance novel *Franklin Evans* (1842) and a number of short stories, but probably also the "This-is-what-you-shall-do" energy of many passages in *Leaves of Grass* (1855 LG v–vi). Emerson, on the other hand, has usually been seen as having remained outside organized, collective reform movements: his refusal to join Brook Farm is the best known example. Yet there is evidence for Emerson's implication in the discourses of these reform efforts and the vocabulary of the human body they deployed, providing additional proof of their pervasiveness. Many of these movements share an interest in the restoration of the integrity of the individual, often as a means to social and spiritual regeneration. Whether the call was for temperance, quasi-vegetarian diets, or hydropathic therapies to relieve or prevent disease, antebellum reform movements often started from a belief that the individual body must be purified as a means, ultimately, of revivifying the larger body politic.[1]

Within these discourses, images of enslaved bodies provide would-be reformers with a ubiquitous analogy for the current physical or psychological state of a "free" citizenry that nevertheless needs to invest in self-improvement as a means of restoring "self-mastery." It is not, therefore, surprising to read in Whitman's *Franklin Evans* about "the strength of the chains which bind" the drunkard to his bottle, or, in the epigraph to chapter 13, these lines attributed to a Mrs. Embury: "Be free! not chiefly from the iron chain, / But from the one which passion forges, be / The master of thyself!" (EPF 181, 192). If at first glance this passage seems as if it might seek out some less conflicted language within which to frame its rallying cry for temperance—that is, a language less fatally dependent on the image of a "chain"—any such gestures are derailed by the last clause's charge to self-*mastery*, and so the passage serves ultimately to demonstrate merely the rule rather than any exception: that slavery provides the central defining language through which the temperance movement gains its adherents and explains its goals. As Ronald Walters makes clear, "temperance writers pictured alcohol as a form of tyranny, resembling slavery in depriving people of their ability to act as morally responsible creatures. Giving in to it meant destruction of one's autonomy" (128). Glenn Hendler provides further evidence for this alignment between embodiment and enslavement when he notes that "representations of the bloated, red-faced, lustful, uncontrolled male inebriate, both in literature and in [temperance society] experience meetings, made him the most vividly embodied figure in antebellum fiction and public life, except perhaps for the black slave with whom he was often compared" ("Bloated" 127). This representational overlap between the bodies of the inebriated and of the enslaved becomes even more important when considered below in relation to Whitman's crucial months spent as an editor in New Orleans.

The novel *Franklin Evans* is even bolder in its depiction of the alliances between slavery and temperance, especially as its central character travels south and comes into contact with the practices of plantation slavery. For the most part this is carried out by means of a subplot in which Evans obsesses over, marries, and ultimately betrays an enslaved African woman named Margaret who is owned by Bourne, Evans's new friend and the plantation owner. Witnessing Evans's intemperate desires for Margaret, Bourne at once frees her and gives her to Evans, which would seem inextricably to link the novel's temperance interests to the parallel concern with the loss of self-mastery that slavery essentially represents. It may also represent an author who is not entirely in control of the slippery discourses at hand—though the slipperiness of their juxtaposition is largely my point. This is something Whitman's well-known disclaimer about his composition of the novel—"Their offer of cash payment was so tempting—I was so hard up at the time—that I set to work at once ardently on it (with the help of a bottle of port or what not)" (*wwwc* 1: 93)—also tends to emphasize.

In *Franklin Evans* drink alone is "The Great Master" (*epf* 175), and it alone rules the plot. Drink destroys Evans's chances for happiness with his first wife Mary (ch. 9), and when she dies she is called "the innocent victim of another's drunkenness" (*epf* 176). Thus, when faced with the enslaved, "innocent victims" of Bourne, "the Great Master" on this plantation and his dear friend, Evans can do nothing more than ventriloquize his friend's self-interested apology for slave-holding:

> Perhaps it may hardly be the appropriate place here, to remark upon the national customs of this country; but I cannot help pausing a moment to say that Bourne, as he saw with his own eyes, and judged with his own judgment, became convinced of the fallacy of many of those assertions

which are brought against slavery in the south. He beheld, it is true, a large number of men and women in bondage; but he could not shut his eyes to the fact, that [the slaves] would be far more unhappy, if possessed of freedom. (EPF 202)

It is significant that the narrative should be self-conscious here about "intruding" a remark on "the national customs," because it is at just this moment that Evans moves onto Bourne's plantation and becomes enamored of the enslaved creole woman Margaret. That is, this is precisely the moment when the novel must, as it were, inoculate itself from permitting slavery—rather than intemperance-as-slavery—from entering the narrative as the impetus behind its reformist agenda. With these lines, slavery "itself" is banished from the narrative—after all, the slaves are better off enslaved rather than "possessed" of freedom—a "fact" that frees up the narrative to pursue its sole interest in intemperance as a form of "white slavery."

Indeed, as Karen Sánchez-Eppler has noted, the novel even describes "intoxication itself as an issue of color" (Touching 58); it describes an inebriated Evans as a darker Evans, even as it darkens the creole Margaret while making her behavior more animal-like when she jealously stalks as "prey" another woman of whom the narrator has become enamored (as he is wont to do). Whereas no apologies can be omitted, nor any possibilities for adjustment and incremental change denied, to the intemperate Evans, there is no possibility that the creole woman Margaret can be reformed, possessing as she does what the narrator calls "a remnant of the savage" (EPF 224) under a logic that confirms something like once-a-slave-always-a-slave.[2]

Banishing the slave-in-fact in favor of the slave-to-drink also permits the novel's alignment of intemperance and homoeroticism, a structuring relation that emerges in a single comprehensive passage:

That very afternoon, Bourne, who was a justice of the peace, united myself and the creole [Margaret] in matrimony. The certificate of manumission also was drawn out and signed, and given into Margaret's own hand. A couple of apartments in the homestead were assigned to her use—and I signalized this crowning act of all my drunken vagaries, that night, by quaffing bottle after bottle with the planter. (EPF 207)

A careful reader has been prepared for these substitutions of Bourne for Margaret and of drinking for sex because Evans foregrounds the growing intensity of his bond with Bourne, one that has from the start taken place over numerous bottles of wine: "So intimate did we at length become, and so necessary to one another's comfort, that I took up my residence in his house . . ." (*EPF* 203). When the traditional consummation of the heterosexual wedding night is replaced by a night of alcoholic indulgence between two men, one finds an early example in Whitman's corpus of the alignments in this reform-saturated culture of homoeroticism *and/as* intemperance. These alignments recur in another more famous account of the circulation and recirculation of erotically charged fluids between men discussed below—that of the twenty-eight bathers in "Song of Myself"; it might suffice here simply to recall Michael Warner's pithy remark about *Franklin Evans*: "when he is talking about alcohol . . . Whitman often seems to be thinking about something else" ("Drunk" 31).

Toasting the marriage, Bourne and Evans celebrate as well a clean escape from the risk that the central character's miscegenist marriage poses to the novel's reliance on slavery as "mere" metaphor because Margaret the "impure" creole wife does not have the luxury of such mere metaphoricity. The fear that the practices of slavery might enter the novel as a genuine concern available for the same reformist energies as Evans's story of inebriation are put aside as quickly as Margaret is left to her own rooms following the marriage ceremony, while the two men figuratively consummate the restored unity of the novel's central thrust. Bourne and Franklin might from this perspective be seen as celebrating not simply a marriage perfectly triangulated in a textbook exchange "between men" but the novel's success at this pivotal moment in distancing Margaret and the racial concerns her role as wife raises. The men's conspicuous consumption ("quaffing bottle after bottle") emphasizes the novel's reaffirmation of its primary focus on the dissipations of intemperance without any thematic shift into the conceivably parallel concerns of abolition.

Quite to the contrary, Evans the title character is impulsively, intemperately swept up into a slave economy; he is at least as charmed by his new wife as he is by her owner's power to bestow her upon him, even as the power implicit in the plantation economy is its own pleasure:

> My residence and walks about the plantation, made me familiar with all its affairs; and I even took upon myself, at times, the direction of things, as though I were upon my own property. I cannot look back upon this period of my life without some satisfaction. . . . (*EPF* 203)

Later, to please a new love, Evans will give away as a servant his wife Margaret's brother, reasoning "why should I not do with my own property as I liked?" (EPF 212). The slave-to-drink will be freed at novel's end—in the words of the triumphant and visionary cheer that sets Franklin Evans once and for all on the straight and narrow path, "The Last Slave of Appetite is free, and the people are regenerated!" (EPF 223)—but not the slave-in-fact. So dependent is the novel (and temperance more broadly) that it only intermittently, if at all, recognizes slavery as itself in need of reform, and by novel's end it can sustain the reform of intemperance only because it has come so fully to inhabit the rhetoric of chattel slavery. Joyce Appleby has explained with great acuity the process that seems to be at work here. Writing of the place of slavery in the American political worldview at the turn of the nineteenth century, she notes "what was vital to the success of the [Jeffersonian] Republicans was not abolition but rather their being able to divorce slavery from their social vision" (*Capitalism* 102).

The Poetic Temperament

Emerson's interest in the capacities and the purification of the individual is well known and a focus he shared with at least some antebellum reform efforts. Where Emerson parted company was at the prospect of the collective: he makes clear his distrust of communal projects and of the effectiveness of reform organizations in his lecture on "New England Reformers" from March 1844:

> But . . . [to] men of less faith . . . concert appears the sole specific of strength. I have failed, and you have failed, but perhaps together we shall not fail. . . . I have not been able either to persuade my brother or to prevail on myself, to disuse the traffic or the potation of brandy, but perhaps a pledge of total abstinence might effectually restrain us. . . . What is the use of the concert of the false and the disunited? There can be no concert in two, where there is no concert in one. When the individual is not *individual*, but is dual; when his thoughts look one way, and his actions another; . . . when with one hand he rows, and with the other backs water, what concert can be? (LAE 598–99)[3]

This reluctance to join renders all the more remarkable the ways in which one of Emerson's most influential essays, "The Poet," participates in the discursive conjunction between slavery and temperance that links this high canonical, transcendental essay to Whitman's "lowbrow" efforts in a novel like *Franklin*

Evans. Emerson's essay, like Whitman's fiction, bears the traces of reform in its concern with the purification of the body depicted specifically in the rhetoric of abolition. Of course one of the central propositions of Emerson's essay—"The sublime vision comes to the pure and simple soul in a clean and chaste body" (*LAE* 460)—derives as well from Emerson's ascetic origins in the traditions of New England Puritanism, but the essay here and elsewhere is simultaneously speaking the language of temperance and its abolitionist diction. Employing the same verbal alliances as Whitman's temperance novel, Emerson writes in "The Poet": "With what joy I begin to read a poem, which I confide in as an inspiration! And now my chains are to be broken . . ." (*LAE* 451); these are lines that could almost serve as epigraphs to Whitman's novel, like those by Mrs. Embury considered earlier. Such similarities emblematize the broader discursive contexts out of which literary history selects its representative and canonical authors, though these may share in discursive terms a great deal with the authors and texts left behind and separated out.

Even more striking than these verbal links between temperance and abolition is the essay's discussion that directly connects libation to poetic liberation. The quest for the latter leads men to the former, Emerson argues:

> This is the reason why bards love wine, mead, narcotics, coffee, tea, opium, the fumes of sandal-wood and tobacco, or whatever other species of animal exhilaration. All men avail themselves of such means as they can, to add this extraordinary power to their normal powers. (*LAE* 460)

Not long after the explanation, however, comes the condemnation:

> Hence a great number of such as were professionally expressors of Beauty, as painters, poets, musicians, and actors, have been more than others wont to lead a life of pleasure and indulgence; all but the few who received the true nectar; and, as it was a spurious mode of attaining freedom, as it was an emancipation not into the heavens, but into the freedom of baser places, they were punished for that advantage they won, by a dissipation and deterioration. . . . The spirit of the world, the great calm presence of the creator, comes not forth to the sorceries of opium or of wine. (*LAE* 460)

The passage merits comment for its strongly moralistic tone and its invocation of age-old religious syllogism, in appropriately antiquated syntax ("comes not forth"), that sinners will have their just rewards. Still, this component of the passage is firmly rooted in the tradition of temperance; Emerson's sketch of "dissipation and deterioration" reads like a plot summary of *Franklin Evans*. Even more, it sounds like lines from a contemporaneous poet Emerson could not have known—one Emily Dickinson of Amherst—who seems also to have been intoxicated by the discursive spirits of the call to temperance:

> I taste a liquor never brewed—
> From Tankards scooped in Pearl—
>
> . . .
>
> Inebriate of Air—am I—
> And Debauchee of Dew—
> (poem 214)

Like Emerson, Dickinson's retreat from public engagement—culminating in a self-imposed exile for approximately the last fourteen years of her life—seems to have protected her no more completely than did Emerson's aversion to collective commitments from registering in her language the shared discursive flux and alignments of her age.

Emerson's own imbeddedness in these discourses becomes only clearer as his discussion proceeds:

> So the poet's habit of living should be set on a key so low and plain, that the common influences should delight him. His cheerfulness should be the gift of the sunlight; the air should suffice for his inspiration, and he should be tipsy with water. (LAE 461)

What is this but an exhortation to a better life lived free of the chains of alcoholic and other artificial stimulants, but spoken in a different key—one in which "poetry" and "The Poet" designate the pinnacle of the individual's potential, and always at least implicitly a form of self-mastery? "This emancipation is dear to all men" (LAE 463), Emerson writes, and his formulation seems uncannily precise in ways he may not have imagined: women have at best an irregular and inconsistent place in his rhetoric, while enslaved men and women have no place at all. "Emancipation" is a vital word joining slavery and temperance discourses; but what is striking about this language drawn from the brutal facts of slave-holding and slave-trading is the extent to which Emerson and Whitman are able to invoke it seemingly without recognizing any concrete sense of the practices that lie at its source. Before taking up additional texts by

Whitman and Emerson in turn, however, I want to consider briefly a document that would seem, at least from within a certain disciplinary perspective, to exist at some remove from the concerns raised by antebellum reformers. To do so also helps to demonstrate the ways in which the distinctions drawn by literary historians may be productively blurred, as in chapter 1's reconsideration of Federalist and Anti-Federalist literary-political production.

Abraham Lincoln's speech at Gettysburg, as Garry Wills has argued, redefined America's national commitment to equality by relocating the country's founding principles in the Declaration of Independence, rather than in the Constitution over which the Civil War was, ostensibly, in the process of being fought. The Emancipation Proclamation, issued eleven months before Lincoln's dedication of the Gettysburg cemetery, had the equally significant, and perhaps preparatory, effect of making less possible the un-self-conscious deployment of the rhetorics of enslavement and/as abolition. Two paragraphs from the final Proclamation issued at Washington underwrite this suggestion:

> And by virtue of the power, and for the purpose aforesaid, I do order and declare that all persons held as slaves within said designated States, are, and henceforward shall be free; and that the Executive government of the United States, including the military and naval authorities thereof, will recognize and maintain the freedom of said persons.
>
> And I hereby enjoin upon the people so declared to be *free to abstain* from all violence, unless in necessary self-defence; and I recommend to them that, in all cases when allowed, they labor faithfully for reasonable wages. (Lincoln 425, emphasis added)

How striking that so significant a document in the period's unfolding struggle for black citizenship should demonstrate (in the second paragraph quoted) an alignment between temperance and the discourses constituting the citizen and juridical subject. If it is paradoxical to have one's freedom to labor proclaimed rather than assumed, or to have one's inalienable rights guaranteed only through the intervention of the combined military forces of the state(s), it is doubly so when that freedom is at the very moment of its instantiation circumscribed within the temperance-inflected rhetoric of bourgeois subjection. Here, Lincoln's hailing of the black individual replicates what this section has been attempting to detail: that the privileged marker of freedom in this antebellum period—as well as the surest sign of self-mastery and self-possession—is taken to be the freedom "to abstain."[4]

A brief passage that appeared in the New Orleans *Daily Crescent* during the months Whitman worked there foregrounds precisely this insistence on self-management under even the most contradictory circumstances:

> Saw a negro throw a large stone at the head of his mule, because it would not pull an empty dray—wished I owned the negro—wouldn't treat him as he treated the mule, but make him a present of a cow-skin, and make him whip himself. . . . [5]

Condensing in its few lines a whole range of interrelated issues, this passage reproduces the cultural logic I have been attempting to unfold: that the best slaveholder is the slaveholder-within, the slaveholder-as-self.[6] No amount of coercion, however equivocated, can be spared in dispensing this lesson. Thus the speaker wishes he owned the slave, insists he would not abuse him, but then assures his readers that the result would be the same in either case—the slave will be whipped, only he will himself have been taught to do the whipping.[7] Michael Warner has encapsulated the driving paradox: "Controlling your body *had* made you temperate. Now it made you free" ("Drunk" 32). On that point, Emerson, Whitman, Lincoln, and their contemporaries seem to have been in complete agreement.

"The expression of a wellmade man"

Any exploration of the relation between Whitman's poetry and slavery in the United States must take into account Betsy Erkkila's fundamental observation about the prominence of slavery at what may be for Whitman a formally and generically constitutive moment. As Erkkila explains,

> When in his notebook Whitman breaks for the first time into lines approximating the free verse of *Leaves of Grass*, the lines bear the impress of the slavery issue:
>
> > I am the poet of slaves, and of the masters of slaves
> > I am the poet of the body
> > And I am[.]
> > > (*Political Poet* 50)

These lines are particularly significant for the way they hold in unsteady but no less certain relation the issues of physicality and the institution of slavery at the heart of the present investigation. According to the passage's inchoate logic, poetic identity is constituted in relation to both slavery and corporeality, while the third line may raise the stakes still more by constituting essential, un-qualified existence ("I am") in relation to them as well. In any event, the last line exhibits a noteworthy oscillation, announcing self-containment and utter in-terpretive plenitude at the same time as fragmentation and ambiguity—the former in its invocation of the Deity of the Old Testament ("I am that I am."), and the latter through the absence of any sense-making punctuation, end-stopped or otherwise.

These links between the body, slavery, and poetry are somewhat clarified by a passage that would become part of section 13 of the poem eventually titled "Song of Myself." In order to understand how this seven-line description of "The negro [who] holds firmly the reins of his four horses" functions in rela-tion to the representations of bodies elsewhere in Whitman's first edition, it needs to be read in relation to a nearby passage that has received considerably more critical attention. The account of the "twenty-eight bathers" that de-scribes a woman watching a frolicking band of naked young men has become central for many critics interested in the inscriptions in *Leaves of Grass* of Whitman's homosexuality:

> Twenty-eight young men bathe by the shore,
> Twenty-eight young men, and all so friendly,
> Twenty-eight years of womanly life, and all so lonesome.
>
> She owns the fine house by the rise of the bank,
> She hides handsome and richly drest aft the blinds of the window.
>
> Which of the young men does she like the best?
> Ah the homeliest of them is beautiful to her.
>
> Where are you off to, lady? for I see you,
> You splash in the water there, yet stay stock still in your room.
>
> Dancing and laughing along the beach came the twenty-ninth bather,
> The rest did not see her, but she saw them and loved them.
>
> The beards of the young men glistened with wet, it ran from their long
>   hair,
> Little streams passed all over their bodies.

An unseen hand also passed over their bodies,
It descended tremblingly from their temples and ribs.

The young men float on their backs, their white bellies swell to the
　　sun . . . . they do not ask who seizes fast to them,
They do not know who puffs and declines with pendant and bending
　　arch,
They do not think whom they souse with spray.

　　　　　　　　　　(1855 LG 19–20)

Robert K. Martin reads this passage as one in which Whitman, constrained
by cultural phobias, expresses his homoerotic interest in the young men by
displacing it onto the voyeuristic woman, thereby participating in the scene
vicariously (*Homosexual Tradition* 18–21). More recently, Michael Moon has
expanded Martin's reading by noting the passage's doubly transgressive nature:
its inscription at the same time—Moon refrains from selecting either at the
expense of the other—of transgressive homoerotic desire between men and of
active female desire on the part of the woman who imaginatively joins the
young men in their sexually energetic romp (45).[8] As Moon argues, "Alongside
the officially prohibited representation of a man feeling, enacting, and fulfilling
his desire for other men, Whitman posits the hardly less transgressive representation of a woman doing the same thing" (45).

In keeping with this study's recurring interest in the original, material forms
in which texts by Emerson and Whitman circulated—and so cued by Moon's
preposition, "alongside"—this analysis attends to the details of the untitled and,
significantly, unsectioned text of the first edition of *Leaves of Grass* in which the
"twenty-eight bathers" passage first appeared. It was not, after all, until 1867
that this episode became the self-contained section 11. In the 1855 edition, there
were no section boundaries and no titles to distinguish the poems from one
another, and while these are well-rehearsed details of Whitman's first edition
(in part from the discussion in chapter 2), their ramifications for this context
have been less fully reckoned. In the case of the passages under consideration
here, the "edges" of "self-contained" passages like the twenty-eight bathers now
taken for granted were in the first edition, at the very least, blurred.[9]

The eventual demarcation of the account of the "twenty-eight bathers" as a
separate section has enabled a process of critical reification that makes the
passage available as a distinct site for a wide range of psychosexual readings, but
at the expense of the materiality of the original edition within which the pas-

sage first appeared. In a process that is at its core circular, more reifying read-ings of the passage serve to reinforce its decontextualized density, which then makes the passage even more available for isolating critical readings. Conse-quently, it is salutary to reconsider the passage as it appeared in 1855, while at the same time calling for a more precise historical location of the readers for whom particular aspects of Whitman's texts might operate in particular ways. In the case of the "twenty-eight bathers" passage, precisely the transgressive nature of its homoerotic display *as we understand it* might be lost on readers in 1855, who would easily identify in the scene what Moon rightly calls "a large, rowdy, congenial swimming-hole party," but who might miss the "erotic lin-ings" (45–46) in the terms that a critic today, like Moon, would delineate them.

Readers in 1855 might miss the transgressiveness for two reasons, then. First, because the passage is itself literally transgressive; in the 1855 edition it (to the extent "it" exists as such) reaches into the text around it at start and end because of the absence of section numbers that mark the borders, and enforce the integrity, of its episodic space. Without these borders it is a good deal less certain which passages were salient, or discrete, to contemporaneous readers who read, again, without a critical tradition that assists readers, especially scholarly ones, in locating the passages that merit critical scrutiny.

Second, as I have argued elsewhere,[10] the categories within which present-day readers and critics categorize these sexual representations—for the most part, within the binaries homosexual/heterosexual and public/private—are categories that are not operative in 1855, which leaves the possibility that there is nothing in these passages to be "prohibited," because the categories are not in place within which to judge Whitman's representations and so find them sus-pect or transgressive.[11] Unable to align the male erotics of the passage within a binarized homosexual/heterosexual differentiation, readers in 1855 may well have missed what Moon so carefully elucidates; if this is correct, then the male homoerotics that have so captivated recent critics may have gone unread for being *unreadable* in 1855 on *our* terms.

Cathy Davidson has remarked (in *Revolution and the Word*) on the difficulty of recovering reader responses to eighteenth-century novels, and the possibility of such recovery is no less complex in the case of Whitman's poetry. One partic-ularly detailed "reader's report" of *Leaves of Grass*, however, dated 1 March 1882, and composed by one particularly interested group of readers, offers evidence that to a large degree substantiates the argument given above. When Boston District Attorney Oliver Stevens attempted to suppress publication of the 1881, seventh edition of *Leaves of Grass*, his list of lines to be expunged uniformly encompasses what could only be categorized as sexually explicit or ambiguously sexual—ambiguous, that is, with regard to the particular acts being depicted, but not with regard to the genders of the participants.[12] His list does not specifically target male homoeroticism; in fact, it does not demand that a single word from the "Calamus" series be excluded. If it targets any dimension of *Leaves* disproportionately, the list aims at representations of female sexuality, including two lines from the "twenty-eight bathers."[13] At the very least, this recognition may qualify Moon's assertion about the "officially prohibited" status of homoerotic representation; as the Boston D.A.'s list attests, these sanctioned repressions are nascent and by no means uniform, rather than categorical.[14]

If readers in 1855 were unlikely to see, or to see universally, transgressive homoeroticism in the scene, it is possible to sketch an alternative understanding of the scene that these readers may have been more likely to achieve. Drawing on alliances between the rhetorics of slavery and antebellum temperance movements, the story of "the twenty-ninth bather" is for all intents and purposes a story of liberation that frees the "handsome and richly drest" woman from the confines of her home, where she watches the men like a prisoner from behind "the blinds of the window."[15] And the space into which this woman is released is indubitably one of bodily intemperance, marked especially strongly in the account's last line: "They do not think whom they souse with spray." "Souse" carries a definitional strand dating to the seventeenth century synonymous with our current slang term "soused," which denotes a state of inebriation; similarly, "spray" in the nineteenth century could refer to a drunken spree or frolic.[16] Thus the men play and the woman participates, however vicariously, in a scene that overlaps with nineteenth-century depictions of intemperate revelry, an unthinking and anonymous "sousing" centered on a "spray" that is at once water, alcohol, and semen. In that way the twenty-eight bathers passage evokes some of the same erotic ambiguities as lines from "The Sleepers" which suggest fellatio, and which also depend on an available correspondence between sexual pleasure and alcoholic indulgence:

The cloth laps a first sweet eating and drinking,
Laps life-swelling yolks . . . . laps ear of rose-corn, milky and just
    ripened:
The white teeth stay, and the boss-tooth advances in darkness,

And liquor is spilled on lips and bosoms by touching glasses, and the
    best liquor afterward.
                (1855 LG 72)

Temperance, then, functions complexly in Whitman's writings, marking not
only the dangerous obverse to the much-desired state of self-mastery (as in
Franklin Evans), but also a valorized and liberatory possibility as well.

    If the transgressiveness of the bathing scene may not have been read in the
terms that critics have recently assumed—that is, if it was read, on the one hand,
as a homoerotically charged, but not for that reason particularly transgressive,
swimming-hole party, and, on the other, by the Boston D.A. as an exhibition of
indecent and distinctly unfeminine sexual desire—the verse-paragraph about
"the negro" that occurs eight lines later may be significantly and tellingly less
ambiguous:

The negro holds firmly the reins of his four horses . . . . the block swags
    underneath on its tied-over chain,
The negro that drives the huge dray of the stoneyard . . . . steady and
    tall he stands poised on one leg on the stringpiece,
His blue shirt exposes his ample neck and breast and loosens over his
    hipband,
His glance is calm and commanding . . . . he tosses the slouch of his hat
    away from his forehead,
The sun falls on his crispy hair and moustache . . . . falls on the black of
    his polish'd and perfect limbs.

I behold the picturesque giant and love him . . . . and I do not stop
    there,
I go with the team also.
                (1855 LG 20)

There is a representation of immediacy in these lines that contrasts vividly with
the highly mediated depiction of the bathing party. There, the presentation of
the male bodies is elaborately framed as a box within a box: readers gain access
to the male bodies through the gaze of the half-hiding woman: "Which of the
young men does *she* like the best?" And this mediation takes another form as
well, since the event is described through a speaker who is at least as interested
in detailing the reactions and experiences of the woman, even if Moon is correct and the scene hinges on "a grammatically transvestite moment halfway

through" in which the speaker exchanges places with the woman, "without necessarily having merged *her* into himself" (42, 43). The complexity involved in detailing the textual dynamics between subject positions and object positions has lately come to be seen as part of the erotic charge: by the end of the section, just who is, after all, doing what to whom? But this is a complexity that may come with a price, one that can best be calculated by means of its stark contrast to the relatively direct account of "the negro."

In short what is so striking—disarmingly so, if the slender amount of critical attention these lines have received is any indication—is the utter simplicity of this account. "The negro" in all his self-possession and strength appears immediate (unmediated) and present to our eye as to the speaker's. This is of course the illusion of the extended Whitmanian catalogs—that they are, as suggested in chapter 3, somehow "pure" representation—and in this regard the description of "the negro" might usefully be contrasted with one of Moon's most intriguing suggestions about the passages describing the twenty-eight young men:

> No unconsidered metonym, the "unseen hand" of the closing lines . . . is also a sign of the poet's projected physical presence among the twenty-eight bathers as well as among his readers in general. It is a sign of the hand of the writer unseen by the reader, who has only the print on the page to signify the desire to provide affectionate physical presence which impels Whitman's writing—or, one might say, only the print on the page *and* the elaborate eroticized image of writing contained in the closing lines of the passage, . . . [the poet] covering them [the young men's "white bellies"] with the "pendant and bending arch" of his "flowing" script. (46)

The lines about "the negro" may lack any of the metonymic intricacies that Moon uncovers, but in place of the "unseen hand" there is an "eye" (again, the illusion of unmediated vision and representation) that merges with the "I" of the poet in one particularly resonant way: for this portrait of "the negro" leading his team resembles nothing so much as the frontispiece engraving of Whitman that faced the title page in both the 1855 and 1856 editions of *Leaves* (see figure 4). That is, there is no inscription of the writing process in the latter passage about "the negro" at work, but in its stead a self-referentiality, insofar as this description functions as a caption for the portrait that the reader would have seen on opening the book for the first time: "His blue shirt exposes his ample neck and breast and loosens over his hipband, / His glance is calm and

FIGURE 4. Steel engraving by Samuel Hollyer of a daguerreotype by Gabriel
Harrison, which served as the frontispiece in the first two editions of *Leaves
of Grass* (1855 and 1856). Courtesy Special Collections, Northwestern University
Library.

commanding . . . . he tosses the slouch of his hat away from his forehead."[17] Karen Sánchez-Eppler, in noting this resemblance, remarks how "the slave at auction provides the quintessential instance of what it means for one's identity to be entirely dependent upon one's body." For this reason, she writes, "to a significant degree Whitman's fundamental image of the body remains that of the slave" (55)—though it is perhaps unclear whether "the negro" working in the stoneyard is enslaved or free—and she refers to this description's uncanny resemblance to the frontispiece as "the first instance of the book's complex and self-conscious strategies of self-incarnation" (56). These insistent efforts to complicate the relations between self, author, reader, and text in *Leaves of Grass* can be stated most economically in the refrain "Who touches this, touches a man."[18]

Eric Lott specifies some of the complexities of this self-representation by situating Whitman's *Leaves* within the amalgam of racial and class discourses and practices that coalesce in the performances of blackface minstrelsy. As Lott details, Whitman was a great lover of minstrel shows in 1840s New York City (78); for this reason his writings are productively situated within the incipient urban working-class cultures of Manhattan where "popular entertainments in which race was foregrounded yielded up a sense of unrest waiting to be tapped at its class source" (87). Restoring Whitman's writings to the specific racialized contexts of the antebellum cityscape affords an opportunity to witness Whitman's implication in the complicated discursive intersections between race and class in the urban North.

Indeed, there may be no more precise measure of the position of Whitman's writings in this nascent working-class milieu than their bipolar oscillations around the issues of slavery and of African Americans more generally: what Lott so provocatively calls "love and theft." On the one hand, this cross-racial, "blackface" identification between the frontispiece portrait and the account of "the negro" at work might be viewed within an always tentative alliance between working-class blacks and whites across the racial divide.[19] But one will also find in Whitman's writing just the opposite possibility, as Lott notes; a Whitman who asks rhetorically, and in passing, in a *Brooklyn Daily Times* editorial of May 1858, "Besides, is not America for the whites?" (*I Sit* 190), and a Whitman the intensity of whose concern for the white working-class exhibited in "The Eighteenth Presidency!" only intensifies in the decade preceding the Civil War. To all of this add the care for the runaway slave in the 1855 edition (about which more below). As Lott summarizes: "Whitman is a salutary reminder that there is no simple correspondence between individual racial feeling, cultural predisposition, and political ideology" (79).[20] Furthermore, there may be no simple correspondences to be found between these disparate viewpoints over the course of a lifetime.

This only becomes clearer as the section about "the negro" and his team moves beyond the cross-racial self-representation already noted, and toward explicit interracial affection and bonding, for when at last the "I" appears overtly in the passage, it does so as the subject of an utterance that takes "the negro" as its beloved direct object: "I behold the picturesque giant and love him." As such, the speaker observing "the negro" stands in parallel relation to the speaker who watches the woman watch the bathing young men: "The rest did not see her, but she saw them and loved them." But the speaker who observes "the negro" does not "stop there," he says, with either simply beholding or simply loving. Rather he says he "goes with the team also," thereby announcing his decision to stay with the man, for reasons that the next verse-paragraph (and later additions to it) reveal to be at the heart of the speaker's agenda:

> In me the caresser of life wherever moving, backward as well as forward
>   sluing,
> To niches and junior bending, not a person or object missing,
> Absorbing all to myself and for this song.[21]

Thus the two episodes establish parallel positions between the speakers who behold all the many "objects" of their gaze. It may also be important to note that the speaker's going with the "team" puts him in a subordinated, objectified position in relation to "the negro" who "holds firmly the reins" and "drives" them—a pronominal grouping that now may include the horses *and* the speaker by episode's end. In this reading the "team" "absorbs" the speaker as he had earlier "absorbed" them, a power-sharing arrangement that may bespeak as well an erotically charged and potentially sadomasochistic dynamic that partly constitutes this speaker's "love" for "the negro." This is a possibility that grows even more resonant because the twenty-eight bathers scenario is framed on the other (preceding) side by the encounter between the speaker and a runaway slave, whom the speaker cares for and assists on his escape to the North: "And gave him a room that entered from my own . . ." (1855 LG 19). Thus is the swimming party literally framed by these homoerotic and importantly interracial episodes.

When the speaker "goes" with the team, however, it deflates the exclusivity of his admiration for "the negro," potentially collapsing it into a version of human/animal subjection, or at the very least, a hierarchical relation, in which the speaker is complexly implicated because of the self-reflexivity of his relation to "the negro" in the first place. This hierarchical relation may recall an element of the runaway slave passage which Jonathan Arac has discussed, that "the slave remains an object by means of which the narrator is morally empowered" ("Vernacular" 46). Later in the book "the negro" may make a reappearance, this time fully transformed in a fantasy of mastery that the speaker had until now carried out only analogically:

A gigantic beauty of a stallion, fresh and responsive to my caresses,
Head high in the forehead and wide between the ears,
Limbs glossy and supple, tail dusting the ground,
Eyes well apart and full of sparkling wickedness . . . . ears finely cut and
    flexibly moving.

His nostrils dilate . . . . my heels embrace him . . . . his well built limbs
    tremble with pleasure . . . . we speed around and return.

I but use you a moment and then I resign you stallion . . . . and do not
    need your paces, and outgallop them,
And myself as I stand or sit pass faster than you.

(1855 LG 35)

Edwin Haviland Miller writes somewhat incongruously of these lines: "After the I dominates and pleasures the stallion . . . he has no more to prove and abandons the horse" (*Mosaic* 109). But the "fresh and responsive" sexual encounter between the speaker and the horse also marks one of the parameters for writing interracial erotic encounters within a context suffused by scientific racism's alignment of Africans with animals along the structuring hierarchies of what the (European) Renaissance first labeled a Great Chain.[22] These are representations that allow space for what we are seeing here: variations on a theme of self-mastery that Whitman's erotic play demonstrates and that includes as well a kind of role playing (first the speaker and then "the negro" is identified with the horses), spinning out variations where sexuality and race meet at the site(s) of the lover's enslaved body/the enslaved lover's body. For within the phrenology- and temperance-inflected discourses of self-management in the antebellum period, desire is first and foremost a matter of self-control and of willful self-mastery, and these dual demands are a great part of what makes Whitman's journey south so consequential a trip in the late 1840s.[23]

Whitman's Big Easy

The passage depicting "the negro" functions not only backwards, as it were, in relation to the frontispiece engraving; rather, it carries rhetorical effects forward into the 1855 volume as well. These effects appear especially prominently in the single poem that most definitively takes as its subject the representation of the body; untitled in 1855, this poem becomes "I Sing the Body Electric" by the time of its revised appearance in the 1867, fourth edition. The poem's revisions encapsulate many of the most significant components of the relationship between representations of slavery and of the body in the early editions of *Leaves of Grass*.

The untitled first version of "I Sing the Body Electric" in the 1855 edition "enlists the reader in the defense of black personhood," as Betsy Erkkila has written (*Political Poet* 126), by means of the speaker's intervention in "A slave at auction!":

> I help the auctioneer . . . . the sloven does not half know his business.
> Gentlemen look on this curious creature,
> Whatever the bids of the bidders they cannot be high enough for
>   him . . . .
>   (*1855 LG* 80–81)

The slave auction represents not only "the defilation of the human body by the institution of slavery" (127), as Erkkila makes clear, but also the defilation of the human body *as* the institution of slavery along the lines that the previous discussion of temperance has begun to bring into perspective. More than simply the most visible and most politically charged cultural site at which the degradations of slavery are exhibited, the slave auction also represents one of the relatively few arenas for the public display and the literal commodification of the human body in antebellum culture. It is thus no mere coincidence in "I Sing the Body Electric" that the speaker's inventory of the body's parts in the poem commences after he appropriates the role and the voice of the auctioneer ("Gentlemen . . ."); it is rather an expression of a peculiar antebellum cultural logic that locates the representability of the body at the site of the slave market *apart from* any potentially contradictory investment this poem or any other text might make with regard to, or in condemnation of, these practices.

For this reason, it is important to reconsider the time between February and May 1848 that Whitman spent in New Orleans working as an exchange editor[24] at the *Daily Crescent*, because it is during these months that he would have experienced first hand the sights and sounds of the country's largest slave market, where perhaps 100,000 slaves changed hands before the Civil War.[25] Here he would have seen, as did copious other visitors, the display of the bodies of enslaved men and women for sale at auction, paraded on the sidewalks and the streets or "stay[ing] stock still" on display in front of the slave pens where they were temporarily housed.

It may be a gauge of just how uninformed about the embodied particularities of Southern slavery Whitman was before his time in New Orleans that he depends in *Franklin Evans* (1842) on Charles Dickens's account of a plantation house from *American Notes* (1842) as an epigraph for chapter 15.[26] But in New Orleans Whitman and his brother Jeff (Thomas Jefferson Whitman) lived and worked mere blocks from the city's central slave markets (see figure 5); moreover, as Walter Johnson illustrates, "the lively traffic in information and influence that joined the slave traders to the hotels and bars where travelers and traders gathered and discussed their business suggests that the practice of trading slaves far outreached the cluster of pens publicly identified as 'the slave market'" (52). The Whitman who arrived in New Orleans was an itinerant who walked widely and who quite likely penned pieces for the *Crescent* with titles like "Sketches of the Sidewalks and Levees, With Glimpses into the New Orleans Bar (rooms)," and "A Walk About Town By A Pedestrian," in which the resonant account of "a negro" made to whip himself first appeared, and which may now suggest a wholly different sense of the "help" which the speaker provides the auctioneer in "Body Electric."[27]

This is also a Whitman who likely spent time in the barrooms that adjoined the auction blocks, worrying over the excessive consumption of mint juleps and other spirits in such a hot climate (Rubin 186), someone who would have been exposed not simply to the humid weather but to what Joseph Roach describes as "the very normality of the slave trade in the performance of daily life in New Orleans" (*Cities* 213). Everywhere Whitman walked he would likely have been reminded of slavery's ubiquity, its influence not only on the prospects of the white workingmen of the North and the South whose interests he defended in a 1 September 1847 editorial in the *Brooklyn Daily Eagle*, but also its life-and-

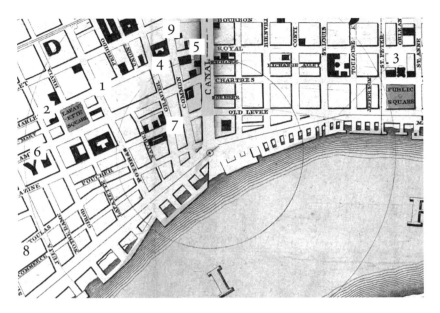

FIGURE 5. Detail from "Norman's plan of New Orleans & environs, 1845," showing locations central to Whitman's life in the city during his visit of 1848. Courtesy Geography and Map Division, Library of Congress.

LEGEND

1. Corner of St. Charles and Poydras—lodging of first night's stay
2. General location of Tremont House—known to be located near St. Charles Theater and across from the offices of the *Crescent* on St. Charles Ave.
3. WW and Jeff visit French Quarter and "French Church" [the Cathedral of St. Louis]
4. Office of Pierson & Bonneval, Auctioneers
5. Grand Salon at the St. Charles Hotel
6. WW picture taken at Maguire's Daguerreotype, 6 Camp Street
7. Bank's Arcade—Pierson & Bonneval slave auctions
8. St. Mary's Market
9. Rusconi's Book Depot

death stakes for the African and African-descended men and women whose attributes were hawked and whose prices were negotiated in public view at the same time that their eyes could be met (or not) and their fates lamented (or not) by passersby.[28]

There is a long tradition in Whitman studies focusing on the importance of New Orleans in Whitman's development as a poet, and since at least 1905, much speculation has centered on the possibility of a romance there with a woman.[29] In place of what has often been a barely shrouded quest for Whitman's hetero-sexuality, I want to argue that New Orleans be renewed as a site of particular importance for understanding the constellation of discourses that pronounce Whitman's homoerotic sexual desire. This is not, of course, the same as arguing for New Orleans as the site of Whitman's coming out of the closet as a homo-sexual, for, as numerous historians have demonstrated, neither homo- nor heterosexuality yet existed as a social role or identity in mid-nineteenth-century America. But the particular shape of Whitman's erotic desire, inflected by both temperance and by important cross-racial representation and identifications, is usefully read in relation to these few important months spent in New Orleans. It seems unlikely that unambiguous factual evidence of Whitman's genital sexual activity with a woman, so desired by one strand of the Whitman critical heri-tage, will be discovered in the New Orleans months. In its stead I am arguing that the discursive nexus of visible bodies and slavery (including the scopophilic description of bodies that auctions both sanctioned and depended on) plays a formative role very like the one so long ascribed to that fanciful New Orleans heterosexual romance.[30] Besides the freedom of this relatively young Whitman's first sustained trip away from his Brooklyn home, New Orleans permits an immersion in enslaved and racialized embodiment, and in male bodies in crisis, that Whitman takes back with him, importing these northward as central structures evident in his later published writing.[31]

These possibilities grow even more suggestive because New Orleans was a city in which the wounded and striving male bodies that so arrested Whitman's attention during the Civil War (and surely the runaway slave in the 1855 edition is a version of this as well) have some of their counterparts in the black male bodies at auction. This important feature of what this Southern city offered Whitman is only reinforced by recalling its role as "an armed camp, a staging area, and a hospital depot" during the Mexican-American War; as Whitman and his brother took up residence there, "recruits continued to arrive from the interior and bivouacked in open fields or pitched tents in Lafayette Square until steamers carried them along with teamsters and quartermasters to Vera Cruz. Every ship returning from that port brought sick and wounded veterans who filled all hospital beds while healthy victors paraded and accepted honors and hospitality" (Rubin 186–87). Indeed, one of the articles that Whitman as exchange editor selected for the *Daily Crescent* was a report that the House of Representatives had authorized "Barracks for Invalid Soldiers" wounded in Mexico; the report emphasizes that "a thousand of our poor fellows . . . will be saved" (18 May 1848).

My argument builds on two central aspects of Kirsten Silva Gruesz's important discussion of Whitman in the South. Gruesz argues in the first place that "the Hispanized realm of mid-century New Orleans . . . heightens Whitman's already nascent sense of embodiment as a poetic strategy of erotic nationalism" (121). Moreover, spending time in the South magnifies Whitman's "profound ambivalence" about Manifest Destiny and links this "to his perceptions of the subjugated, racialized body—both the enslaved black one and the conquered brown one" (121). Whitman's New Orleans writings bear out these conclusions, in ways that have yet to be fully investigated.

One of Whitman's first contributions to the *Crescent* upon his arrival in New Orleans, "The Mississippi at Midnight," reveals something of what is at stake in restoring this erotic and racial context to Whitman's pre-*Leaves* years. Here is the poem in its entirety:

How solemn! sweeping this dense black tide!
    No friendly lights i' the heaven o'er us;
A murky darkness on either side,
    And kindred darkness all before us!

Now, drawn near the shelving rim,
    Weird-like shadows suddenly rise;
Shapes of mist and phantoms dim
    Baffle the gazer's straining eyes.

River fiends, with malignant faces!
    Wild and wide their arms are thrown,
As if to clutch in fatal embraces
    Him who sails their realms upon.

Then, by the trick of our own swift motion,
    Straight, tall giants, an army vast,

Rank by rank, like the waves of ocean,
> On the shore march stilly past.

How solemn! the river a trailing pall,
> Which takes, but never again gives back;
And moonless and starless the heavens' arch'd wall,
> Responding an equal black!

Oh, tireless waters! like Life's quick dream,
> Onward and onward ever hurrying—
Like Death in this midnight hour you seem,
> Life in your chill drops greedily burying!

> (EPF 43)

The poems foregrounds race from its opening line—"How solemn! sweeping this dense black tide!"—and its importance ultimately depends on the speaker's taking on (as one of his "changes of garments" [1855 LG 39]) the imagined perspective of a fugitive slave. Thus the poem transmutes Whitman's trip "down the river" to New Orleans (away from the known parameters of his life in Brooklyn) into the plea of a speaker who is attempting to escape through what the poem calls a "kindred darkness" (4).

The poem alternates between depictions of the landscape's blackness as "kindred" and as an enemy that hides (possibly only imagined) obstacles to his escape. Thus there are "no friendly lights" (2) and "a murky darkness on either side" (3). Stanza 3 introduces the possibility of "River fiends" who would "clutch in fatal embraces," a scenario that looks at first like an early version of the running fugitive slave and the dogs clamoring after him in the 1855 Leaves.[32] In its attention to these potentially erotic "fatal embraces," however, the poem simultaneously invokes the amorous temptations this voyager to parts unknown may also risk: once again the racial and the sexual overlap. Indeed, a later revision of the poem seizes on these sexual temptations with a polemical vigor that the editors call "painfully didactic" (EPF 43n):

But when there comes a voluptuous languor,
> Soft the sunshine, silent the air,
Bewitching your craft with safety and sweetness,
> Then, young pilot of life, beware.

> (EPF 43)

The earlier, *Daily Crescent* version of the poem keeps these racial and sexual temptations both at bay and in rhetorical play:

River fiends, with malignant faces!
> Wild and wide their arms are thrown,
As if to clutch in fatal embraces
> Him who sails their realms upon.

"Fatal embraces" carries some of the erotic charge Michael Warner has found in *Franklin Evans*, especially that novel's attempts "simultaneously to articulate pleasure and to manage it. . . . Fatal pleasure, but also *Oh, fatal pleasure*" ("Drunk" 32). In the interplay between the sexual and the racial, one finds in the poem the incoherence of a "fatality" (with echoes, perhaps, of a biblical, sexual "death") that from another point of view may be the possibility most earnestly desired.[33]

As the journey continues, the poem next depicts "an army vast," "Straight, tall giants" whom the speaker is somehow able to avoid "by the trick of our own swift motion." "Rank by rank" the soldiers ashore glide past in a landscape completely darkened and masculinized, and unaware of the speaker's escape just out of reach. The escape climaxes in the penultimate stanza:

How solemn! the river a trailing pall,
> Which takes, but never again gives back;
And moonless and starless the heavens' arched wall,
> Responding an equal black!

Here the poem makes its most forceful gesture toward its uncanny equation between the journey Whitman has just taken and the one the speaker in the poem experiences. In part this equivalence is carried out by the poem's repeated depiction of the landscape—shore, river, sky—in terms of blackness, a recurring trope that comes to seem a particularly insistent and broadly *racialized* pathetic fallacy, mirroring the darkness of what the poem projects as an "equal[ly] black" speaker: precisely a "kindred darkness." Moreover, so momentous is this interpellative gesture—this ventriloquism of the point of view of a fugitive black slave—that the poem itself thematizes the transmigration of voice with the crucial line "Responding an equal black!"

In a poem like this, Whitman, in Beach's pithy formulation, "brings the fact of slavery into his own space—that of his body and soul and of the larger republic they represent" (82).[34] Barely two weeks after arriving in New Orleans, Whitman's poetic persona has absorbed the possibility of writing from the complicated perspective of an enslaved black man who might also experience a voyage on the Mississippi, though one with utterly higher stakes. The editors of the Whitman standard edition conclude that the early *Crescent* version of the poem gives "the impression that the poet is sincerely reporting his emotional reaction to a real experience" (EPF 42 n.1); what is not quite certain is just whose experiences the poem chronicles, just what kinds of ventriloquism its speaker performs in the name of that "kindred darkness all before us!"

Whit(e)man

When Whitman returns to New York from New Orleans and begins to publish the *Brooklyn Freeman*, the one copy that survives is positively suffused with the issue of slavery, as its very title makes clear. In the words of volume 1, number 1, issued Saturday, 9 September 1848, "Hardly anyone who takes the trouble to look two minutes at our paper will need being told, at any length, what objects we have in view. . . . we shall oppose, under all circumstances, the addition to the Union, in future, of a single inch of *slave land*. . . ."[35] From the perspective of the controversies over naming opened out in chapter 1, it is interesting to read on the paper's first page, under the heading "Our Enmity to the South":

> It was a tolerably cunning trick of those, in Congress, who would propa-
> gate slavery through new territories, to speak of "the *South*," as wishing
> this, and determined on that, and threatening the other. What do they
> mean by "the South"? Do they mean that any other portions of the white
> population except the slave owners, traders and breeders, have so sol-
> emnly determined upon standing out for what they call their "rights," of
> establishing slavery in fresh lands? Do they mean that the hundreds of
> thousands of white farming men, mechanics, artificers, professional per-
> sons, clerks, &c., who do *not* own slaves, take this matter so much at
> heart?

Here is a Whitman attentive to the politics of naming, to the correspondent invisibility and/or inadequate representation in the collective noun "the South" of those white men whose livelihoods suffer as long as elite Southerners have at their disposal an endless supply of enslaved black laborers whose welfare or social progress they need not consider.[36]

The first issue of the newspaper also reprints extended extracts from Martin Van Buren's "last best Letter," as evidence for the paper's endorsement of him as the Free Soil presidential candidate in the 1848 election. At the helm of his own paper Whitman continues to practice the trade of the exchange editor, responsible for the cutting and pasting that made every antebellum newspaper an amalgamation of multiple printed texts: out of many, one. And the same front page of this inaugural issue reprints from Jefferson's writings on slavery, though its pronouncing Jefferson "in the literal sense of the word, an *abolitionist*" may seem little short of absurd given the current understanding about Jefferson's relation to his slaves—not simply his paternity of Sally Hemings's children, but his failure to free most of his slaves in his will, such that [those] "he had vowed to protect as a benevolent father were sold to the highest bidder" (Ellis 347).

Nevertheless it is not difficult to understand the selection Whitman makes from Jefferson's writings; in Jefferson, Whitman finds a Founding Father who shares his concern about intemperate behavior as among slavery's most deleterious effects on whites:

> There must doubtless be an unhappy influence on the manners of our people produced by the existence of slavery among us. The whole commerce between master and slave is a perpetual exercise of the most boisterous passions. . . . Our children see this, and learn to imitate it. . . . If a parent could find no motive . . . for restraining the *intemperance* of passion toward his slave, it should always be a sufficient one that his child is present. (*Freeman*, front page, emphasis added)

Once again slavery is a crisis for white people, in this instance because it trains those who witness its practices likewise to indulge their unreasonable passions and to lose control. This is the intemperance at slavery's core, and its irony was captured in the juxtaposition in the pages of nearly every issue of the *Daily Crescent*, which devoted columns to the growing membership rolls of the Washingtonian Temperance Societies virtually alongside its advertisements for slave auctions.

I want to argue that these print conjunctions objectify the binarized discourses through which, in part, Whitman the lifelong printer imagined eroticism and sexual desire. They provided him, along with phrenology—which, like reform movements in the nineteenth century of all stripes, emphasized balance and self-control—a fundamental vocabulary for his experiences of embodiment and sensuality. (Here we might recall the report of his own phrenological examination that Whitman included in the 1856 edition of *Leaves of Grass*.)[37]

This focus on balance and self-control recurs in entries in an 1855–56 notebook that stress "perfect calmness and sanity":

> Idea to pervade largely / Eligibility—I, you, any one/ eligible to the conditions / or attributes or advantages / of any being, no matter / who,—/ 3ᵈ. Feb. Make no puns / funny remarks / Double entendres / "witty" remarks / ironies / Sarcasms / —only that which / is simply earnest, / meant,—harmless / to any one's feelings / —unadorned / unvarnished / nothing to / excite a / laugh / silence / silence / silence / laconic / taciturn (*1855–56 Notebook* 8)

This entry's insistence on first universality and then simplicity and equanimity—the "unadorned . . . unvarnished"—bears a remarkable similarity to one that occurs in a later notebook that has become best known for the code through which Whitman seems to have referred to his boyfriend of the 1860s, Peter Doyle:

> Cheating, childish abandonment of myself, fancying what does not really exist in another, but is all the time in myself alone—utterly deluded and cheated by *myself* & my own weakness—Remember where I am most weak, & most lacking. Yet always preserve a kind spirit & demeanor to 16. But Pursue Her No More. A cool, gentle, (less demonstrative) *more* UNI-FORM DEMEANOR—give to poor, help any,—be indulgent to the criminal & silly and low persons generally & the ignorant—but SAY little—make no explanations—give no confidences—never attempt puns, or plays upon words, or utter sarcastic comments, or (under ordinary circumstances) hold any discussions or arguments. (quoted in Holloway, "Affairs" 481)[38]

The entry struggles with perception and projection ("fancying what . . . is all the time in myself alone"), though the question of the greatest "weak"-ness provides the entry's focus: the issue is emotions out of sync, and the lines inscribe a plan for restoring a lost emotional and affective equilibrium. Moreover, the excerpt demonstates only a very slim line between the emotional or the presumably "private" and the strictures or rules for what must be construed as "public" writing. Taken together the two excerpts reveal the slippages—both within and between them—around the issues of affection, desire, and right writing. Self-control and temperate behavior of the kind Jefferson lamented in relation to slavery is at the very center of the sexuality and desire articulating itself here: Whitman the desiring compositor composing himself, writing a self into affectionate self-composure. New Orleans, a slave culture that by definition loses its composure and indulges its passions, accentuates what Fowler eventually pinpointed in Whitman: "a certain reckless swing of animal will." The struggle with (against?) balance and self-control articulated through phrenology and temperance fiction represents a prominent part of what gets written into the desiring selves that speak homoeroticism in *Leaves of Grass*.[39] This is "simmering" and "boiling" of a wholly different kind, and New Orleans importantly adds race to the mix.[40]

After three months at the heart of America's slave economy, the control and containment of slavery becomes for Whitman the one, the only political issue that warrants his attention:

> Free Soilers! Radicals! Liberty Men! all whose throats are not quite tough enough to swallow Taylor or Cass! come up and subscribe for the '*Daily Freeman!*' . . . Let us see whether we can't make both Whig and Democratic Old Hunkerism reel in Kings county.

Whitman's immersion in the performance of daily life in New Orleans is transformative—in ways explicitly political, as the pages of the *Freeman* make clear—as well as discursively instrumental. Forged at the coincident sites of racial embodiment and a culturally pervasive attention to intemperance, Whitman's poetry stages erotic relations across racial lines more frequently than has usually been noted. These representations inscribe the traces of an erotic and cross-racial performativity that New Orleans would have proffered on a daily basis; in perhaps no other American city could Whitman have been schooled so handily in the dual and dueling contradictions of desire and self-mastery in a place that everywhere denied the possibility of relations across the racial line, even as it staged such possibilities on its public streets everywhere and every day. The sites and sounds of these recurrent events thus may offer a previously unrecognized source for the sexual charge explicit in Whitman's body-parts catalogs by considering them now as versions of the thousands of physical examinations that preceded the closure of chattel transactions. As Walter Johnson suggests, "The careful stories buyers used to explain their actions [in examining the bodies of slaves under consideration for purchase] were revealing denials. . . . For white men, examining slaves, searching out hidden body parts, running hands over limbs, massaging limbs and articulating pelvic joints, probing wounds and scars with fingers, was erotic" (149).

"I Sing the Body Electric" becomes an even more salient poem when viewed from a perspective that restores Whitman's time in New Orleans as a necessary condition of its composition, especially in light of the shift between the first and second versions of the poem, from "A slave at auction!" to "A man's body at auction!" The disappearance of the direct reference to the slave in the 1856 version corresponds, however, to the addition of the lines in which the speaker famously catalogs body parts:

> . . . Wrist and wrist-joints, hand, palm, knuckles, thumb,
> forefinger, finger-balls, finger-joints,
> Broad breast-front, curling hair of the breast, breast-bone,
> breast-side,
> Ribs, belly, back-bone, joints of the back-bone. . . . [41]

This 1856 version of the poem is probably the most familiar, and it is also the one—including the listing of body parts, and the generic designation of the "man" at auction—in which, extending Erkkila's commentary, the egalitarian thrust of the poem is most powerfully delivered. That is, now it is simply a "man" that is being "auctioned," and the use of the generic category equates free whites and enslaved blacks and thereby redoubles the impact of an already powerful statement defending the humanity of blacks.

But it may also be the case that the shift toward "man" is double-edged, that the omission of the word "slave" is tacitly recalled in an antebellum logic that equates embodiment and blackness in the first place. The irony here would operate in a way similar to what Karen Sánchez-Eppler has remarked with regard to Whitman's claims for universal humanity, especially insofar as these emerge in his ventriloquized auctioneer's cry: "Within there runs his blood. . . . the same old blood. . . . the same red running blood":

> From the auction block an appeal to blood too easily recalls the bloody backs of whipped slaves. In the lore of plantation slavery, as in all racist discourses, blood is precisely where race dwells, and the genealogy and value of light-skinned slaves is traditionally measured in drops of black and white blood. . . . Whitman's chorus of merger and inclusion repeats the bloody, physical differentiations of plantation life. (*Touching Liberty* 57)

In the same way, the poem's invocation of "a man at auction" attempts to evade, but may be unable to avoid, re-inscribing embodiment itself as the defining function and characteristic of racial identity and blackness.

My central contention, however, pertaining to the function of slavery as a lens that consolidates representations of the body can best be demonstrated by turning to "Enfans d'Adam 2"—the poem that immediately precedes "Body Electric" in its 1860 incarnation—and the way it conjoins the auction scenario with an erotically charged escapade:

> The slave's body for sale—I, sternly, with harsh voice,
>   auctioneering,
> The divine list, for myself or you, or for any one, making,
> The face—the limbs—the index from head to foot, and what
>   it arouses,
> The mystic deliria—the madness amorous—the utter
>   abandonment,
> (Hark, close and still, what I now whisper to you,
> I love you—O you entirely possess me,
> O I wish that you and I escape from the rest, and go utterly
>   off—O free and lawless,
> Two hawks in the air—two *fishes swimming* in the sea not
>   more lawless than we;) . . . .
>   ("Enfans d'Adam 2"; *1860 LG* 289, emphasis added)

These lines explicitly link the body of the slave with the "index from head to foot" that appears in the very next poem: thus the alignments I have been describing have come full circle. The 1855 versions give the "slave at auction" without the catalog, while the 1856 edition has the listing but with "slave" changed to the potentially generic "man." Here, in 1860, the site of the body/slavery alliance has moved to the poem previous to "Body Electric," in which the possibility of "the divine list" grows directly from the reference to "the slave's body for sale." And where did such slave sales occur? The rotunda of the St. Louis Hotel—a few blocks from Whitman's first lodgings in New Orleans—served as what a contemporaneous guide calls "the principal auction mart, where slaves, stocks, real estate, and all other kinds of property were sold from noon to 3:00 P.M.": Roach refers to this site as "a kind of homosocial pleasure dome with overlapping commercial and leisure attractions" ("Spectacles" 54–55).[42]

The speaker's relation to "the slave's body" connects directly to the homo-social dynamics that occur later in the 1860 edition:

> We two boys together clinging,
> One the other never leaving,
>
> . . .
>
> With birds singing—With *fishes swimming*—With trees
>   branching and leafing,
> Cities wrenching, ease scorning, statutes mocking . . . .
>
>   ("Calamus 26"; *1860 LG* 369, emphasis added)

The repeated phrase across poems and poetic clusters demonstrates the sugges-tive and potentially mobile place "the slave" occupies with regard to the depic-tions of homosociality in the 1860 edition, even as the original 1855 passage about "the negro" and his horse team now looks an incipient form of the homoeroticism that becomes in 1860 the explicit subject matter of "Calamus."

Even taken as an isolated instance, however, the dynamics in "Enfans d'Adam 2" are positively striking: from "the slave's body" to "the index," to delcarations of sensual pleasure ("the index . . . and what it arouses . . ."), and of love and commitment ("O I love you . . . O I wish that you and I es-cape . . ."). The allusions to "escape" and "possession" ("O you entirely possess me") reveal the close connection between rhetorics of liberation drawn from temperance discourses and another essential aspect of Whitmanian poetics, especially in the 1860 edition: sexual liberation, the liberation of the body to enjoy sensual pleasures.

Moreover, it is important to note that the slave's escape from the auction and from slavery (in "Enfans d'Adam 2") is made parallel to, and simultaneous with, the speaker's escape *into* sexual liberation and the exercise of the body. Likewise the slave's dispossession of himself as slave produces an erotic dis-possession, again, on the part of the speaker ("I love you—O *you entirely possess me*"). Discourses of erotic attraction, love, and enslavement intertwined here operate in peculiar and not necessarily predictable ways. One might expect, for example, if only from the example of the twenty-eight bathers, that the viewer would be the owner of the object viewed, but here it is the socially and visually disempowered object of the speaker's erotic gaze who possesses *him*. Thus slav-ery literally inhabits, takes over, possesses Whitman and his erotic discourse.

From this overdetermined instance it would be difficult to overstate how complexly conjoined are the multiple languages of slavery, temperance, embodiment, and homoeroticism—not only here, but over the whole course of these themes' variegated transmutations beginning in the years before 1855, that watershed year for what we could perhaps do no better than to call Whitman's poetic corpus.

Self-Same Power

The significance of antebellum discourses of temperance for Emerson's "The Poet" examined earlier makes newly clear the value in taking Emerson at his (historicist) word when he explains transcendentalism as "Idealism as it appears in 1842" (*LAE* 193). Seeking to restore the historicity of Emerson's essays, we find that "The Poet" is of course no isolated case; "Experience" also demonstrates Emerson's entanglement in antebellum figurations of embodiment through slavery's corporealized practices. Materiality as it appears in this essay takes many forms: for example, the text itself, and the body of a child. But the material grounding of "Experience" in 1844, the year of its first publication, emerges most powerfully by restoring to the essay its dependence on rhetorics associated with the contradictions of American slavery.

It is not simply the title of Emerson's essay that locates it in terms of a relation to, or an engagement with, the material world. This engagement is signaled as well by the essay's very first sentences:

> Where do we find ourselves? In a series of which we do not know the extremes, and believe that it has none. (*LAE* 471)

Appearing in a volume titled *Essays: Second Series*, "series" is powerfully self-referential, emphasizing at the very start the process of reading, insofar as a reader does not know the "extremes" of either the essay or the volume, having just begun to read. Moreover, "series" has the additional effect of emphasizing the concrete text the reader holds in his hands, and so makes overt the temporal and even the spatial locations at which this reader's reading is taking place. In a word, the essay's opening links speaker and reader ("Where do *we* find ourselves?") and foregrounds not simply the act of reading but the places and the material texts that the activity of reading encompasses. The effect is almost Whitmanian.

Of course "series" also refers to the inscrutable position "we" occupy with respect to the diminished past behind and the horizons of an indiscernible future ahead:

> We wake and find ourselves on a stair; there are stairs below us, which we seem to have ascended; there are stairs above us, many a one, which go upward and out of sight. (LAE 471)

The image of stairs partially climbed, like the series of essays a reader has just begun ("Experience" is the second of nine essays in the 1844 volume), grounds even more thoroughly the opening of "Experience" in the concrete materiality of quotidian life. This grounding is particularly appropriate, too, because the essay soon introduces one of its primary topics: the ineradicable fact of Emerson's son Waldo's death at the age of five, about two years before the essay was published.

"Ineradicable" may more accurately describe some of the critical accounts of the relationship between Waldo's death and Emerson's essay than it does Emerson's own account. Nevertheless, the word introduces well one particularly provocative reading of Emerson's essay, by Sharon Cameron:

> "Experience" is an elegy, an essay whose primary task is its work of mourning, and, in light of that poorly concealed fact, it is surprising that critics have consistently spoken of the child as only one of several causes equal in their provocation of listlessness and despair. In those few discussions in which Waldo's death is acknowledged to have special status, it is still not seen as it crucially must be: the occasion that generates in a nontrivial way all other losses that succeed it. (211)

Besides encompassing, in Cameron's reading, the full range of losses that the essay itemizes, Waldo's death reveals itself the site of a potent confrontation with the competing demands of the material and the spiritual. As such, the essay furnishes a particularly useful occasion for observing how the claims for transcendence endemic to Emerson's writings are brought to voice, and by extension, how inextricably the textualities of the political and the literary interweave themselves within the warp and woof of even so ostensibly "personal" an essay as this one on the death of a child.

Waldo's death seems "ineradicable" to some Emerson scholars, Cameron among them, but the speaker in the essay's best-known lines is at some pains to make clear that, for him, precisely the opposite is the case:

> In the death of my son, now more than two years ago, I seem to have lost a beautiful estate,—no more. I cannot get it nearer to me. If tomorrow I should be informed of the bankruptcy of my principal debtors, the loss of

my property would be a great inconvenience to me, perhaps, for many years; but it would leave me as it found me,—neither better nor worse. So it is with this calamity: it does not touch me: some thing which I fancied was a part of me, which could not be torn away without tearing me, nor enlarged without enriching me, falls off from me, and leaves no scar. It was caducous. (*LAE* 473)

Cameron invokes Freud on mourning to discover grief's presence in these reiterated declarations of absence.[43] Even in the context of the speaker's lamentation, however, the word "caducous" vividly represents a quintessentially Emersonian relation to embodiment, since something that was "caducous" was once physically, palpably joined, but has since faded away, leaving no trace of its previous state. Thus this single word carries in another form the fundamental exchange at the heart of Emerson's epistemology and exhibited in a range of representative samplings from across his corpus: "All reflexion goes to teach us the strictly emblematic character of the material world" ("English Literature: Introductory," *EL* 1: 224); "The visible creation is the terminus or the circumference of the invisible world" (*Nature*, *LAE* 25). What is caducous has successfully transmigrated from physicality and visibility to spirituality and invisibility, and to precisely that extent Waldo's death may also represent the desired culmination toward which the striving in Emerson's essays repeatedly directs its readers: "*That* is morning, to cease for a bright hour to be a prisoner of this sickly body, and to become as large as nature" ("Literary Ethics" [1838]; *LAE* 102).

These analogies between the loss of an "estate" and the loss of a child might be read in historical terms as symptoms of the functional equivalences between persons and objects, and between children and objects, that slavery as an institution makes available in antebellum America. Indeed, as Philip Fisher has argued, part of the work of sentimentalism's obsession with the child and the slave in antebellum writings is "the extension of full and complete humanity to classes of figures from whom it has been socially withheld" (*Hard Facts* 99). Moreover, human beings and objects are conflated and exchanged in the day-to-day operating assumptions of the slave market; in Whitman's poem, the auction block functions as the originary site for the exhortation of both the slave's personhood and the shared particularities of human corporeality. Similarly, Waldo's death reckoned in terms of property gained and lost reflects the culturally easy accessibility and substitutability of these terms. The passage may even offer a glimmer, in an unintended way, of the capitalist, plantation practices in which white slave-masters fathered, owned, and sold their own slave-children as moveable chattel quantifiable on estate inventories.

Within such a historical or economic framework, the hard fact of Waldo's physical demise undergoes an unexpected transformation, one which confronts a dominant Emersonian conviction that cessation signifies release and spiritualized reunion. The most prominent signs of this shift occur at identifiable sites of contradiction where the speaker reverses the position from which the essay opens—yearning for what he calls a "rough rasping friction" (LAE 472)—and draws instead on a language that derogatorily links physicality to the spirit-negating constraints of slavery. Thus the speaker rails against science in general and physicians in particular: "The physicians say, they are not materialists; but they are" (LAE 475); one can perhaps hear a note of desperation in the stunning simplicity (a mere reversal) of the coun.charge.[44] This is for Emerson the salient point—that spirit is its own proof and requires no materialized confirmation: "But the definition of *spiritual* should be, *that which is its own evidence*" (LAE 475).

Still, how revealing is the movement from "physicians" and "scientists" to another, and now perhaps familiar, vocabulary within which physicality is envisioned, for no sooner does the speaker discredit them than he singles them out for a particularly vehement denunciation: they are all "theoretic kidnappers and slave-drivers" who falsely and arbitrarily insist on "the links of the chain of physical necessity" (LAE 475–76). The speaker's craving for an intense physical encounter—for the rough friction or some alternative to Waldo's merely "caducous" slipping away—has in these lines their fullest retraction. This is in part because the alignment of materiality with enslavement across the Emersonian corpus makes not only Waldo's death, but also his embodied life, the site of an epistemological crisis. It is, in a word, the fact of Waldo's (materialized) life that needs to be processed and transmuted in "Experience" as much as his death must be.

This denigration and attempted expulsion of the physical in "Experience" (and in experience) has its parallel in the other text that takes Waldo's death as its ostensible origin: Emerson's elegiac poem "Threnody." In that poem David Porter has described a "hidden allegory" that sets "about abstracting . . . with the purpose of converting the death to a usable idea" (32), a movement from the physical fact toward the universal and the spiritual that makes the poem an inscription of the Emersonian poet's mission. (And indeed, by poem's end, as

Porter observes, Waldo is eulogized, like Milton's Lycidas, as a lost, budding poet.)[45] In "Experience" the alignment between physicality and enslavement makes of Waldo's death, but also Waldo's life, a contradictory locus from the epistemological consequences of which the speaker-father must necessarily (using the term advisedly) escape.

This movement is reiterated by the essay's inscription of another life-or-death dilemma, for while it is clearly too late for Waldo, it is not for these swimmers in need of assistance:

> A sympathetic person is placed in the dilemma of a swimmer among drowning men, who all catch at him, and if he give so much as a leg or a finger, they will drown him. They wish to be saved from the mischiefs of their vices, but not from their vices. . . . A wise and hardy physician will say, *Come out of that*, as the first condition of advice. (*LAE* 490)

By the curious logic of its inclusion within "Experience," this passage analogizes the dying Waldo to these drowning men, and, by extension, would seem to provide the essay's speaker ("a swimmer") an opportunity to "save" his "son." It is an opportunity about which the essay records only uncertainty, however, and for reasons that "The deep Heart" reiterates in "Threnody" in the form of rhetorical questions:

> Light is light which radiates,
> Blood is blood which circulates,
> Life is life which generates,
> And many-seeming life is one,—
> Wilt thou transfix and make it none?
> Its onward force too starkly pent
> In figure, bone and lineament?
>   (Emerson, *Selections* 434)

The rhetorical question "Experience" frames is this: Is it not possible that Waldo is better off in the cherished, dematerialized state he now occupies and has achieved, as "deep Heart" impatiently explains, and not for the first time? Unlike the physicians the speaker railed against a few pages earlier, this other physician who stands, or swims, apart is specifically *not* tied to "the links of the chain of physical necessity," symbolized by the bodies of the drowning men. Rather he is described as "wise and hardy": not only is he sufficiently insightful regarding the larger stakes in play, but he also possesses a kind of (etymological) "hardy"-ness that makes him resistant to the claims of the "rough, rasping friction" in the form of the drowning men "who all catch at him." Which is to say that at best the essay's speaker only half craves the "friction" with which the essay opens, and the shift in subject positions in this crucial passage—from "a sympathetic person"/"swimmer" to "a wise and hardy physician"—encapsulates the essay's vexed epistemic dilemma.

Remarking on the controversial and best-known lines from "Experience," including the allusion to Waldo's demise as the loss of "a beautiful estate," Richard Poirier has remarked that "it can of course be said, and therefore repeatedly has been, that these comparisons are 'shocking' or 'heartless' or 'cold' or 'confusing' " (*Poetry* 61). Readings of "Experience" that find it insufficiently emotional, or that seek out an affective dimension in it that would approximate more closely the experience of grief the essay presumably *should* enunciate, fail fully to account for the vexed status of physicality that the essay takes Waldo's death as an occasion to examine.

Considered in these terms, physicality in Emerson's epistemology may leave no uncomplicated position from which grief can be so familiarly or reassuringly expressed. One sees this in what is often read as a passage in *Nature* about Emerson's brother Charles's death:

> When much intercourse with a friend has supplied us with a standard of excellence, and has increased our respect for the resources of God who thus sends a real person to outgo our ideal; when he has, moreover, become an object of thought, and, whilst his character retains all its unconscious effect, is converted in the mind into solid and sweet wisdom,—it is a sign to us that his office is closing, and he is commonly withdrawn from our sight in a short time. (*LAE* 31)[46]

The lives of even the most beloved are subject to "conversion"—a word that marks another example of the transmutation (here, transubstantiation?) of keywords in Anglo-American religious, cultural, and political life. However conversion signified for Emerson's ministerial forefathers, in Emerson's epistemology it limns the necessity of breaking the bounds of material encumbrance in favor of the possibilities of purely spiritual release. When readers find the accounts of grief insufficient in "Experience" they are responding to ambivalences that go to the very heart of Emersonian epistemology. As Fisher explains, we live in a world that is indebted to the cultural work achieved by texts like

Stowe's *Uncle Tom's Cabin*, which helped to naturalize the humanity of both slave and child.[47] But Emerson's essay, with its vexed relation to embodiment, cannot easily meet these readerly demands or expectations. This leaves the curious possibility that an analogue for the speaker's relation to the ultimate, if uncanny, tragedy of embodiment in "Experience" may be a character like Sethe in Toni Morrison's (admittedly anachronistic) *Beloved*—at least as much as anything Stowe's work epitomizes at the site of the sentimental child. Sethe's murder spares her child the tragedy of embodiment literalized as enslavement; Emerson's ambivalence about just what it means that Waldo lived, and did so (as do we all) necessarily delimited by the bounds of an embodiment-as-enslavement, accounts for the emotional ambivalences critics have noted in "Experience" with clarity, but sometimes without quite knowing what to make of them.[48]

From this perspective, the pronoun "that" in the wise and hardy physician's command (*"Come out of that"*) denotes not simply the water but the state of physicality itself. And to the extent of the difference—from the "slave-driver," corporeally bound physician discussed earlier, to this one, standing alone and apart—the rhetorical achievements of "Experience" may be called a success: the situation of the drowning men functions to transmute Waldo's death and permits the speaker to restore the primacy of the spiritual over any other claims. He has seemingly paid heed to his own advice.

What's more, Waldo's involuntary death of scarlet fever and the speaker's absent-present mourning are both rewritten in the swimmers passage as versions of a willful fall into "vice." Thus disease and mourning are linked at this fluid site, as both the speaker's mourning and his failure to mourn are inscribed as a kind of wallowing, like the drowning men, and like the fall into a kind of intemperate vice. Vice is equivalent to the fall into embodiment and creation itself, about which the essay records a precisely Blakean, excruciating ambivalence: "It is," the speaker recalls, "very unhappy, but too late to be helped, the discovery we have made that we exist" (*LAE* 487).

The ending of "Experience," echoing the call to arms that concludes "The American Scholar," exposes rather clearly the costs of these confrontations with the crisis of embodiment. The body—Waldo's body, the swimmers' bodies—that had been aligned with the enslaved or the kidnapped becomes instead the occasion for affirming once more the possibilities of decorporealized "Man Thinking":

Patience and patience, we shall win at the last. We must be very suspicious of the deceptions of the element of time. It takes a good deal of time to eat or to sleep, or to earn a hundred dollars, and a very little time to entertain a hope and an insight which becomes the light of our life. We dress our garden, eat our dinners, discuss the household with our wives, and these things make no impression, are forgotten next week; but in the solitude to which every man is always returning, he has a sanity and revelations, which in his passage into new worlds he will carry with him. Never mind the ridicule, never mind the defeat: up again, old heart!—it seems to say,—there is victory yet for all justice; and the true romance which the world exists to realize, will be the transformation of genius into practical power. (LAE 492)

Reading allegorically—that is, from the material toward its spiritual analogues, as we are asked to do constantly in Emerson's writings—it is difficult not to see in the image of "a hope and an insight" that becomes "the light of our life" for "a very little time" an emblem for Waldo himself, appropriately ethereal and spiritualized and so able to fit into the newly restored Emersonian worldview.

There is nevertheless a rhetorical price to be paid for these transmutations. These emerge in the slip away from the language of certainty found in "The American Scholar" toward a language marred by the possibility that decorporealized vision, of the kind encountered while "crossing a bare common," is not renewed, but rather only perpetually deferred. The passage just excerpted begins assuredly enough, its call for "Patience and patience, we shall win at the last" resounding like the charge for "patience" near the end of the earlier address. But much else at the close of "Experience" deflates this assurance and defers the compensation, as the possibility of mere sensory delusion interrupts the exhortation—"it *seems* to say"—and the spiritual promises drift in some ill-defined future tense: ". . . there is victory *yet* . . . and the true romance—*will be*. . . ." Whereas "The American Scholar" closes on a note of unmitigated, collective triumph ("We will walk on our own feet; we will work with our own hands; we will speak our own minds"), what may most palpably linger at the finish of the latter essay is "ridicule" and "defeat"—ignored, unminded, but not obliterated.

Emerson asks us here at the end of "Experience" to be satisfied once again with the deferral of "practical power," in favor of the "genius" we can presumably have now. In a sense this choice recapitulates one that American literary criticism as it emerges from F. O. Matthiessen has often followed: a deferral of the "practical power" that, for example, Matthiessen invested in his activist life but abstracted from his criticism in favor of an explication, more often than not, of unencumbered "genius."[49] This chapter, and this book, propose alternative modes of reading that refuse this deferral, in part by offering alternatives to the persistent Emersonian pressure to read in the end always allegorically.[50] To read against that imperative is to insist on the instrumentality not simply of "practical power" but of the supposedly otherworldly, or unworldly, abstraction called "genius"—including, for example, its embodiment as "The Poet" monumentalized in Emerson Hall. What emerges from such resistances is the outline of a different critical practice and a different Renaissance, the disciplinary parameters of which appear newly permeable, and the writings of which are everywhere implicated in projects of world-making begun in the eighteenth century (and long before). Such is the history of representation. Only by insisting on such instrumentality can anything like the worlds Matthiessen sought during his lifetime to bring to fruition come about.

NOTES

❦

Introduction

1 *Department of Commerce et al. v. United States House of Representatives et al.*, 119A
Sup. Ct. 765, 768 (1998).

2 On the Bill of Rights as a condition of ratification, however unofficial, see Kammen
xix; Currie 110–15; and Matthews 152–57. See also that document's preamble: "THE
Conventions of a number of the States, having at the time of their adopting the
Constitution, expressed a desire, in order to prevent misconstruction or abuse of its
powers, that further declaratory and restrictive clauses should be added: And as
extending the ground of public confidence in the Government, will best ensure the
beneficent ends of its institution[,] RESOLVED. . . . "

3 It is important to note Adams's disavowal of mob violence in this letter to Jefferson,
its omission of the tarring and feathering of loyalists and of events like the Boston
Tea Party, which turns the Revolution into an almost purely mental phenomenon.
These omissions reveal the importance of work by scholars like Michael Prokopow,
whose accounts of the sometimes bloody fate of loyalists during the Revolutionary
era importantly complements and sometimes contests that of, for example, Bernard
Bailyn in *Ideological Origins of the American Revolution*. Likewise Robert Ferguson
includes in his interpretation of American Enlightenment those other acts so vital
to the "forgotten ritual of the Revolution": "spectacle and display"; Ferguson describes, for example, the ingenuity with which the Sons of Liberty masterminded the
death of an obscure street urchin to turn it into "the largest funeral ever seen in
the New World" (8–9) just two weeks before "The Boston Massacre," an event
similarly reconstructed and exploited and re-represented (cf. Paul Revere's famous
engraving).

4 Cf. Jefferson to Madison: "A constitutive act . . . which leaves some previous articles
unnoticed, and raises implications against others, a declaration of rights becomes
necessary by way of supplement" (quoted in Irons 69–70).

5 "Each state retains its sovereignty, freedom, and independence, and every power,

jurisdiction, and right, which is not by this Confederation expressly delegated to the United States, in Congress assembled."

6 The 1990s saw a range of U.S. Supreme Court decisions striking down federal legislation as usurpations of oversight and legislative purviews reserved by the Constitution to the separate states; see Greenhouse, "The Justices Decide Who's in Charge." These decisions, of course, bear at best a curious relation to the Supreme Court decision that brought the 2000 presidential election to its untimely end.

7 On Shays, see the anthology edited by Gross.

8 See Warner, *Republic*, and "Whitman Drunk"; also Robertson, ch. 2, "Oral Speech on the Printed Page."

9 On continuing voting rights abuses, see Nixon, "Turning Back the Clock."

10 NPR's *Morning Edition*, 30 Nov. 1998, "Supreme Court Hears Census Case," Nina Totenberg reporting.

11 Fisher Ames, Massachusetts Ratifying Convention, 15 Jan. 1788, in *The Founders Constitution*, ed. Philip B. Kurland and Ralph Lerner, vol. 1, ch. 13, document 28, online, 14 Dec. 2000; available at http://press-pubs.uchicago.edu/founders/documents/v1ch13s28.html.

12 It is worth noting that the NPR commentator's "virtual" is about "making up" people, while the Founders' "virtual" has more to do with "filtering" or "diluting" the people's opinions.

13 "Thus it appears that the liberties, happiness, interests, and great concerns of the whole United States, may be dependent upon the integrity, virtue, wisdom, and knowledge of 25 or 26 men.—How unadequate and unsafe a representation!" (*DC* 1: 542).

14 "The election for members of the convention was held at so early a period and the want of information was so great, that some of us did not know of it until after it was over, and we have reason to believe that great numbers of the people of Pennsylvania have not yet had an opportunity of sufficiently examining the proposed constitution." The passage goes on to do the math with reference to just how many citizens voted for the men who adopted the Constitution (*DC* 1: 531).

15 Joyce Appleby finds a similar situation in the generation immediately following independence: Americans, she writes, possessed "the intensely felt need to create a union from the disparate groups that formed their country. Americans knew that the ideal of a commonwealth was one king, one church, and one tongue. The Revolution had offered patriots the rhetorical opportunity to treat America's social diversity as a summons to a new kind of nationhood, but a successful War for Independence did not supply the shared sentiments, symbols, and social explanations necessary for an integrative national identity. . . . What seems remarkable in retrospect is that so many members of the first generation deliberately reflected upon their situation" (*Inheriting* 240).

16 On Matthiessen's politics, see Arac, "F. O. Matthiessen," Cheyfitz, "Matthiessen's *American Renaissance*," and Grossman, "Canon."

17 For a recent summary, see the introduction to Powell's *Ruthless Democracy*, 5–7. On the exclusion of Poe, who was, Matthiessen writes, "bitterly hostile to democracy," see AR xii n. 3.

18 See the preface to Ziff, *Writing* ix–xi; also Warner, *Letters* 122. For period usage, Brown (*Knowledge Is Power* 205) cites the description of a compelling interlocutor "on all subjects" as "a man of literature."

19 To name only two examples of this important revisionist work in feminist criticism and women's writing: Jane Tompkins's *Sensational Designs* (1985), and Nina Baym's influential essay, "Melodramas of Beset Manhood: How Theories of American Fiction Exclude Women Authors" (1981).

20 One could expand this question of virtual representation to include the literary-historical notion of the canon that has so energized literary studies during the last three decades. John Guillory in *Cultural Capital* has been one of the most prescient commentators on the status of the representative as it has infused these debates over standard and alternative canonicity. His reminder that there is no simple alignment between the curricular inclusion of texts by underrepresented or minority authors and the distribution of either political power or access to literacy and to educational institutions importantly complicates how it is we think about the work that remains to be accomplished following the expansion of the academic literary canon.

21 "The one common denominator of my five writers, uniting even Hawthorne and Whitman, was their devotion to the possibilities of democracy" (AR ix).

22 Twenty years ago Hedges noted, while considering the literary consequences of the myth of American exceptionalism, that these eighteenth-century writings, along with pre–American Renaissance texts more generally, evince "a deeper literary significance . . . in the tension between the exorbitance of the new nation's pretensions to political, moral, and intellectual enlightenment and its fears and suspicions, conscious and unconscious, that its claims were not fully justified. . . . This is a tension that pervades much of the writing of the period, whether strictly political and utilitarian or more obviously imaginative" (109).

23 For these reasons, the term "American Renaissance" should be read wherever it appears in this book as "under erasure."

24 Likewise Buell in *New England Literary Culture* analyzes across Neo-Classical and Romantic divisions in order to highlight "the definition of poetic strategies common . . . to the period as a whole" (107).

25 Castronovo helps us to periodize Emerson's impatience with monumentality by reminding us of Webster's 1825 address at the Bunker Hill Monument cornerstone

ceremony. "We are among the sepulchres of the fathers," Webster said, hoping that "the thousands of Americans gathered in front of him would disregard time and skip across the years to recover the storied viability of democratic origins" (*Fathering* 128). Only a decade later such a return seems less viable for a nation already under pressure from a range of groups marginalized at the nation's founding (women, slaves, unpropertied men), and for Emerson, whose commitments tended always toward the individual against the claims of collectivity (those "thousands of Americans").

26 From Emerson's "The Poet": "For poetry was all written before time was, and whenever we are so finely organized that we can penetrate into that region where the air is music, we hear those primal warblings, and attempt to write them down . . . " (*LAE* 449).

27 See Williams, "The Romantic Artist," ch. 2 in *Culture and Society*.

28 This book thus differs from Reynolds's *Beneath the American Renaissance* both methodologically and in terms of its archive. These differences can be elucidated in relation to one of that book's introductory goals: "To study the cross-influences and dynamics between the major and minor writers is to participate in the democratic spirit of the major authors themselves, all of whom in various ways expressed their profound debt to lesser writers" (4). By contrast, *Reconstituting the American Renaissance*, though it concentrates on two "major" authors, does so in part to interrogate the "representativeness" such canonical judgments carry. Moreover, this book assumes "democratic spirit" to be a much contested term in the period, while explicating discursive resemblances and distinctions without reference to canonical status ("beneath," "major," "minor," "lesser") and across a range of texts and literary periods as these have been traditionally understood.

29 Writing in the preface to his epic poem *The Columbiad* (1807), Joel Barlow suggests even the lofty conventions of the epic may not be sufficiently elevated for America's narrative: "The Columbiad is a patriotic poem; the subject is national and historical. Thus far it must be interesting to my countrymen. But most of the events were so recent, so important and so well known, as to render them inflexible to the hand of fiction. The poem, therefore, could not with propriety be modelled after that regular epic form which the more splendid works of this kind have taken, and on which their success is supposed in great measure to depend. The attempt would have been highly injudicious; it must have diminished and debased a series of actions which were really great in themselves and could not be disfigured without losing their interest" (v–vi).

30 Cole offers provocative evidence of Mary Moody Emerson's formative role in shaping Emerson's relation to the body and to transcendence more generally, as well as an account of the gender implications of such pedagogy (109–10).

"Standing on the bare ground, — my head bathed by the blithe air, & uplifted into infinite space, — all mean egotism vanishes. I become a transparent Eyeball."

——. "The Making of an American Prophet: Emerson, His Audiences, and the Rise of the Culture Industry in Nineteenth-Century America." *The American Historical Review* 92 (June 1987): 597–620. Rpt. in Buell, *Emerson: A Collection* 77–100.

——. "The Prisonhouse of Emerson." *American Quarterly* 43 (Mar. 1991): 110–18.

Chai, Leon. *The Romantic Foundations of the American Renaissance.* Ithaca: Cornell University Press, 1987.

Chapman, Mary, and Glenn Hendler, ed. *Sentimental Men: Masculinity and the Politics of Affect in American Culture.* Berkeley: University of California Press, 1999.

Charvat, William. "A Chronological List of Emerson's American Lecture Engagements: Part III." *Bulletin of the New York Public Library* 64 (1960): 606–10.

——. *Literary Publishing in America, 1790–1850.* Philadelphia: University of Pennsylvania Press, 1959.

——. *The Origins of American Critical Thought, 1810–1835.* 1936. New York: A. S. Barnes, 1961.

——. *The Profession of Authorship in America, 1800–1870.* Ed. Matthew J. Bruccoli. Columbus: Ohio State University Press, 1968.

Chauncey, George, Jr. "From Inversion to Homosexuality: Medicine and the Changing Conceptualization of Female Deviance." *Salmagundi* 58–59 (1982–83): 114–46.

Cheyfitz, Eric. "Matthiessen's *American Renaissance*: Circumscribing the Revolution." *American Quarterly* 41 (June 1989): 341–61.

——. *The Trans-Parent: Sexual Politics in the Language of Emerson.* Baltimore: Johns Hopkins University Press, 1981.

Cmiel, Kenneth. *Democratic Eloquence: The Fight over Popular Speech in Nineteenth-Century America.* Berkeley: University of California Press, 1990.

Colacurcio, Michael J. "The American-Renaissance Renaissance." *New England Quarterly* 64 (Sept. 1991): 445–93.

Cole, Phyllis. *Mary Moody Emerson and the Origins of Transcendentalism: A Family History.* New York: Oxford University Press, 1998.

Cornell, Saul. *The Other Founders: Anti-Federalism and the Dissenting Tradition, 1788–1828.* Chapel Hill: University of North Carolina Press for Omohundro Institute of Early American History and Culture, 1999.

Coviello, Peter. "Intimate Nationality: Anonymity and Attachment in Whitman." *American Literature* 73.1 (Mar. 2001): 85–120.

Cowley, Malcolm. Introduction. *Walt Whitman's* Leaves of Grass: *The First (1855) Edition.* Ed. Cowley. 1959. New York: Penguin, 1986.

——. "Walt Whitman: The Miracle." *The New Republic* (18 Mar. 1946): 385–88.

Crain, Caleb. *American Sympathy: Men, Friendship, and Literature in the New Nation.* New Haven: Yale University Press, 2001.

Creech, James. *Closet Writing/Gay Reading: The Case of Melville's* Pierre. Chicago: University of Chicago Press, 1993.

Crèvecoeur, J. Hector St. John de. *Letters from an American Farmer*. 1782. Ed. Susan Manning. New York: Oxford University Press, 1997.

Culler, Jonathan. *On Deconstruction: Theory and Criticism after Structuralism*. Ithaca: Cornell University Press, 1982.

Currie, David P. *The Constitution in Congress: The Federalist Period, 1789–1801*. Chicago: University of Chicago Press, 1997.

[Dalrymple, Sir John.] *The Rights of Great Britain Asserted Against the Claims of America*. Philadelphia: Bell, 1776.

Davidson, Cathy N. *Revolution and the Word: The Rise of the Novel in America*. Oxford: Oxford University Press, 1986.

Delehanty, Randolph. *Ultimate Guide to New Orleans*. San Francisco: Chronicle, 1998.

de Marly, Diana. *Fashion for Men: An Illustrated History*. London: B. T. Batsford, 1989.

D'Emilio, John, and Estelle B. Freedman. *Intimate Matters: A History of Sexuality in America*. New York: Harper and Row, 1988.

"Democracy and Literature." *United States Magazine and Democratic Review* 11.50 (Aug. 1842): 196–200.

Denning, Michael. *Mechanic Accents: Dime Novels and Working-Class Culture in America*. New York: Verso, 1987.

Derrida, Jacques. *The Ear of the Other: Otobiography, Transference, Translation*. Ed. Christie McDonald. Trans. Peggy Kamuf. Lincoln: University of Nebraska Press, 1988.

——. *Limited Inc*. Evanston: Northwestern University Press, 1988.

de Tocqueville, Alexis. *Democracy in America*. Trans. George Lawrence. Ed. J. P. Mayer. New York: Harper Perennial, 1988.

Devotion, Ebenezer. *The examiner examined. A letter from a gentleman in Connecticut, . . . : intitled, The claim of the colonies to an exemption from internal taxes imposed by authority of Parliament, examined*. New London, Conn.: Timothy Green, 1766. Early American imprints, 1st series, no. 10281.

Dickens, Charles. *American Notes for General Circulation*. 1842. New York: Penguin, 1985.

Dickinson, Emily. *Complete Poems*. Ed. Thomas H. Johnson. Boston: Little, Brown, 1960.

Dimock, Wai-chee. *Empire for Liberty: Melville and the Poetics of Individualism*. Princeton: Princeton University Press, 1989.

——. "Scarcity, Subjectivity, and Emerson." *Revisionary Interventions into the Americanist Canon*. Ed. Donald Pease. Durham: Duke University Press, 1994. 83–99.

Donald, David Herbert. *Lincoln*. New York: Simon and Schuster, 1995.

Dougherty, James. *Walt Whitman and the Citizen's Eye*. Baton Rouge: Louisiana State University Press, 1993.

Douglass, Frederick. *Narrative of the Life of Frederick Douglass An American Slave*. 1845. New York: Signet, 1968.

Dowling, William C. *Literary Federalism in the Age of Jefferson: Joseph Dennie and the Port Folio, 1801–1812.* Columbia, SC: University of South Carolina Press, 1999.

Duke University Library. *Catalogue of the Whitman collection in the Duke University Library, being a part of the Trent Collection given by Dr. and Mrs. Josiah C. Trent, compiled by Ellen Frances Frey.* Durham: Duke University Library, 1945.

Eagleton, Terry. *The Ideology of the Aesthetic.* Cambridge, MA: Basil Blackwell, 1990.

——. *Marxism and Literary Criticism.* Berkeley: University of California Press, 1976.

Elkins, Stanley, and Eric McKitrick. *The Age of Federalism: The Early American Republic, 1788–1800.* New York: Oxford University Press, 1993.

Elliot, Jonathan, ed. *The Debates in the Several State Conventions on the Adoption of the Federal Constitution, as Recommended by the General Convention at Philadelphia in 1787.* 5 vols. 1787. Philadelphia: J. B. Lippincott, 1941.

Ellis, Joseph. *American Sphinx: The Character of Thomas Jefferson.* New York: Vintage, 1998.

Ellmann, Richard, and Robert O'Clair, eds. *The Norton Anthology of Modern Poetry.* 2nd ed. New York: Norton, 1988.

"The Emerson Mania." Review of *Essays*, by R. W. Emerson. *The Living Age* 23.88 (24 Nov. 1849): 344–50.

Emerson, Ralph Waldo. *The Complete Sermons of Ralph Waldo Emerson.* Ed. Albert J. von Frank et al. 4 vols. Columbia: University of Missouri Press, 1989–.

——. *Complete Works.* Centenary Edition. Ed. Edward Waldo Emerson. 12 vols. Boston: Houghton Mifflin, 1903–4.

——. *The Early Lectures of Ralph Waldo Emerson.* Ed. Stephen Whicher et al. 3 vols. Cambridge: Belknap Press of Harvard University Press, 1960–72.

——. *Emerson in His Journals.* Selected and edited by Joel Porte. Cambridge: Belknap Press of Harvard University Press, 1982.

——. *Emerson's Antislavery Writings.* Ed. Len Gougeon and Joel Myerson. New Haven: Yale University Press, 1995.

——. *Essays and Lectures.* Ed. Joel Porte. New York: Library of America, 1983.

——. *Essays: First and Second Series.* Ed. Joel Porte. New York: Vintage Library of America, 1990.

——. *The Journals and Miscellaneous Notebooks of Ralph Waldo Emerson.* Ed. William H. Gilman, et al. 16 vols. Cambridge: Belknap Press of Harvard University Press, 1960–82.

——. *Nature (1836).* Ed. Kenneth Walter Cameron. New York: Scholars' Facsimiles and Reprints, 1940.

——. *Representative Men.* Text established by Douglas Emory Wilson. Introd. Andrew Delbanco. Cambridge: Belknap Press of Harvard University Press, 1996.

——. *Selections.* Ed. Stephen E. Whicher. Boston: Houghton Mifflin, 1960.

Erkkila, Betsy. "Emily Dickinson and Class." *American Literary History* 4 (spring 1992): 1–27.

——. *Walt Whitman among the French.* Princeton: Princeton University Press, 1980.

——. *Whitman the Political Poet.* New York: Oxford University Press, 1989.

Erkkila, Betsy, and Jay Grossman, eds. *Breaking Bounds: Whitman and American Cultural Studies.* New York: Oxford University Press, 1996.

Ferguson, Robert A. *The American Enlightenment, 1750–1820.* Cambridge: Harvard University Press, 1997.

——. *Law and Letters in American Culture.* Cambridge: Harvard University Press, 1984.

Fiedler, Leslie A. *Love and Death in the American Novel.* Rev. ed. New York: Stein and Day, 1982.

——. "Come Back to the Raft Ag'in, Huck Honey!" 1948. Rpt. in *An End to Innocence: Essays on Culture and Politics.* Boston: Beacon, 1952. 142–51.

Fischer, David Hackett. *The Revolution of American Conservatism.* New York: Harper and Row, 1965.

Fisher, Philip. *Hard Facts: Setting and Form in the American Novel.* New York: Oxford University Press, 1987.

——, ed. *The New American Studies: Essays from* Representations. Berkeley: University of California Press, 1991.

Fishkin, Shelley Fisher. *From Fact to Fiction: Journalism and Imaginative Writing in America.* Baltimore: Johns Hopkins University Press, 1985.

Fliegelman, Jay. *Declaring Independence: Jefferson, Natural Language, and the Culture of Performance.* Stanford: Stanford University Press, 1993.

——. Introduction. *Wieland, or The Transformation.* By Charles Brockden Brown. New York: Penguin, 1991. vii–xlii.

——. *Prodigals and Pilgrims: The American Revolution Against Patriarchal Authority, 1750–1800.* Cambridge: Cambridge University Press, 1982.

Folsom, Ed. " 'Affording the Rising Generation an Adequate Notion': Whitman in Nineteenth-Century Textbooks, Handbooks, and Anthologies." *Studies in the American Renaissance* (1991): 345–74.

——. "Appearing in Print: Illustrations of the Self in *Leaves of Grass.*" Greenspan, *Cambridge Companion* 135–65.

——. "The House That Matthiessen Built." *Iowa Review* 20 (1990): 162–80.

——. *Walt Whitman's Native Representations.* Cambridge: Cambridge University Press, 1994.

——, ed. *Walt Whitman: The Centennial Essays.* Iowa City: University of Iowa Press, 1994.

Fone, Byrne R. S. *Masculine Landscapes: Walt Whitman and the Homoerotic Text.* Carbondale: Southern Illinois University Press, 1992.

Foner, Eric. *Free Soil, Free Labor, Free Men: The Ideology of the Republican Party Before the Civil War.* New York: Oxford University Press, 1970.

——. *A Short History of Reconstruction.* New York: Harper and Row, 1990.

——. *Tom Paine and Revolutionary America*. New York: Oxford University Press, 1977.

——, ed. *The New American History*. Philadelphia: Temple University Press, 1997.

Foster, Hannah Webster. *The Coquette*. 1797. Ed. Cathy N. Davidson. New York: Oxford University Press, 1986.

Foster, Vanda. *A Visual History of Costume: The Nineteenth Century*. New York: Drama Book, 1986.

Foucault, Michel. *Discipline and Punish*. Trans. Alan Sheridan. New York: Vintage, 1995.

——. *The History of Sexuality. Volume 1: An Introduction*. Trans. Robert Hurley. New York: Vintage, 1980.

——. *The Order of Things: An Archaeology of the Human Sciences*. New York: Vintage, 1973.

——. "What Is An Author?" *The Foucault Reader*. Ed. Paul Rabinow. New York: Pantheon, 1984. 101–20.

Fredrickson, George M. *The Inner Civil War: Northern Intellectuals and the Crisis of the Union*. 1965. Urbana: University of Illinois Press, 1993.

Furtwangler, Albert. *The Authority of Publius: A Reading of the* Federalist *Papers*. Ithaca: Cornell University Press, 1984.

Fuss, Diana. *Essentially Speaking: Feminism, Nature, and Difference*. New York: Routledge, 1989.

Gardner, Jared. *Master Plots: Race and the Founding of American Literature, 1787–1845*. Baltimore: Johns Hopkins University Press, 1998.

Gilmore, Michael T. *American Romanticism and the Marketplace*. Chicago: University of Chicago Press, 1985.

——. "The Literature of the Revolutionary and Early National Periods." *The Cambridge History of American Literature*. Vol. 1, *1590–1820*. Gen. ed. Sacvan Bercovitch. New York: Cambridge University Press, 1994.

Goddu, Teresa A. *Gothic America: Narrative, History, and Nation*. New York: Columbia University Press, 1997.

Gohdes, Clarence. "Some Remarks on Emerson's *Divinity School Address*." *American Literature* 1.1 (Mar. 1929): 27–31.

Gonnaud, Maurice. *An Uneasy Solitude: Individual and Society in the Work of Ralph Waldo Emerson*. Trans. Lawrence Rosenwald. Princeton: Princeton University Press, 1987.

Gougeon, Len. *Virtue's Hero: Emerson, Antislavery, and Reform*. Athens: University of Georgia Press, 1990.

Gougeon, Len, and Joel Myerson, eds. *Emerson's Anti-Slavery Writings*. New Haven: Yale University Press, 1995.

Gould, Philip. "Remembering Metacom: Historical Writing and the Cultures of Masculinity in Early America." Chapman and Hendler 112–24.

Graff, Gerald. *Professing Literature: An Institutional History*. Chicago: University of Chicago Press, 1987.

Greenspan, Ezra. *Walt Whitman and the American Reader*. Cambridge: Cambridge University Press, 1990.

——, ed. *The Cambridge Companion to Walt Whitman*. New York: Cambridge University Press, 1995.

Grey, Robin. *The Complicity of Imagination: The American Renaissance, Contests of Authority, and Seventeenth-Century English Culture*. Cambridge: Cambridge University Press, 1997.

Gross, Robert A., ed. *In Debt to Shays: The Bicentennial of an Agrarian Rebellion*. Charlottesville: University Press of Virginia, 1993.

Grossman, Allen. "The Poetics of Union in Whitman and Lincoln: An Inquiry Toward the Relationship of Art and Policy." Michaels and Pease 183–208.

Grossman, Jay. " 'A' is for Abolition?: Race, Authorship, *The Scarlet Letter*." *Textual Practice* 7.1 (spring 1993): 13–30.

——. "The Canon in the Closet: Matthiessen's Whitman, Whitman's Matthiessen." *American Literature* 70.4 (Dec. 1998): 799–832.

——. " 'The evangel-poem of comrades and of love': Revising Whitman's Republicanism." *American Transcendental Quarterly* 4 (Sept. 1990): 201–18.

Gruesz, Kirsten Silva. *Ambassadors of Culture: The Transamerican Origins of Latino Writing*. Princeton: Princeton University Press, 2001.

Guillory, John. "Canonical and Non-Canonical: A Critique of the Current Debate." *English Literary History* 54 (fall 1987): 483–527.

——. *Cultural Capital: The Problem of Literary Canon Formation*. Chicago: University of Chicago Press, 1993.

Gustafson, Sandra M. *Eloquence Is Power: Oratory and Performance in Early America*. Chapel Hill: University of North Carolina Press for Omohundro Institute of Early American History and Culture, 2000.

Gustafson, Thomas. *Representative Words: Politics, Language, and the American Language, 1776–1865*. Cambridge: Cambridge University Press, 1992.

Hall, A. Oakey. *The Manhattaner in New Orleans; or, Phases of "Crescent City" Life*. New York: J. S. Redfield, 1851.

Halperin, David M. *One Hundred Years of Homosexuality and Other Essays on Greek Love*. New York: Routledge, 1990.

Harding, Samuel B. *The Contest Over the Ratification of the Federal Constitution in the State of Massachusetts*. 1896. New York: Da Capo, 1970.

Havelock, Eric A. *Preface to Plato*. Cambridge: Belknap Press of Harvard University Press, 1963.

Hedges, William L. "From Franklin to Emerson." Buell, *Emerson: A Collection* 32–47.

——. "The Myth of the Republic and the Theory of American Literature." *Prospects* 4 (1979): 101–20.

Heimert, Alan, and Andrew Delbanco, eds. *The Puritans in America: A Narrative Anthology*. Cambridge: Harvard University Press, 1985.

Hendler, Glenn. "Bloated Bodies and Masculine Sentiments: Masculinity in 1840s Temperance Narratives." Chapman and Hendler 125–48.

Henkin, David H. *City Reading: Written Words and Public Spheres in Antebellum New York*. New York: Columbia University Press, 1999.

Hochmuth, Marie, and Richard Murphy. "Rhetorical and Elocutionary Training in Nineteenth-Century Colleges." Wallace 153–77.

Hofstadter, Richard. *The American Political Tradition and the Men Who Made It*. New York: Vintage, 1989.

——. *The Idea of a Party System: The Rise of Legitimate Opposition in the United States, 1780–1840*. Berkeley: University of California Press, 1969.

Holloway, Emory. "Walt Whitman in New Orleans." *Yale Review* 5 (Oct. 1915): 166–83.

——. "Walt Whitman's Love Affairs." *The Dial* 69 (Nov. 1920): 473–83.

——. *Whitman: An Interpretation in Narrative*. New York: Knopf, 1926.

Hyde, Alan. *Bodies of Law*. Princeton: Princeton University Press, 1997.

Ingersoll, Thomas N. *Mammon and Manon in Early New Orleans: The First Slave Society in the Deep South, 1718–1819*. Knoxville: University of Tennessee Press, 1999.

Irons, Peter H. *A People's History of the Supreme Court*. New York: Penguin, 2000.

Jameson, Fredric. *The Political Unconscious: Narrative as a Socially Symbolic Act*. Ithaca: Cornell University Press, 1981.

Jefferson, Thomas. *Notes on the State of Virginia*. Ed. William Peden. New York: Norton, 1982.

——. *Public and Private Papers*. Ed. Merrill D. Peterson. New York: Vintage / Library of America, 1990.

Jensen, Merrill, ed. *Tracts of the American Revolution, 1763–1776*. Indianapolis: Bobbs-Merrill, 1967.

Johnson, Walter. *Soul by Soul: Life Inside the Antebellum Slave Market*. Cambridge: Harvard University Press, 1999.

Kaminski, John P. "New York: The Reluctant Pillar." *The Reluctant Pillar: New York and the Adoption of the Federal Constitution*. Ed. Stephen L. Schechter. Troy, N.Y.: Russell Sage College, 1985. 48–117.

Kammen, Michael, ed. *The Origins of the American Constitution: A Documentary History*. New York: Penguin, 1986.

Kaplan, Justin. *Walt Whitman: A Life*. New York: Simon and Schuster, 1980.

Kateb, George. *Emerson and Self-Reliance*. Thousand Oaks, Calif.: Sage Publications, 1995.

——. *The Inner Ocean: Individualism and Democratic Culture*. Ithaca: Cornell University Press, 1992.

Katz, Jonathan. *Gay American History*. New York: Harper and Row, 1985.

Kennedy, W. S. *The Fight of a Book for The World: A Companion Volume to* Leaves of Grass. West Yarmouth, Mass.: Stonecraft Press, 1926.

———. *Reminiscences of Walt Whitman.* London: Alexander Gardner, 1896.

Ketcham, Ralph, ed. *The Anti-Federalist Papers and the Constitutional Convention Debates.* New York: Mentor, 1986.

Kielbowicz, Richard B. "Newsgathering by Printers' Exchanges Before the Telegraph." *Journalism History* 9.2 (summer 1982): 42–48.

Killingsworth, M. Jimmie. *Whitman's Poetry of the Body.* Chapel Hill: University of North Carolina Press, 1989.

Klammer, Martin. *Whitman, Slavery, and the Emergence of* Leaves of Grass. University Park: Pennsylvania State University Press, 1995.

Konvitz, Milton R., and Stephen E. Whicher, eds. *Emerson: A Collection of Critical Essays.* 1962. Westport, Conn.: Greenwood, 1978.

Kramer, Michael P. "Imagining Authorship in America: 'Whose American Renaissance?' Revisited." *American Literary History* 13.1 (spring 2001): 108–25.

———. *Imagining Language in America.* Princeton: Princeton University Press, 1992.

Kramnick, Isaac. "The 'Great National Discussion': The Discourse of Politics in 1787." *William and Mary Quarterly* 45.1 (Jan. 1988): 3–32.

———. Introduction. *The Federalist Papers.* By James Madison, Alexander Hamilton, and John Jay. New York: Penguin, 1988. 11–82.

Krieg, Joann P. *A Whitman Chronology.* Iowa City: University of Iowa Press, 1998.

Larson, Kerry. *Whitman's Drama of Consensus.* Chicago: University of Chicago Press, 1988.

Lasch, Christopher. "Journalism, Publicity, and the Lost Art of Argument." *Gannett Center Journal* (spring 1990): n.p.

Leverenz, David. *Manhood and the American Renaissance.* Ithaca: Cornell University Press, 1989.

Lewis, R. W. B. *The American Adam.* Chicago: University of Chicago Press, 1955.

Lincoln, Abraham. *Speeches and Writings, 1859–1865.* New York: Library of America, 1989.

Looby, Christopher. " 'As Thoroughly Black as the Most Faithful Philanthropist Could Desire': Erotics of Race in Higginson's *Army Life in a Black Regiment.*" *Race and the Subject of Masculinities.* Ed. Harry Stecopoulos and Michael Uebel. Durham: Duke University Press, 1997. 71–115.

———. *Voicing America: Language, Literary Form, and the Origins of the United States.* Chicago: University of Chicago Press, 1996.

Lopez, Michael. "De-Transcendentalizing Emerson." *ESQ* 34 (1988): 77–139.

———. *Emerson and Power.* DeKalb: Northern Illinois University Press, 1996.

Lott, Eric. *Love and Theft: Blackface Minstrelsy and the American Working Class.* Oxford: Oxford University Press, 1995.

Loving, Jerome. *Emerson, Whitman, and the American Muse*. Chapel Hill: University of North Carolina Press, 1982.

——. *Walt Whitman: The Song of Himself*. Berkeley: University of California Press, 1999.

Lynch, Michael. " 'Here is Adhesiveness': From Friendship to Homosexuality." *Victorian Studies* 29 (autumn 1985): 67–96.

Madison, James. *Notes of Debates in the Federal Convention of 1787 Reported by James Madison*. New York: Norton, 1987.

——. *Papers*. Ed. David B. Mattern, et al. Vol. 17. Charlottesville: University Press of Virginia, 1991.

Magee, Michael. "Emerson's Emancipation Proclamations." *Raritan* 20.4 (spring 2001): 96–116.

Main, Jackson Turner. *The Anti-Federalists: Critics of the Constitution, 1781–1788*. Chapel Hill: University of North Carolina Press, 1961.

Manning, William. *The Key of Liberty: The Life and Democratic Writings of William Manning, "A Laborer," 1747–1814*. Ed. Michael Merrill and Sean Wilentz. Cambridge: Harvard University Press, 1993.

Marcus, Greil. "A Hunka' Hunka' Burnin' Text: Greil Marcus on Dead Elvis and Other Pop Icons." Interview. *Lingua Franca* 1.6 (Aug. 1991): 28–32.

Marr, David. *American Worlds Since Emerson*. Amherst: University of Massachusetts Press, 1988.

Martin, Robert K. *The Homosexual Tradition in American Poetry*. Austin: University of Texas Press, 1979.

——. "Whitman and the Politics of Identity." Folsom, *Centennial Essays* 172–81.

Matthews, Richard K. *If Men Were Angels: James Madison and the Heartless Empire of Reason*. Lawrence: University Press of Kansas, 1995.

Matthiessen, F. O. *American Renaissance: Art and Expression in the Age of Emerson and Whitman*. 1941. New York: Oxford University Press, 1968.

Matthiessen, F. O., and Russell Cheney. *Rat and The Devil: Journal Letters of F. O. Matthiessen and Russell Cheney*. Ed. Louis Hyde. Boston: Alyson, 1988.

May, Henry F. *The Enlightenment in America*. Oxford: Oxford University Press, 1976.

Mayfield, John. *The New Nation, 1800–1845*. Rev. ed. New York: Hill and Wang, 1982.

McAleer, John. *Ralph Waldo Emerson: Days of Encounter*. Boston: Little, Brown, 1984.

McCoy, Drew R. *The Elusive Republic: Political Economy in Jeffersonian America*. Chapel Hill: University of North Carolina Press for the Omohundro Institute of Early American History and Culture, 1980.

McCullough, David G. *John Adams*. New York: Simon and Schuster, 2001.

McDowell, Deborah E., and Arnold Rampersad, eds. *Slavery and the Literary Imagination*. Baltimore: Johns Hopkins University Press, 1989.

McFarland, Thomas. *Originality and Imagination*. Baltimore: Johns Hopkins University Press, 1985.

McGann, Jerome J. *A Critique of Modern Textual Criticism*. Chicago: University of Chicago Press, 1983.

——, ed. *Textual Criticism and Literary Interpretation*. Chicago: University of Chicago Press, 1985.

McGill, Meredith L. *American Literature and the Culture of Reprinting 1834–1835*. Philadelphia: University of Pennsylvania Press, 2002.

McWilliams, John. "The Rationale for 'The American Romance.'" *Revisionary Interventions into the Americanist Canon*. Ed. Donald Pease. Durham: Duke University Press, 1994. 71–82.

Melville, Herman. *The Confidence-Man: His Masquerade*. 1852. Ed. Hershel Parker. New York: Norton, 1971.

——. *Moby-Dick*. 1851. New York: Norton, 1967.

Michaels, Walter Benn, and Donald E. Pease, eds. *The American Renaissance Reconsidered: Selected Papers from the English Institute, 1982–83*. Baltimore: Johns Hopkins University Press, 1985.

Middlekauff, Robert. *The Glorious Cause: The American Revolution, 1763–1789*. New York: Oxford University Press, 1982.

Miller, Edwin Haviland. *Walt Whitman's "Song of Myself": A Mosaic of Interpretations*. Iowa City: University of Iowa Press, 1989.

Miller, Perry. "From Edwards to Emerson." Buell, *Emerson: A Collection* 13–31.

——, ed. *The Transcendentalists*. New York: MJF Books, 1950.

Monteiro, George. "Fire and Smoke: Emerson's Letter to Whitman." *Modern Language Studies* 15.2 (spring 1985): 3–8.

Montesquieu, Charles de Secondat, Baron de. *The Spirit of the Laws*. Trans. and ed. Anne M. Cohler, Basia Carolyn Miller, and Harold Samuel Stone. Cambridge: Cambridge University Press, 1989.

Moon, Michael. *Disseminating Whitman: Revision and Corporeality in* Leaves of Grass. Cambridge: Harvard University Press, 1991.

Moretti, Franco. *Signs Taken for Wonders: Essays in the Sociology of Literary Forms*. New York: Verso, 1997.

Morgan, Edmund S. *American Slavery, American Freedom: The Ordeal of Colonial Virginia*. New York: Norton, 1975.

——. "Government by Fiction: The Idea of Representation." *Yale Review* 72 (spring 1983): 321–39.

——. *Inventing the People: The Rise of Popular Sovereignty in England and America*. New York: Norton, 1988.

Morgan, Edmund S., and Helen M. Morgan. *The Stamp Act Crisis: Prologue to Revolu-*

tion. Chapel Hill: University of North Carolina Press for Omohundro Institute of Early American History and Culture, 1995.

Morone, James A. *The Democratic Wish: Popular Participation and the Limits of American Government*. Rev. ed. New Haven: Yale University Press, 1998.

Morrison, Toni. *Beloved*. New York: Plume, 1988.

Mulcaire, Terry. "Publishing Intimacy in *Leaves of Grass*." *ELH* 60.2 (summer 1993): 471–501.

Myerson, Joel, ed. *A Historical Guide to Ralph Waldo Emerson*. New York: Oxford University Press, 2000.

——. *Transcendentalism: A Reader*. New York: Oxford University Press, 2000.

Nathanson, Tenney. *Whitman's Presence: Body, Voice, and Writing in* Leaves of Grass. New York: New York University Press, 1992.

Nedelsky, Jennifer. *Private Property and the Limits of American Constitutionalism*. Chicago: University of Chicago Press, 1990.

Nelson, Dana. *National Manhood: Capitalist Citizenship and the Imagined Fraternity of White Men*. Durham: Duke University Press, 1998.

Nelson, Robert K., and Kenneth M. Price. "Debating Manliness: Thomas Wentworth Higginson, William Sloane Kennedy, and the Question of Whitman." *American Literature* 73.3 (Sept. 2001): 497–524.

Newbury, Michael. *Figuring Authorship in Antebellum America*. Stanford: Stanford University Press, 1997.

Newfield, Christopher. *The Emerson Effect: Individualism and Submission in America*. Chicago: University of Chicago Press, 1996.

Nicloff, Philip L. *Emerson on Race and History: An Examination of English Traits*. New York: Columbia University Press, 1961.

Nixon, Ron. "Turning Back the Clock on Voting Rights." *The Nation* 15 Nov. 1999: 11–17.

Oliver, Peter. *Origin and Progress of the American Rebellion: A Tory View*. 1781. Ed. Douglass Adair and John A. Schutz. Stanford: Stanford University Press, 1961.

Onuf, Peter S. *Jefferson's Empire: The Language of American Nationhood*. Charlottesville: University Press of Virginia, 2000.

Packer, B. L. *Emerson's Fall*. New York: Continuum, 1982.

Paine, Thomas. *The Thomas Paine Reader*. Ed. Michael Foot and Isaac Kramnick. New York: Penguin, 1987.

Patterson, Mark R. *Authority, Autonomy, and Representation in American Literature, 1776–1865*. Princeton: Princeton University Press, 1988.

——. "Emerson, Napoleon, and the Concept of the Representative." *ESQ* 31.4 (1985): 230–42.

Patterson, Stephen E. "The Federalist Reaction to Shays's Rebellion." Gross 101–18.

Pearce, Roy Harvey. *The Continuity of American Poetry*. 1961. Middletown, Conn.: Wesleyan University Press, 1987.

Pease, Donald. "*Moby Dick* and the Cold War." Michaels and Pease 113–55.

———. *Visionary Compacts: American Renaissance Writings in Cultural Context.* Madison: University of Wisconsin Press, 1987.

Persons, Stow. *The Decline of American Gentility.* New York: Columbia University Press, 1973.

Pessen, Edward. *Jacksonian America: Society, Personality, Politics.* Rev. ed. Chicago: University of Illinois Press, 1985.

Phillips, Dana. "Nineteenth-Century Racial Thought and Whitman's 'Democratic Ethnology of the Future.'" *Nineteenth-Century Literature* 49.3 (Dec. 1994): 289–320.

Phillips, Kevin. *The Cousins' Wars: Religion, Politics, and the Triumph of Anglo-America.* New York: Basic, 1999.

Pitkin, Hanna. *Representation.* New York: Atherton, 1969.

Plato. *The Republic.* Trans. Francis MacDonald Cornford. New York: Oxford University Press, 1990.

Pocock, J. G. A. *The Machiavellian Moment: Florentine Political Thought and the Atlantic Republican Tradition.* Princeton: Princeton University Press, 1975.

Poirier, Richard. Introduction. *Ralph Waldo Emerson.* Ed. Poirier. New York: Oxford University Press, 1990. ix–xx.

———. *Poetry and Pragmatism.* Cambridge: Harvard University Press, 1992.

Pole, J. R. *Political Representation in England and the Origins of the American Republic.* New York: St. Martin's, 1966.

———, ed. *The American Constitution For and Against.* New York: Hill and Wang, 1987.

Pollak, Vivian R. *The Erotic Whitman.* Berkeley: University of California Press, 2000.

———. "'In Loftiest Spheres': Whitman's Visionary Feminism." Erkkila and Grossman 92–111.

Porte, Joel. *Emerson and Thoreau: Transcendentalists in Conflict.* Middletown, Conn.: Wesleyan University Press, 1966.

———. *Representative Man: Ralph Waldo Emerson in His Time.* New York: Oxford University Press, 1979.

Portelli, Alessandro. *The Text and the Voice: Writing, Speaking, and Democracy in American Literature.* New York: Columbia University Press, 1994.

Porter, Carolyn. "Are We Being Historical Yet?" *South Atlantic Quarterly* 87 (fall 1988): 743–786.

———. *Seeing and Being: The Plight of the Participant Observer in Emerson, James, Adams, and Faulkner.* Middletown, Conn.: Wesleyan University Press, 1981.

Porter, David. *Emerson and Literary Change.* Cambridge: Harvard University Press, 1978.

Powell, Timothy B. *Ruthless Democracy: A Multicultural Interpretation of the American Renaissance.* Princeton: Princeton University Press, 2000.

Price, Kenneth M. *Whitman and Tradition: The Poet in His Century.* New Haven: Yale University Press, 1990.

Prokopow, Michael John. "To The Torrid Zones: The Fortunes And Misfortunes of American Loyalists in the Anglo-Caribbean Basin, 1774–1801." Ph.D. diss., Harvard University, 1996.

Publius [James Madison, Alexander Hamilton, and John Jay]. *The Federalist Papers.* 1788. Ed. Isaac Kramnick. New York: Penguin, 1988.

Rakove, Jack N. *Original Meanings: Politics and Ideas in the Making of the Constitution.* New York: Knopf, 1996.

Reid, John Phillip. *The Concept of Representation in the Age of the American Revolution.* Chicago: University of Chicago Press, 1989.

——. *Constitutional History of the American Revolution.* Abridged. Madison: University of Wisconsin Press, 1995.

Remini, Robert V. *The Jacksonian Era.* Arlington Heights, Ill: Harlan Davidson, 1989.

Review of "An Address Pronounced at the Opening of the New York Athenaeum, December 14, 1824, by Henry Wheaton." *North American Review* 20 (April 1825): 453–55.

Reynolds, David S. *Beneath the American Renaissance: The Subversive Imagination in the Age of Emerson and Melville.* Cambridge: Harvard University Press, 1989.

——. *Walt Whitman's America: A Cultural Biography.* New York: Knopf, 1995.

Reynolds, Larry J. *European Revolutions and the American Literary Renaissance.* New Haven: Yale University Press, 1988.

Rice, Grantland S. *The Transformation of Authorship in America.* Chicago: University of Chicago Press, 1997.

Richardson, Robert D. *Emerson: The Mind on Fire.* Berkeley: University of California Press, 1996.

Richie, Robert, and Steven Hill. *Reflecting All of Us: The Case for Proportional Representation.* Boston: Beacon, 1999.

Rigal, Laura. *The American Manufactory: Art, Labor, and the World of Things in the Early Republic.* Princeton: Princeton University Press, 1998.

Roach, Joseph R. *Cities of the Dead: Circum-Atlantic Performance.* New York: Columbia University Press, 1996.

——. "Slave Spectacles and Tragic Octoroons: A Cultural Genealogy of Antebellum Performance." *Exceptional Spaces: Essays in Performance and History.* Ed. Della Pollock. Chapel Hill: University of North Carolina Press, 1998. 49–76.

Robertson, Andrew W. *The Language of Democracy: Political Rhetoric in the United States and Britain, 1790–1900.* Ithaca: Cornell University Press, 1995.

Rodgers, Daniel T. *Contested Truths: Keywords in American Politics Since Independence.* New York: Basic, 1987.

Rogin, Michael Paul. *Subversive Genealogy: The Politics and Art of Herman Melville.* Berkeley: University of California Press, 1985.

Rombes, Nicholas. "Cheating with Sound: Imagining Civic Culture in Federalist America." *Arizona Quarterly* 54.4 (winter 1998): 1–24.

Rose, Anne C. *Transcendentalism as a Social Movement, 1830–1850*. New Haven: Yale University Press, 1981.

Rosenfeld, Richard N. "The Adams Tyranny: Lost Lessons from the Early Republic." Rev. of *John Adams*, by David McCullough. *Harper's* (Sept. 2001): 82–6.

——. *American Aurora: A Democratic-Republican Returns*. New York: St. Martin's, 1997.

Rosenwald, Lawrence. *Emerson and the Art of the Diary*. New York: Oxford University Press, 1988.

Ross, Gordon D. "*The Federalist* and the 'Experience' of Small Republics." *Eighteenth-Century Studies* 5 (1972): 559–68.

Rowe, John Carlos. *At Emerson's Tomb: The Politics of Classic American Literature*. New York: Columbia University Press, 1997.

Rubin, Joseph Jay. *The Historic Whitman*. University Park: Pennsylvania State University Press, 1973.

Rusk, Ralph. *The Life of Ralph Waldo Emerson*. New York: Scribner's, 1949.

Saillant, John. "The Black Body Erotic and the Republican Body Politic, 1790–1820." Chapman and Hendler 89–111.

Sánchez-Eppler, Karen. "Temperance in the Bed of a Child: Incest and Social Order in Nineteenth-Century America." *American Quarterly* 47.1 (Mar. 1995): 1–33.

——. "Then When We Clutch Hardest: On the Death of a Child and the Replication of an Image." Chapman and Hendler 64–85.

——. *Touching Liberty: Abolition, Feminism, and the Politics of the Body*. Berkeley: University of California Press, 1993.

Schechter, Stephen L., ed. *The Reluctant Pillar: New York and the Adoption of the Federal Constitution*. Troy, N.Y.: Russell Sage College, 1985.

Schmidgall, Gary. *Walt Whitman: A Gay Life*. New York: Dutton, 1997.

Sealts, Morton M., Jr., and Alfred R. Ferguson. *Emerson's* Nature: *Origin, Growth, Meaning*. 2nd ed. Carbondale: Southern Illinois University Press, 1979.

Sedgwick, Eve Kosofsky. *Between Men: English Literature and Male Homosocial Desire*. New York: Columbia University Press, 1985.

——. *Epistemology of the Closet*. Berkeley: University of California Press, 1992.

Seitz, Brian. *The Trace of Political Representation*. Albany: State University of New York Press, 1995.

Sellers, Charles. *The Market Revolution: Jacksonian America, 1815–1846*. New York: Oxford University Press, 1991.

Sharp, John Roger. *American Politics in the Early Republic: The New Nation in Crisis*. New Haven: Yale University Press, 1993.

Shields, David S. *Civil Tongues and Polite Letters in British America*. Chapel Hill: University of North Carolina Press for Omohundro Institute of Early American History and Culture, 1997.

Shively, Charley, ed. *Calamus Lovers: Walt Whitman's Working-Class Camerados*. San Francisco: Gay Sunshine Press, 1987.

Shumway, David R. *Creating American Civilization*. Minneapolis: University of Minnesota Press, 1994.

Silverman, Kenneth. *A Cultural History of the American Revolution*. New York: Thomas Y. Crowell, 1976.

Simpson, David. *The Politics of American English, 1776–1850*. Oxford: Oxford University Press, 1986.

Simpson, Lewis P. *Mind and the American Civil War: A Meditation on Lost Causes*. Baton Rouge: Louisiana State University Press, 1989.

Siskin, Clifford. *The Historicity of Romantic Discourse*. New York: Oxford University Press, 1988.

——. *The Work of Writing: Literature and Social Change in Britain, 1700–1830*. Baltimore: Johns Hopkins University Press, 1998.

Smith, Barbara Herrnstein. "Contingencies of Value." von Hallberg 5–39.

Smith, Rogers M. *Civic Ideals: Conflicting Visions of Citizenship in U.S. History*. New Haven: Yale University Press, 1997.

Smith-Rosenberg, Carroll. *Disorderly Conduct: Visions of Gender in Victorian America*. New York: Oxford University Press, 1985.

Spengemann, William C. *A New World of Words: Redefining Early American Literature*. New Haven: Yale University Press, 1994.

Stallybrass, Peter, and Allon White. *The Politics and Poetics of Transgression*. Ithaca: Cornell University Press, 1986.

Steele, Jeffrey. *The Representation of the Self in the American Renaissance*. Chapel Hill: University of North Carolina Press, 1987.

Stern, Julia A. *The Plight of Feeling: Sympathy and Dissent in the Early American Novel*. Chicago: University of Chicago Press, 1997.

Stern, Madeleine B. "Emerson and Phrenology." *Studies in the American Renaissance*. Ed. Joel Myerson. Charlottesville: University Press of Virginia, 1984. 213–28.

——. *Heads and Headlines: The Phrenological Fowlers*. Norman: University of Oklahoma Press, 1971.

Storing, Herbert J. *What the Anti-Federalists Were For*. Vol. 1 of *The Complete Anti-Federalist*. 7 vols. Chicago: University of Chicago Press, 1981.

Story, Ronald. *The Forging of an Aristocracy: Harvard and the Boston Upper Class, 1800–1870*. Middletown, Conn.: Wesleyan University Press, 1980.

Sturrock, John, ed. *Structuralism and Since*. Oxford: Oxford University Press, 1979.

Sullivan, Kathleen M. "Madison Got It Backward." *New York Times* 16 Feb. 1999, late ed.: A19.

Symonds, John Addington. *Walt Whitman: A Study*. 1893. New York: AMS Press, 1968.

Teichgraeber, Richard F., III. *Sublime Thoughts/Penny Wisdom: Situating Emerson and Thoreau in the American Market.* Baltimore: Johns Hopkins University Press, 1995.

Thomas, Kendall. " 'Masculinity,' 'The Rule of Law,' and Other Legal Fictions." *Constructing Masculinity.* Ed. Maurice Berger, Brian Wallis, and Simon Watson. New York: Routledge, 1995. 221–37.

Thoreau, Henry David. Walden *and* Civil Disobedience. Ed. Owen Thomas. New York: Norton, 1966.

Tocqueville, Alexis De. *Democracy in America.* Trans. George Lawrence. Ed. J. P. Mayer. New York: HarperCollins, 1988.

Tompkins, Jane P. *Sensational Designs: The Cultural Work of American Fiction, 1790–1860.* New York: Oxford University Press, 1985.

Trachtenberg, Alan. "The Politics of Labor and the Poet's Work: A Reading of 'A Song for Occupations.' " Folsom, *Centennial Essays* 120–32.

Traubel, Horace. *With Walt Whitman in Camden.* 7 vols. Vol. 1: Boston: Small, Maynard, 1906. Vol. 2: New York: D. Appleton, 1908. Vol. 3: New York: Mitchell Kennerley, 1914; rpt. New York: Rowman and Littlefield, 1961. Vol. 4: Philadelphia: University of Pennsylvania Press, 1953. Vol. 5: Carbondale: Southern Illinois University Press, 1964. Vol. 6: Carbondale: Southern Illinois University Press, 1982. Vol. 7: Carbondale: Southern Illinois University Press, 1992.

Trowbridge, John Townsend. "Reminiscences of Walt Whitman." *Atlantic Monthly* Feb. 1902: 163–75.

Van Anglen, Kevin. *The New England Milton: Literary Reception and Cultural Authority in the Early Republic.* University Park: Pennsylvania State University Press, 1993.

von Frank, Albert J. *An Emerson Chronology.* New York: G. K. Hall, 1994.

——. *The Trials of Anthony Burns: Freedom and Slavery in Emerson's Boston.* Cambridge: Harvard University Press, 1998.

von Hallberg, Robert, ed. *Canons.* Chicago: University of Chicago Press, 1984.

Wald, Priscilla. *Constituting Americans: Cultural Anxiety and Narrative Form.* Durham: Duke University Press, 1995.

Waldstreicher, David. "Anti-Foundational Founders: Did Post-Structuralism Fail the Historians, or Did the Historians Fail Post-Structuralism?" Rev. of *The Other Founders,* by Saul Cornell. *American Quarterly* 53.2 (June 2001): 340–48.

Wallace, Karl Richards, ed. *History of Speech Education in America.* New York: Appleton-Century-Crofts, 1954.

Walters, Ronald G. *American Reformers, 1815–1860.* New York: Hill and Wang, 1978.

Warner, Michael. *The Letters of the Republic: Publication and the Public Sphere in Eighteenth-Century America.* Cambridge: Harvard University Press, 1990.

——. *The Trouble with Normal: Sex, Politics, and the Ethics of Queer Life.* Cambridge: Harvard University Press, 2000.

——. "Whitman Drunk." Erkkila and Grossman 30–43.

Warren, James Perrin. *Walt Whitman's Language Experiment*. University Park: Pennsylvania State University Press, 1990.

Warren, Joyce W. *Fanny Fern: An Independent Woman*. New Brunswick, N.J.: Rutgers University Press, 1992.

Watson, Harry L. *Liberty and Power: The Politics of Jacksonian America*. New York: Hill and Wang, 1990.

Weisbuch, Robert. *Atlantic Double-Cross: American Literature and British Influence in the Age of Emerson*. Chicago: University of Chicago Press, 1986.

West, Cornel. *The American Evasion of Philosophy: A Genealogy of Pragmatism*. Madison: University of Wisconsin Press, 1989.

——. "Minority Discourse and the Pitfalls of Canon Formation." *Yale Journal of Criticism* 1 (fall 1987): 193–201.

West, Michael. "Scatology and Eschatology: The Heroic Dimensions of Thoreau's Wordplay." *PMLA* 89 (1974): 1043–64.

Whicher, Stephen E. *Freedom and Fate: An Inner Life of Ralph Waldo Emerson*. Philadelphia: University of Pennsylvania Press, 1953.

White, Hayden. *The Content of the Form: Narrative Discourse and Historical Representation*. Baltimore: Johns Hopkins University Press, 1990.

Whitman, Walt. *An American Primer*. Ed. Horace Traubel. Afterword by Gay Wilson Allen. Stevens Point, Wisc.: Holy Cow! Press, 1987.

——. *Complete Poetry and Collected Prose*. New York: Library of America, 1982.

——. *The Correspondence*. Ed. Edward Haviland Miller. 6 vols. New York: New York University Press, 1961–77.

——. *Early Poems and Fiction*. Ed. Thomas L. Brasher. New York: New York University Press, 1963.

——. *An 1855–56 Notebook Toward the Second Edition of* Leaves of Grass. Introduction and notes by Harold W. Blodgett, foreword by Charles E. Feinberg, and additional notes by William White. Carbondale: Southern Illinois University Press, 1959.

——. *Franklin Evans, or The Inebriate. A Tale of The Times*. 1842. Ed. Emory Holloway. New York: Random House, 1929.

——. *The Gathering of the Forces: Editorials, Essays, . . . by Walt Whitman as Editor of the* Brooklyn Daily Eagle *in 1846 and 1847 . . .* Ed. Cleveland Rodgers and John Black. New York: G. P. Putnam's Sons, 1920.

——. *I Sit and Look Out: Editorials from the* Brooklyn Daily Times. 1932. Ed. Emory Holloway and Vernolian Schwarz. New York: AMS Press, 1966.

——. *Leaves of Grass*. 1st ed. Brooklyn, 1855.

——. *Leaves of Grass*. 2nd ed. Brooklyn, 1856.

——. *Leaves of Grass*. 3rd ed. Boston: Thayer and Eldridge, 1860–61. Facsimile ed. Ithaca: Cornell University Press, 1984.

——. *Leaves of Grass*. Ed. Sculley Bradley and Harold W. Blodgett. New York: Norton, 1973.

——. *Leaves of Grass: The First (1855) Edition*. Ed. Malcolm Cowley. New York: Penguin, 1986.

——. *Leaves of Grass: A Textual Variorum of the Printed Poems*. 3 vols. Ed. Sculley Bradley et al. New York: New York University Press, 1980.

——. *Notebooks and Unpublished Prose Manuscripts*. Ed. Edward F. Grier. 6 vols. *The Collected Writings of Walt Whitman*. New York: New York University Press, 1984–.

——. "The People and John Quincy Adams." 1848[?]. Berkeley Heights, N.J.: The Oriole Press, 1961.

——. *Selected Letters*. Ed. Edwin Haviland Miller. Iowa City: University of Iowa Press, 1990.

——. *Specimen Days and Collect*. 1883. New York: Dover Publications, 1995.

——. *Walt Whitman of the New York* Aurora. Ed. Joseph Jay Rubin and Charles H. Brown. State College, Pa.: Bald Eagle Press, 1950.

——. *Whitman's Manuscripts:* Leaves of Grass *(1860) A Parallel Text*. Ed. Fredson Bowers. Chicago: University of Chicago Press, 1955.

——. *The Wound Dresser: A Series of Letters Written from the Hospitals in Washington During the War of the Rebellion*. Ed. Richard Maurice Bucke. 1898. Folcroft, Pa.: Folcroft Library Editions, 1975.

——. *Uncollected Poetry and Prose of Walt Whitman*. 2 vols. Ed. Emory Holloway. 1921. Gloucester, Mass.: Peter Smith, 1972.

Wider, Sarah. "What Did the Minister Mean: Emerson's Sermons and Their Audience." *ESQ* 34 (1988): 1–21.

Widmer, Edward L. *Young America: The Flowering of Democracy in New York City*. New York: Oxford University Press, 1999.

Wiebe, Robert H. *The Opening of American Society*. New York: Vintage, 1985.

Wilentz, Sean. *Chants Democratic: New York City and the Rise of the American Working Class, 1788–1850*. New York: Oxford University Press, 1984.

——. "Society, Politics, and the Market Revolution, 1815–1848." *The New American History*. Ed. Eric Foner. Philadelphia: Temple University Press, 1990. 51–71.

Willard, Charles B. *Whitman's American Fame: The Growth of His Reputation in America after 1892*. Providence, R.I.: Brown University, 1950.

Williams, Raymond. *Culture and Society: 1780–1950*. New York: Columbia University Press, 1983.

——. *Keywords: A Vocabulary of Culture and Society*. Rev. ed. New York: Oxford University Press, 1983.

——. *Marxism and Literature*. New York: Oxford University Press, 1986.

Wills, Garry. *Explaining America:* The Federalist. Garden City, N.Y.: Doubleday, 1981.

——. *Lincoln at Gettysburg: The Words That Remade America*. New York: Simon and Schuster, 1992.

Wolin, Sheldon S. *The Presence of the Past: Essays on the State and the Constitution*. Baltimore: The Johns Hopkins University Press, 1990.

Wood, Gordon S. *The Creation of the American Republic, 1776–1787*. 1969. Chapel Hill: University of North Carolina Press for Omohundro Institute of Early American History and Culture, 1998.

——. *The Radicalism of the American Revolution*. New York: Vintage, 1991.

Wright, Conrad Edick. *The Transformation of Charity in Postrevolutionary New England*. Boston: Northeastern University Press, 1992.

——, ed. *A Stream of Light: A Sesquicentennial History of American Unitarianism*. Boston: Unitarian Universalist Association, 1975.

Yingling, Thomas. "Homosexuality and Utopian Discourse in American Poetry." Erkkila and Grossman 135–46.

Zagarri, Rosemarie. *The Politics of Size: Representation in the United States, 1776–1850*. Ithaca: Cornell University Press, 1987.

Ziff, Larzer. *Literary Democracy: The Declaration of Cultural Independence in America*. New York: Viking, 1981.

——. *Writing in the New Nation: Prose, Print, and Politics in the Early United States*. New Haven: Yale University Press, 1991.

Zwarg, Christina. *Feminist Conversations: Fuller, Emerson, and the Play of Reading*. Ithaca: Cornell University Press, 1995.

Zweig, Paul. *Walt Whitman: The Making of the Poet*. New York: Basic, 1984.

INDEX

∾

Jay Grossman is assistant professor
of English at Northwestern University. He is the
coeditor of *Breaking Bounds: Whitman and
American Cultural Studies* (1996).

∾

Library of Congress Cataloging-in-Publication Data

Grossman, Jay.

Reconstituting the American renaissance : Emerson, Whitman,
and the politics of representation / Jay Grossman.

p. cm. — (New Americanists)

Includes bibliographical references and index.

ISBN 0-8223-3129-2 (acid-free paper)

ISBN 0-8223-3116-0 (pbk. :

acid-free paper)

1. American literature—19th century—History and criticism.
2. Politics and literature—United States—History—19th century.
3. Representative government and representation—United
States—History—19th century. 4. Representative government
and representation in literature. 5. Emerson, Ralph Waldo,
1803–1882—Political and social views. 6. Whitman, Walt,
1819–1892—Political and social views. 7. United States—Politics
and government—19th century. I. Title. II. Series.

PS217 .P64 G76 2003

810.9'358—dc21   2002153878